JAMESTOWN

M000087628

SIGNATURE READING

LEVEL

J

 Glencoe

New York, New York   Columbus, Ohio   Chicago, Illinois   Peoria, Illinois   Woodland Hills, California

Reviewers

Marsha Miller, Ed.D
Reading Specialist
Elgin High School
1200 Maroon Drive
Elgin, IL 60120

Kati Pearson
Orange County Public Schools
Literacy Coordinator
Carver Middle School
4500 West Columbia Street
Orlando, FL 32811

Lynda Pearson
Assistant Principal
Reading Specialist
Lied Middle School
5350 Tropical Parkway
Las Vegas, NV 89130

Suzanne Zweig
Reading Specialist/Consultant
Sullivan High School
6631 N. Bosworth
Chicago, IL 60626

Cover Image: Donald E. Carroll/Getty Images

ISBN: 0-07-861728-6 (Pupil's Edition)
ISBN: 0-07-861729-4 (Annotated Teacher's Edition)

Send all queries to:
Glencoe/McGraw-Hill
8787 Orion Place
Columbus, OH 43240-4027

4 5 6 7 8 9 113 09 08 07 06

Contents

How to Use This Book

Working Through the Lessons

The following descriptions will help you work your way through the lessons in this book.

Building Background will help you get ready to read. In this section you might begin a chart, discuss a question, or learn more about the topic of the selection.

Vocabulary Builder will help you start thinking about—and using—the selection vocabulary. You might draw a diagram and label it with vocabulary words, make a word map, match vocabulary words to their synonyms or antonyms, or use the words to predict what might happen in the selection.

Strategy Builder will introduce you to the strategy that you will use to read the selection. First you will read a definition of the strategy. Then you will see an example of how to use it. Often, you will be given ways to better organize or visualize what you will be reading.

Strategy Break will appear within the reading selection. It will show you how to apply the strategy you just learned to the first part of the selection.

Strategy Follow-up will ask you to apply the same strategy to the second part of the selection. Most of the time, you will work on your own to complete this section. Sometimes, however, you might work with a partner or a group of classmates.

Personal Checklist questions will ask you to rate how well you did in the lesson. When you finish totaling your score, you will enter it on the graphs on page 217.

Vocabulary Check will follow up on the work you did in the Vocabulary Builder. After you total your score, you will enter it on page 217.

Strategy Check will follow up on the strategy work that you did in the lesson. After you total your score, you will enter it on page 217.

Comprehension Check will check your understanding of the selection. After you total your score, you will enter it on page 217.

Extending will give ideas for activities that are related to the selection. Some activities will help you learn more about the topic of the selection. Others might ask you to respond to the selection by dramatizing, writing, or drawing something.

Resources such as books, recordings, videos, and Web sites will help you complete the Extending activities.

Graphing Your Progress

The information and graphs on pages 216–217 will help you track your progress as you work through this book. **Graph 1** will help you record your scores for the Personal Checklist and the Vocabulary, Strategy, and Comprehension Checks. **Graph 2** will help you track your overall progress across the book. You'll be able to see your areas of strength, as well as any areas that could use improvement. You and your teacher can discuss ways to work on those areas.

The Silent Storm

Building Background

Have you ever been outside during a violent storm? Were you alone or with others? Did the storm come up suddenly and catch you off guard, or did you see it coming too late to get to shelter? Try to put yourself back in that moment. What did it feel like outside? What did you and your companions say or do? What could you see and hear? How did you feel? Record your memories on the concept map below. Then, as you read "The Silent Storm," compare your experience to the boys' adventure.

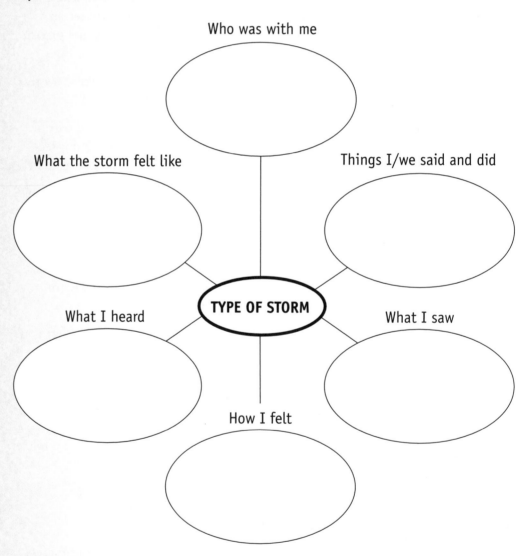

Vocabulary Builder

1. Before you begin reading "The Silent Storm," read the vocabulary words in the margin. Write any of the words that you already know on the appropriate clipboards.

2. Later, as you read the story, find the vocabulary words that you don't know. Read them in context, and decide what they mean. If using context doesn't help, look up the words in a dictionary. Then write each one on the appropriate clipboard.

3. Save your work. You will refer to it again in the Vocabulary Check.

Strategy Builder

Mapping the Elements of a Short Story

- "The Silent Storm" is a short story. A **short story** is a piece of fiction that usually can be read in one sitting. Because it is much shorter than a novel, a short story often has fewer characters and takes place over a briefer period of time.

- One of the main elements of every short story is its **plot**, or sequence of events. In most stories, the plot revolves around a problem (or problems) and what the main characters do to solve it.

- Another element is the **setting**—the time and place in which the story happens. In some stories the setting is a major element. For example, "The Silent Storm" takes place on a mountain during a storm. This setting greatly influences the plot.

- A good way to keep track of what happens in a short story is to record its elements on a **story map**. Study the story map below. It lists and defines the elements that you should look for as you read.

Title (the name of the short story)
Setting (when and where the story takes place)
Main Characters (the people or animals who perform most of the action)
Problem (the puzzle or issue that the main characters must try to solve)
Events (what happens in the story—what the characters do to try to solve the problem)
Solution (the ending, or conclusion, of the story—how the characters finally solve the problem)

barometer

confident

eagerness

excited

exulted

lighthearted

moisture

temperature

urgently

wind chill

CLIPBOARD
Words Related to Weather

CLIPBOARD
Words Related to Feelings

The Silent Storm

by Maureen Crane Wartski

As you begin reading this short story, apply the strategies that you just learned. Keep track of the characters, the setting, and other elements. You may want to underline them as you read.

"Ten degrees above zero, the sun is shining, and the **barometer's** steady," big Buddy Henderson **exulted**. "Yes! We're finally going to make it to the top today."

"It's about time we got lucky," Ben Corwan said. He shared his best friend's excitement. Last year they had planned four times to hike up Algonquin Peak, a difficult mountain in the Adirondacks, and four times their attempts had been scrubbed by bad weather.

Today would be different—but Ben's grin faded as he glanced toward the slight youth who was checking his gear. David Granger was a nice enough kid, but even so, Ben wasn't so sure that Buddy's younger cousin should have come along on this demanding hike.

The other member of their team, Whit Nakanishi, was a fellow senior at Randall High School and the only one of them who'd trekked to the top of Algonquin Peak. He, Ben, and Buddy had hiked up Mount Marcy— the highest peak in the "Daks"— together. They knew they could rely on one another, but—

Once again, Ben glanced at David. Not only was Buddy's visiting cousin only 15, but he was also hearing-impaired.

Whit had pointed out that not being able to hear might cause David problems along the way, but Buddy was **confident** that his cousin could handle himself.

"Dave's done a lot of hiking," he said. "Besides, he's all **excited** about climbing Algonquin Peak with us. How could I tell him he couldn't go?"

Whit had been satisfied, but Ben's eyes remained troubled as he watched the youngster checking his crampons, the saw-toothed footgear that grips ice. Algonquin Peak looked so massive and unfriendly, Ben thought. Could Buddy be *sure* that his cousin could make the grade?

Just then David broke into a grin. He struck the back of his left fist with his clenched right hand, then raised both open palms to the side. "That's the sign for 'mountain,'" Buddy interpreted. "Dave's asking when we're going to get the show on the road."

Whit took the lead position. He was followed by David, then Buddy, and Ben brought up the rear. The day was cold but crystal clear, and as they climbed the steep trail, the three friends talked and joked with one another.

David didn't take part in the **light-hearted** banter, and Ben felt bad for him. Though the younger boy could read lips, there was little chance for face-to-face conversation along the increasingly steep grade.

He must be feeling left out of things, Ben thought. When the group stopped to put on crampons and drink water, Ben offered David some trail mix. The youth smiled broadly,

and moved his hand to and away from his mouth.

"That means 'thank you,'" Buddy explained. He added: "Hey, are you guys going to chow down all day? We've got a mountain to climb."

 Stop here for the Strategy Break.

Strategy Break

If you were to stop and begin a story map for "The Silent Storm" so far, it might look like this:

Title: The Silent Storm

▼

Setting: a cold day on Algonquin Peak, a difficult mountain in the Adirondacks

▼

Main Characters: Buddy Henderson, Ben Corwan, David Granger (Buddy's cousin), Whit Nakanishi

▼

Problem: The boys want to climb to the top of Algonquin Peak, but Ben is worried that the trip will be too demanding for David.

▼

Events: 1. As the boys prepare for their climb, Ben worries about David's ability to make it.
2. David signs to Buddy to "get the show on the road," and the boys begin their climb.
3. The group stops, and Ben offers David some trail mix.

▼

To be continued . . .

As you continue reading, keep paying attention to the events in this short story. You will use some of them to complete the story map in the Strategy Follow-up.

Go on reading to see what happens.

Now the terrain became more difficult. Progress slowed, and talk quieted. After considerable time Whit announced, "We're coming to the tree line."

They stepped out of the trees as he spoke, and before them rose a snow-dusted slope devoid of plant life. Sometime in its history Algonquin Peak's crown had been seared by fire, and no growth had taken root on its inhospitable slope.

David was wide-eyed as he stared upward. "It looks awesome, doesn't it?" Ben exclaimed.

David signed rapidly, and Buddy translated: "He says he can't wait to get up to the peak."

"What you're looking at is just a false peak," Whit warned. "The real peak isn't far behind it, though."

"So what are we waiting for?" Ben demanded. "Let's do it!"

Now that they had left the trees, winds were stronger and the cold more intense. As he followed the others, Ben automatically checked for cairns—piles of rocks that marked the trail to the summit. On a mountain like Algonquin, to leave the established trail could be dangerous.

Their **eagerness** to get to the top made the climb feel easier. "That wasn't bad," Ben exulted when they topped the false peak. "Now for the real thing—"

He broke off as he saw Buddy wince in pain. "Are you hurt?"

"I twisted my ankle back along the way," Buddy groaned. "I thought I could walk it off, but the fool thing's getting worse." He tried to smile as he added, "Guess I'll have to stay here and watch you guys make it to the top."

"We might not get there either," Whit said grimly. "Look at the sky."

Storm clouds were rolling over the surrounding peaks. Ben checked his barometer, and his heart sank when he saw that barometric pressure was dropping. A falling barometer meant that a storm was coming.

Ben shivered. Now that they'd stopped moving, he realized how cold and gusty it was. With the **wind chill**, the **temperature** had dropped by at least 20 degrees. It must be 10 below zero—no wonder the **moisture** in his nose had turned to ice particles.

"Do we go down?" he asked reluctantly.

"Yes, we've got to get to the tree line fast. It's already starting to snow." Whit had to shout to make himself heard above the wind. "Best unsheathe your ice axes," he added. "Remember to stay close. Come on, Buddy. I'll give you a hand down."

Their descent should have been rapid, but wind-whipped snow made it hard to see. Ben staggered as a vicious gust hit him; then he saw David stumble. But it wasn't the wind that had caused the youth to fall. Ben realized that David's left crampon strap had loosened.

"Wait," Ben shouted as David began to pull off his mittens.

Without mittens, a hiker's hands would freeze. Experience had taught Ben to wear polypropylene liners and wool mittens under outer mittens. Even with gloves, his hands felt icy as he knelt to right David's crampon.

Thanks, David signed as Ben straightened up, but there was no time for politeness. **Urgently**, Ben gestured David down the mountainside.

They had to catch up with the others. The trouble was that, blinded and deafened by the now gale-force winds, Whit and Buddy hadn't realized that Ben and David had fallen behind.

Visibility was almost zero, and without Whit's leadership, Ben wasn't sure of the way back. Vainly he searched for the cairns. If he could only spot one—

His thoughts sheared away as his foot slipped from under him. He'd hit a layer of glare ice that his crampons couldn't grip.

As he began to slide, Ben instinctively used his ice ax. His attempt to self-arrest didn't work—all the pick of his ax did was to unloosen a few bits of frozen rock. Wind strangled a scream back into Ben's throat as he slid belly-down into the heart of the storm.

Ben snapped open his eyes. Miraculously he'd stopped sliding, and now he saw why. Alerted by the falling stones, David had looked up, seen what was happening, and managed to throw himself on top of his companion. The younger boy's weight had arrested Ben's slide.

"That was quick thinking," Ben gasped.

He broke off as David tried to get up then doubled up in pain. Ben realized that his crampon had caught the younger boy in the ankle. Even worse, with the storm obscuring the trail markers, there was no way of knowing if they were on the right path. Nor could they stay put, for there was no shelter.

If we stay out here, we'll freeze. As if in answer to Ben's thought, the wind shifted momentarily, and he caught a brief glimpse of a cairn up ahead. It was immediately obscured by wind-blown snow, but Ben could have whooped with joy.

"It's all right; I know the way down," he cried to David, but his voice was lost in the storm. All he could do was gesture forward.

Though obviously in pain, the younger boy followed Ben's lead down the slope. As they descended the storm began to let up. The cairns were easier to spot now; the going was easier. Suddenly, David caught Ben's arm and pointed. Not far below loomed the tree line, and a dark shape was climbing up. Whit was coming back to search for them.

"We made it!" Ben exulted. He started to wave at Whit but turned as David clasped his arm a second time. Smiling sadly, David was touching his chest and then gesturing toward the cloud-shrouded Algonquin Peak. His clenched hand moved from his chin down in a thumbs-up sign, and then made another swift gesture.

Ben recalled the hand sign for the mountain that David had used earlier. "You're right," he agreed. "It beat us this time."

Then he too made the sign for mountain, tapped David's and his own chest, and nodded vigorously. It wasn't real signing, but from David's smile, Ben knew he had definitely gotten his message across.

Someday the two of them were going to conquer Algonquin Peak—together. ●

Strategy Follow-up

Now complete the story map for "The Silent Storm." (Use a separate sheet of paper if you need more room to write.) Start with Event 4. Parts of the events have been filled in for you.

Problem: The boys want to climb to the top of Algonquin Peak, but Ben is worried that the trip will be too demanding for David.

▼

Event 4: The terrain becomes more difficult, and Buddy

▼

Event 5: When storm clouds roll over and the barometric pressure and temperature drop,

▼

Event 6: David falls when

▼

Event 7: Ben pulls off his mittens and

▼

Event 8: When Ben hits ice and begins to slide,

▼

Event 9: Ben glimpses a cairn and

▼

Solution: When the boys make it to the tree line, Ben "signs" to David that

✓Personal Checklist

Read each question and put a check (✓) in the correct box.

1. In Building Background, how well were you able to use your concept map to help you imagine what the boys experienced?
    ☐ 3 (extremely well)
    ☐ 2 (fairly well)
    ☐ 1 (not well)

2. By the time you finished reading this story, how many words were you able to put on the appropriate clipboards?
    ☐ 3 (8–10 words)
    ☐ 2 (4–7 words)
    ☐ 1 (0–3 words)

3. How well were you able to complete the story map in the Strategy Follow-up?
    ☐ 3 (extremely well)
    ☐ 2 (fairly well)
    ☐ 1 (not well)

4. How well do you understand why Ben was concerned about David's ability to make the climb?
    ☐ 3 (extremely well)
    ☐ 2 (fairly well)
    ☐ 1 (not well)

5. How well do you understand why Ben changes his mind about David?
    ☐ 3 (extremely well)
    ☐ 2 (fairly well)
    ☐ 1 (not well)

Vocabulary Check

Look back at the work you did in the Vocabulary Builder. Then answer each question by circling the correct letter.

1. Which of these words suggests a pleasant, contented feeling?
    a. excited
    b. urgently
    c. lighthearted

2. Which of these words names a tool that is used to measure air pressure?
    a. barometer
    b. wind chill
    c. moisture

3. Which words are all related to weather?
    a. temperature, urgently, wind chill
    b. barometer, moisture, temperature
    c. lighthearted, confident, temperature

4. Which words are all related to feelings?
    a. confident, wind chill, lighthearted
    b. barometer, urgently, moisture
    c. eagerness, excited, exulted

5. The story says that "Ben exulted when they topped the false peak." What does *exulted* mean in this context?
    a. cheered
    b. moaned
    c. sobbed

Add the numbers that you just checked to get your total score. (For example, if you checked 3, 2, 3, 2, and 1, your total score would be 11.) Fill in your score here. Then turn to page 217 and transfer your score onto Graph 1.

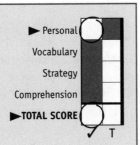

► Personal
Vocabulary
Strategy
Comprehension
►TOTAL SCORE

Check your answers with your teacher. Give yourself 1 point for each correct answer, and fill in your Vocabulary score here. Then turn to page 217 and transfer your score onto Graph 1.

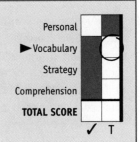

Personal
► Vocabulary
Strategy
Comprehension
TOTAL SCORE

Strategy Check

Review the story map that you completed in the Strategy Follow-up. Then answer these questions:

1. What happens when storm clouds approach and the barometric pressure and temperature change?
   a. The boys stop to put on crampons and drink water.
   b. The boys are forced to go back down the mountain.
   c. Ben hits some ice and begins sliding on his stomach.

2. What causes David to fall?
   a. Ben knocks him down as he slides down the mountain.
   b. David twists his ankle while climbing the rough terrain.
   c. David's left crampon strap loosens, and he stumbles.

3. How does David stop Ben from sliding?
   a. He uses his ice ax to arrest the slide.
   b. He throws himself on top of Ben.
   c. He tightens Ben's left crampon strap.

4. What does Ben see that allows him to find his way down the slope?
   a. a cairn
   b. a crampon
   c. the tree line

5. Why does Ben "sign" to David that someday the two of them will conquer Algonquin Peak together?
   a. After David saves him, Ben realizes that David is very capable of making the climb.
   b. Ben is very angry with David and wants to race him to the top of the mountain.
   c. Now that the four of them have made it to the top, Ben wants to go again with David.

Comprehension Check

Review the story if necessary. Then answer these questions:

1. Why does Ben think that David might have problems climbing Algonquin Peak?
   a. David is smaller than the others.
   b. David is hearing-impaired.
   c. David goes to a different school.

2. Why does Ben offer David some trail mix?
   a. He thinks David must be feeling left out.
   b. All that Ben ever thinks about is food.
   c. Ben wants to learn the sign for "thank you."

3. Which boy is the most experienced climber?
   a. Ben
   b. Buddy
   c. Whit

4. Why does Ben right David's crampon for him?
   a. He knows that if David takes off his mittens, his hands will freeze.
   b. He's trying to make up to David for not wanting him on the hike.
   c. He wants to let David see just what an experienced hiker he is.

5. What do you think Ben learned from his experience on the mountain?
   a. David's hearing impairment doesn't keep him from being a good hiker.
   b. A hearing-impaired person is a better hiker than a hearing person.
   c. Fifteen-year-old boys are too young to go mountain climbing.

Check your answers with your teacher. Give yourself 1 point for each correct answer, and fill in your Strategy score here. Then turn to page 217 and transfer your score onto Graph 1.

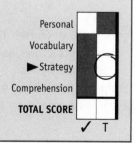

Check your answers with your teacher. Give yourself 1 point for each correct answer, and fill in your Comprehension score here. Then turn to page 217 and transfer your score onto Graph 1.

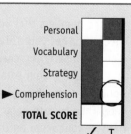

Extending

Choose one or more of these activities:

RESEARCH MOUNTAIN CLIMBING

With one or more partners, learn something about mountain climbing and present it to your class in the form of a poster. Your poster should display pictures of different aspects of the sport, such as:

- necessary equipment, with labels explaining how it is used
- famous climbers, with short paragraphs describing their accomplishments
- favorite or particularly challenging mountains, with maps showing their locations

If there is a sporting goods store or sports facility in your area with a wall that can be climbed, you might give it a try. If possible, take photos for the poster, showing your team members using some of the equipment or techniques.

INVESTIGATE HELP FOR THE HEARING-IMPAIRED

Find out how people with hearing impairments handle everyday situations. For example, how do they use telephones? How do they enjoy movies or television programs? Are any animals trained to help people who cannot hear, as seeing-eye dogs help people who cannot see? Besides using library resources or the ones listed on this page, interview students at your school who are hearing-impaired.

LEARN TO SIGN AND/OR SIGN A FAIRY TALE

Using some of the books listed on this page, learn the basics of signing and demonstrate several words and phrases for your class. Or, if you prefer, sign part of a familiar story. Several books that show how to sign fairy tales for young children are listed in the resources.

Resources

Books

Allen, Linda Buchanan, and Susan Cooley. *High Mountain Challenge: A Guide for Young Mountaineers.* Appalachian Mountain Club Books, 1989.

Anderson, H. C., Harry Bornstein, tr., and Marianne Collins-Ahlgren. *The Ugly Duckling: Signed English.* Clerc, 1974.

Armentrout, David. *Outdoor Adventures.* Rourke Books, 1998.

Bornstein, Harry, and Karen Luczak Saulnier. *Goldilocks and the Three Bears: Told in Signed English.* Gallaudet University Press, 2002.

————. *Little Red Riding Hood: Told in Signed English.* Gallaudet University Press, 2002.

————. *Signing—Signed English: A Basic Guide.* Crown, 1988.

Shelly, Susan, and Jim Schneck. *The Complete Idiot's Guide to Learning Sign Language.* Alpha, 1998.

Web Sites

http://where.com/scott.net/asl/
This site features a visual guide to the alphabet in American Sign Language.

http://www.searchforcare.com/library/articles/in_home_care/inhc0002.html
Read the article "Independent Living for the Hearing-Impaired" on this Web page.

http://www.ukshopuk.com/hnt/trips/guides/guidtran.html
This Web site offers advice for beginning mountain climbers and information on climbing equipment.

Videos/DVDs

Communicating with the Hearing Impaired: An Introductory Course in American Sign Language. Films for the Humanities and Sciences, 1991.

High Five! Fables and Fairy Tales. Sign Media, 1994.

LESSON ❷ Alex, the Talking Parrot

bigger

different

difficult

easy

few

first

last

learn

many

same

smaller

teach

Building Background

From the title of this article, you might not expect to learn anything remarkable about Alex, the talking parrot. After all, aren't parrots known for talking? So, before you begin to read, take a minute to consider what might make a talking parrot remarkable. Then complete the sentences below.

1. My usual notion of parrots is that they are_____
    _____.

2. To me, a talking parrot would be remarkable if it _____
    _____.

3. I predict that Alex will be remarkable because _____
    _____.

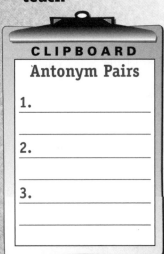

CLIPBOARD

Antonym Pairs

1. _____
   _____

2. _____
   _____

3. _____
   _____

Vocabulary Builder

1. Study the vocabulary words in the margin. Each word is half of a pair of antonyms—words with opposite meanings.

2. Write the antonym pairs on the clipboards. Then, as you read the article, underline any other antonym pairs that you find.

3. Save your work. You will refer to it again in the Vocabulary Check.

CLIPBOARD

Antonym Pairs

4. _____
   _____

5. _____
   _____

6. _____
   _____

Strategy Builder

Summarizing Nonfiction

- **Nonfiction** is writing that gives readers facts and information about a particular subject, or topic. The **topic** is what the piece of writing is all about.

- Every piece of nonfiction follows a particular pattern of organization. The most common patterns are listed in the margin. The pattern of "Alex, the Talking Parrot" is description. **Descriptions** usually tell who or what something is, what it does, or how and why it works.

- Sometimes when you read nonfiction, you're given a lot of information at once. To keep the information straight—and to remember it better—you might stop from time to time and summarize what you've read. When you **summarize** a section of text, you list or retell the most important ideas in your own words.

- Read the following paragraph from an article about parrots. Then read how one student summarized it.

CLIPBOARD

Most Common Organizational Patterns of Nonfiction

_____

_____

_____

_____

_____

> There are many different kinds of parrots in the world. The ones that many people keep as pets are parakeets and lovebirds. Other kinds of parrots are macaws, which are the largest parrots. They live in Central and South America and have long tails, very large bills, and brightly colored feathers. Cockatoos live in Australia and New Guinea. Most of them are white, with crests of long yellow feathers on their heads. Some parrots are really unusual. For example, hanging parrots, which live in southeastern Asia, sleep upside down just like bats. Other unusual parrots are keas, which perch on tourists' cars in New Zealand and beg for food!

Summary:
There are many different kinds of parrots. Parakeets and lovebirds are the ones people keep as pets. Macaws are the largest parrots. Cockatoos have yellow crests on their heads. Hanging parrots are unusual because they sleep upside down like bats, and keas perch on tourists' cars and beg.

Alex, the Talking Parrot

by Dorothy Hinshaw Patent

As you read the first part of this article, think about how you might summarize it. Jot down your ideas on a separate sheet of paper. When you get to the Strategy Break, you can compare your summary with the sample provided.

Parrots that are trained to talk often say silly things like "Polly want a cracker." Although these birds have learned to imitate the sounds that make up the words, they don't really know what they're saying. But there is one parrot who speaks more than a hundred words and actually understands their meanings. He is an African gray parrot named Alex.

Dr. Irene Pepperberg, a scientist at the University of Arizona, has worked with Alex for nineteen years. Teaching Alex to speak and understand wasn't **easy** at **first**. He had to **learn** one word at a time. Irene and an assistant would **teach** Alex by showing him what a word meant. Irene would hold up an object, saying "What's this?" Her human partner would give the word—"pasta," for example—while Alex watched. Irene would praise her partner, then ask Alex the name for the object. When he got it right, Irene would praise him and give him the object to play with as a reward.

It took Alex **many** weeks to learn his first word. After that, each new word became easier and easier for him.

Why did Irene spend so much time getting a parrot to talk? Scientists like Irene are interested in discovering how intelligent animals are and how their brains work. But studying animal intelligence has always been **difficult**, partly because animals haven't been able to communicate clearly with humans. Teaching Alex to speak words that he understands has let Irene talk to him directly. She can ask him questions, and he can answer them in English. In this way, Irene is finding out what sorts of things Alex's brain can do. She has found that parrots are much smarter than scientists used to think. The word "birdbrain," which means someone who isn't very smart, certainly doesn't apply to Alex.

 **Stop here for the Strategy Break.**

Strategy Break

Did you jot down your summary as you read? If you did, see if it looks anything like this:

Teaching Alex to speak and understand wasn't easy at first. Dr. Irene Pepperberg had to teach the parrot one word at a time. It took Alex many weeks to learn his first word, but after that, it became easier. Irene spent so much time getting Alex to talk because she's interested in discovering how smart animals are and how their brains work. Teaching Alex to speak words that he understands has allowed Irene to ask questions and Alex to answer. By talking with Alex, Irene can find out what sorts of things his brain can do. She now knows that parrots are much smarter than scientists used to think.

 Go on reading.

Alex can identify over forty kinds of objects, five different shapes, five materials, and seven colors, and he can use his knowledge to solve problems and answer questions. For example, from a group of objects, he can pick out the number of things of a certain color, up to the number six. He can also make comparisons, such as **bigger** or **smaller** and **same** or **different**, between objects.

"Want wheat!" Alex says loudly. Irene explains to him that she doesn't have any shredded wheat for him. "How about some crackers, Alex?" she asks.

"No, no—want wheat!" he replies.

Because it's time for them to work, Irene ignores his request and shows Alex a tray with simple objects scattered over it—a yellow plastic key, a green wooden square, a five-cornered piece of yellow felt, a gray rawhide rectangle, a yellow paper triangle, a red plastic square, and a blue Play-Doh square.

"What material green, Alex?" Irene asks.

Alex glances over the assortment, then answers, "Wood!" in his clear but croaky parrot voice.

"Good birdie," says Irene as she nuzzles him and hands him the green square. Alex nibbles at it for a moment, then drops it.

"How many yellow?" asks Irene.

Alex takes his time, looking over the bright, colorful display on the tray.

"Three," he answers.

Irene praises him again. "Good boy, good birdie," she says as she hands him the yellow key to play with.

Alex mouths the key, nibbling at it gently before dropping it.

"Wanna go shoulder," he announces.

"O.K., you can come onto my shoulder," answers Irene. She puts out her hand. Alex climbs aboard, and she puts him on her shoulder. He rubs his head against Irene's cheek. "Do you want some corn?" asks Irene.

"Soft corn," answers Alex, and Irene holds out her hand with a **few** kernels on it. Alex carefully takes one kernel into his mouth and eats.

Alex has shown us that birds like parrots can understand categories such as shape, color, and size. They can solve problems and recognize numbers. Before Alex came along, scientists did not believe that animals with such small brains could do these things.

Alex uses his ability to talk outside of work sessions, too. At the end of the day, Irene tells Alex she is leaving.

"I'm going to dinner now," she says. "You be good."

"You be good," Alex answers.

"See you tomorrow," says Irene.

"Bye," says Alex.

"Bye," she responds.

"I love you," croaks Alex.

Irene's **last** words as she goes out the door are "I love you, too." ●

Strategy Follow-up

On a separate sheet of paper, summarize the rest of this article. Use your own words. Be sure to list only the most important ideas, and skip unnecessary details.

✓Personal Checklist

Read each question and put a check (✓) in the correct box.

1. How well do you understand the information presented in this article?
   - ☐ 3 (extremely well)
   - ☐ 2 (fairly well)
   - ☐ 1 (not well)

2. In Building Background you predicted why Alex would be remarkable. How well does your prediction match the reasons that the article describes?
   - ☐ 3 (extremely well)
   - ☐ 2 (fairly well)
   - ☐ 1 (not well)

3. In the Vocabulary Builder, how well were you able to list antonym pairs on the clipboards?
   - ☐ 3 (extremely well)
   - ☐ 2 (fairly well)
   - ☐ 1 (not well)

4. In the Strategy Follow-up, how well were you able to summarize the rest of this article?
   - ☐ 3 (extremely well)
   - ☐ 2 (fairly well)
   - ☐ 1 (not well)

5. How well would you be able to explain why Irene and other scientists believe that Alex has improved our understanding of parrots' intelligence?
   - ☐ 3 (extremely well)
   - ☐ 2 (fairly well)
   - ☐ 1 (not well)

Vocabulary Check

Look back at the work you did in the Vocabulary Builder. Then answer each question by circling the correct letter.

1. Which antonym pair describes sizes?
   - a. *bigger* and *smaller*
   - b. *first* and *last*
   - c. *teach* and *learn*

2. Which antonym pair describes amounts?
   - a. *difficult* and *easy*
   - b. *different* and *same*
   - c. *many* and *few*

3. If you could add another pair of antonyms to the clipboards in the Vocabulary Check, which pair would you add?
   - a. *smart* and *intelligent*
   - b. *colors* and *materials*
   - c. *ask* and *answer*

4. The article says that teaching Alex to speak and understand wasn't easy at first. What are the antonyms of the words *easy* and *first*?
   - a. *different* and *many*
   - b. *difficult* and *last*
   - c. *learn* and *smaller*

5. Which examples best illustrate the antonyms *teach* and *learn*?
   - a. Irene and her assistant
   - b. Irene and Alex
   - c. Irene and another scientist

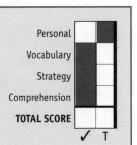

Add the numbers that you just checked to get your Personal Checklist score. Fill in your score here. Then turn to page 217 and transfer your score onto Graph 1.

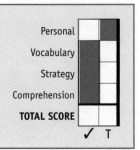

Check your answers with your teacher. Give yourself 1 point for each correct answer, and fill in your Vocabulary score here. Then turn to page 217 and transfer your score onto Graph 1.

Strategy Check

Look back at the summary you wrote. Then answer these questions:

1. Which sentence best summarizes the first paragraph right after the Strategy Break?
   a. Alex can pick out the number of things of a certain color, up to the number six.
   b. Alex can answer questions about the shapes, materials, colors, and sizes of over 40 objects.
   c. Alex can tell which objects are bigger and smaller or the same and different.

2. Which sentence best summarizes the process that Alex and Irene follow when they work?
   a. Irene asks Alex questions about different objects, and Alex answers them.
   b. Alex asks Irene questions about different objects, and Irene answers them.
   c. Alex tells Irene what foods he wants to eat, and Irene gives them to him.

3. Which sentence summarizes what Irene does when Alex answers a question correctly?
   a. Irene praises Alex and gives him some wheat.
   b. Irene praises Alex and hands him the object he has identified.
   c. Irene praises Alex and tells him she loves him.

4. Which detail should you not have included in your summary?
   a. Alex nibbles at the square and then drops it.
   b. "Want wheat!" Alex says loudly.
   c. Both of the above are unnecessary details.

5. Which sentence best summarizes what Alex has shown scientists?
   a. Parrots can understand categories, solve problems, and recognize numbers.
   b. Parrots have much larger brains than scientists ever thought possible.
   c. Both of the above.

Comprehension Check

Review the selection if necessary. Then answer these questions:

1. How is Alex remarkable?
   a. He can use the English language to communicate his thoughts.
   b. He uses words in English instead of bird calls to call his mate.
   c. He can imitate the pronunciations of more than 100 English words.

2. How did Dr. Pepperberg teach Alex to speak with understanding?
   a. She said the same word all day long so that Alex could repeat it.
   b. She and her assistant showed Alex what words actually meant.
   c. She promised Alex rewards if he would say what she said.

3. Why did Dr. Pepperberg teach Alex to speak with understanding?
   a. She wanted to prove it could be done.
   b. She wanted to find out what sorts of things his brain could do.
   c. She wanted to provide a model for people who want talking birds.

4. Which of the following is *not* mentioned as a skill that Alex has learned?
   a. spelling words
   b. counting objects
   c. naming colors

5. What is one thing that Alex has proved?
   a. That birds are not the only animals that can use language.
   b. That birds are just as intelligent as humans.
   c. That parrots are much smarter than scientists used to think.

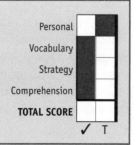

Check your answers with your teacher. Give yourself 1 point for each correct answer, and fill in your Strategy score here. Then turn to page 217 and transfer your score onto Graph 1.

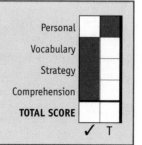

Check your answers with your teacher. Give yourself 1 point for each correct answer, and fill in your Comprehension score here. Then turn to page 217 and transfer your score onto Graph 1.

Extending

Choose one or both of these activities:

LEARN MORE ABOUT PARROTS

Did you know that there are more than 300 species of parrots? With a partner or two, investigate as many species as you can by using the resources listed on this page, as well as visiting pet shops. Draw or copy pictures of several kinds of parrots. You could cut out pictures from magazines or catalogs, copy pictures from reference books, or draw or take pictures of the parrots in pet stores. Paste the pictures on large index cards. On the back of each card, include as much as the following information as possible:

- type of parrot
- where that type of parrot lives
- how long it lives
- how big it gets
- its distinguishing features and/or habits
- what is known about its intelligence and ability to learn language

Share your cards with the rest of the class. If any other students have made cards too, you might want to put all your cards together and bind them into a booklet that you keep in your classroom or school library.

RESEARCH APES THAT USE SIGN LANGUAGE

In several studies, apes have been taught to communicate with people through the use of sign language. Some of these apes have even taught signing to other apes. (See the books and video about Koko listed on this page.) Investigate these studies by yourself or as part of a team. Present your findings in an oral report or, if working with a team, through a panel discussion.

Resources

Books

León, Vicki. *Parrots, Macaws, and Cockatoos.* Bird Life. Silver Burdett Press, 1995.

McNulty, Faith. *With Love from Koko.* Scholastic, 1990.

Naigh, Marshall. *A Beginner's Guide to Parrots.* TFH Publications, 1986.

Patent, Dorothy Hinshaw. *Alex and Friends: Animal Talk, Animal Thinking.* Discovery. Lerner, 1998.

Patterson, Francine. *Koko's Kitten.* Bt Bound, 1999.

———. *Koko's Story.* Scholastic, 1988.

Wentworth, William. *Parrots as a New Pet.* TFH Publications, 1993.

Wolter, Annette. *Parrots: How to Take Care of Them and Understand Them.* Barron's Educational Series, 1992.

Web Sites

http://www.alexfoundation.org/
This is the Web site of the Alex Foundation, which funds Dr. Pepperberg's research into parrot intelligence.

http://www.kakapo.net
Use this Web site to learn about the kakapo, an unusual flightless parrot that lives in New Zealand.

http://www.koko.org/world/
This Web site focuses on the efforts to teach human language to Koko, a female gorilla.

Videos/DVDs

Alex the Grey. Wasatch Avian Education Society, circa 1996.

Koko: A Talking Gorilla. Home Vision Entertainment, 2001.

Koko's Kitten. Gorilla Foundation. Churchill Films, 1989.

Do Animals Think?

colony

communicate

complicated

copy

group

hard

instinct

know

mimic

pattern

talk

understand

Building Background

Have you ever talked to an animal? At some time or other, almost everyone has. Of course, we don't expect animals to answer—in words, anyway. So why do we do it? Perhaps it's because we think that animals can understand what we're saying; we think they *think*. But do they? The article you are about to read explains what scientists have discovered about if and how certain animals think. What do you predict it will say?

Vocabulary Builder

1. Study the vocabulary words in the margin. Each word is half of a pair of synonyms—words with the same or similar meanings.

2. Write the synonym pairs on the clipboards. Then, as you read the article, underline any other synonym pairs that you find.

3. Save your work. You will refer to it again in the Vocabulary Check.

CLIPBOARD

Synonym Pairs

1. _____

2. _____

3. _____

CLIPBOARD

Synonym Pairs

4. _____

5. _____

6. _____

Strategy Builder

Outlining Main Ideas and Supporting Details

- An **informational article** is a type of nonfiction that gives facts and details about a particular topic. The **topic** of an article is often mentioned in its **title**. For example, "Do Animals Think?" is about animals—or more specifically, if and how animals think.

- Many information articles are **descriptions** that are organized into **main ideas** and **supporting details**. These ideas and details help explain or support the topic. In the article you are about to read, the main ideas are stated in the boldfaced **headings**. The supporting details are given in the paragraphs below the headings.

- There are several ways to keep track of main ideas and details as you read an informational article. As you learned in Lesson 2, one way is to summarize them. Another way is to outline them. Some **outlines** use a system of Roman numerals (I, II, III, and so on), capital letters, and Arabic numerals (1, 2, 3, and so on).

- Read the following paragraph from an article about German Shepherd dogs. Then read how one student outlined the main ideas and details.

German Shepherds Make Good Work Dogs
German Shepherds have many qualities that make them good work dogs. For one thing, they are the right size. They are quite large, which makes them strong. And with their big chests, they can get enough wind to run for a long time. They also have a thick coat of fur that protects them in bad weather and helps them stay clean. They are very alert and smart, so they are easy to train. And they are calm and patient with their owners.

Outline:

I. German Shepherds have many qualities that make them good work dogs.

   A. They are the right size.

      1. They're large, which makes them strong.

      2. Their big chests allow them to run for a long time.

   B. They have a thick coat of fur.

      1. It protects them in bad weather.

      2. It helps them stay clean.

   C. They are very alert and smart, so they're easy to train.

   D. They are calm and patient with their owners.

Do Animals Think?

As you read the first part of this article, apply some of the strategies that you just learned. Look for the main ideas and supporting details in this description, and think about how you might outline them.

At times, your pet may appear to be deep in thought. But don't let that pose fool you. Animals often do things that may make you *think* they're thinking.

Thinking about thinking is tricky, because thinking isn't something you can see. It goes on inside the brain. We **know** when *we're* doing it. But who can tell if an animal is thinking? It's not easy.

For example, check out the animal actions below. Do they show that the animals are thinking—or not thinking? What do *you* think? (We'll tell you later what scientists think.)

- A bird builds a nest that's just right for its eggs and babies.
- An octopus uses its arms to open a jar with food inside.
- A lion sneaks around behind its prey and then chases it toward another lion that's hiding and waiting.
- A salmon returns from the ocean to the same stream where it hatched.

What Is Thinking?

It may be easier to first explain what thinking *isn't*. For example, it isn't needed for things animals do automatically—like when a beaver dams a stream with sticks, mud, and grasses.

The beaver is making a pond, but it didn't learn how to do that. It doesn't think about doing it, either. Some animals just do what they do—kind of like robots—and they do it the same way every time. Scientists call this kind of behavior **instinct**.

But what about when an animal *does* learn to do something? Is that thinking? For example, you can teach a dog to give you its paw and "shake hands" for a treat. Even a worm can learn to follow a maze! But most scientists don't believe that the worm—or even the dog—is thinking when it learns such tricks.

A sheepdog at work, though, is a different story. One of the dog's jobs is to single out one sheep from a flock. The dog knows how to do that because it was trained.

But say the sheep doesn't want to leave the flock. It moves this way or that, or tries to duck behind another sheep. The dog must figure out a plan and keep changing that plan until it "outsmarts" the sheep, cutting it away from the others. Many people would agree that the sheepdog must be thinking about what it's doing.

Thinking Tests

For a long time, scientists didn't study animal thinking. Most of them didn't believe that animals *could* think. They thought humans were the only thinking animals.

Now more scientists are studying this subject. But it's very **hard** to prove things that no one can see or measure. So some scientists decided to take a look at brains.

Is bigger better? No. Cow brains are bigger than dog brains, but that doesn't make cows smarter than dogs. And squirrels have some of the biggest brains of all for their body size. But squirrels aren't even close to being the smartest animals in the world. So the size of a brain may give some clues about brain power, but it doesn't prove anything.

Other scientists study thinking by watching how animals solve problems. They watch animals in the wild. Or they set up thinking tests in a lab.

For example, a scientist might put some food just out of an animal's reach. One kind of animal may grab a stick and use it to slide the food over. Another kind might not be able to figure out a way to get the food. Some scientists think animals that have lots of problems to solve must be smarter than animals with simple lives.

Scientists also study certain kinds of behavior for clues about thinking. They watch for three things: whether animals use tools, how they act with each other, and how they **communicate**.

 Stop here for the Strategy Break.

Strategy Break

If you were to create an outline for this article so far, it might look something like this:

I. What thinking is—and isn't
   A. Thinking isn't instinct.
      1. Instinct is when animals do things automatically, like robots.
   B. Real thinking is when animals must figure out a plan in order to solve a problem.
II. More scientists are now studying whether animals think.
   A. Some scientists looked at animals' brains.
      1. They discovered that bigger ≠ smarter.
   B. Other scientists watch how animals solve problems—both in the wild and in labs.
      1. Some scientists think that animals that have lots of problems to solve must be smarter than animals with simple lives.
   C. Some scientists study certain kinds of animal behavior.
      1. They watch whether animals use tools.
      2. They watch how animals act with each other.
      3. They watch how animals communicate.

As you continue reading, keep paying attention to the main ideas and supporting details. At the end of this article, you will use some of them to complete an outline of your own.

Go on reading.

Here's a closer look. . . .

Tool Time

People use lots of tools. We eat with forks and knives. We write with pens and pencils. We build with hammers and nails. There's just no end to the kinds of tools humans make and use.

But some other animals use tools too. The sea otter uses a stone to hammer open shellfish. An elephant uses a stick to scratch its back. And there's a kind of bird that uses a twig or cactus spine to poke out hidden insects.

Besides people, chimpanzees are the most famous tool-users. Like the bird, they use twigs to "fish" for insects. They also can make sponges out of leaves, use sticks and stones to crack open nuts, and wave branches around to scare off enemies.

Many scientists say tool use can be a sign of thinking—but not always. For instance, sea otters use their "hammers" out of instinct. They all do it—and they all do it the same way—even if they've never seen it done before.

But chimps seem to think about the tools they use. And they don't all use the same kinds of tools or use them in the same way.

For example, one chimp might notice some nuts and start looking around for a stick. It may check out several sticks and pick a certain one. Then it tries to crack a nut with it. If the stick doesn't do the trick, the chimp might change the stick somehow, pick out a different stick, or get a stone instead. Another chimp might discover that putting the nut on a rock first makes it easier to crack. This kind of problem solving is a good clue that thinking is going on.

Getting Along

Some animals spend most of their lives alone. But others live in **groups**. An ant **colony**, for example, is made up of many, many ants. They all work together to find and store food, raise young, and keep the colony safe from enemies.

These ants seem to lead very **complicated** lives, but scientists would say that they're not thinking. Why? Because everything the ants do is just a **pattern**, an instinct. And they can't change that pattern, even if they need to.

Wolves live and work in groups too. They play together and howl together. They warn each other about trouble and help each other babysit. They also hunt together. Working as a team, they can track, chase, and kill prey much larger than themselves, such as moose.

Many scientists would say that, unlike the ants, wolves *do* think. That's because wolves can make plans and change their behavior, depending on what's going on around them.

Animal Talk

Many animals communicate, or **"talk"**—with sounds, odors, colors, "body language," and other signals. Communication helps animals get along with each other and survive.

For example, honey bees do a dance in the hive that "tells" other bees where to find food. And birds sing songs that say, "This is *my* place!" Most scientists would say that this kind of "talking" is automatic and doesn't take any thinking.

Other animals, such as wolves and whales, use many different sounds and signals. Are these animals able to tell each other what's on their minds—the same way that people do with language? Do they think about what they're "saying"? Some scientists think so, but most agree that there's no way to tell for sure.

We *know* that human language takes thinking. So some scientists have tried to see what animals can do with our language. For example, a few apes have been taught sign language. The scientists who work with them say the apes seem to **understand** how the words work together. The apes sometimes even make up their own sentences. These could be clues that the animals are thinking.

And then there's Alex. Alex is an African gray parrot. Like any parrot, he can **mimic** the human voice. But

this is one parrot that just might know what he's talking about!

Alex seems to understand and use human words in the correct way—not just **copy** them. That makes some people feel that Alex—and the apes that use sign language—must be thinking animals.

So, Think About It

What did you decide about the animals in the beginning of this article? Well, the bird and salmon are using instinct. Their behaviors are amazing, but they stay the same, no matter what. The lion and the octopus are most likely thinking. Why? Because each is carrying out some kind of plan to solve a problem. And if things were different, they could change their plans and solve their problems in different ways.

Many people think certain animals—such as whales and dolphins, monkeys and apes, wolves and dogs, crows and jays—are especially smart. But each might be smart at some things and not at others. It all depends on the lives they lead.

More and more scientists are coming up with new ways to study animal brain power. They often disagree. But many are sure that we humans aren't the only thinkers. And that leaves us with plenty to think about! ●

Strategy Follow-up

Work alone or with a partner, and on a separate sheet of paper, complete an outline for the sections of this article called "Tool Time," "Getting Along," and "Animal Talk." When you are finished, compare your outline with those of other students. Do your outlines contain similar information? Why or why not? Revise your outline if necessary.

✓Personal Checklist

Read each question and put a check (✓) in the correct box.

1. How well do you understand the information presented in this article?
    - ☐ 3 (extremely well)
    - ☐ 2 (fairly well)
    - ☐ 1 (not well)

2. In Building Background, how well did you predict what the article would say about how animals think?
    - ☐ 3 (extremely well)
    - ☐ 2 (fairly well)
    - ☐ 1 (not well)

3. In the Vocabulary Builder, how well were you able to list synonym pairs on the clipboards?
    - ☐ 3 (extremely well)
    - ☐ 2 (fairly well)
    - ☐ 1 (not well)

4. How well were you able to complete the outline in the Strategy Follow-up?
    - ☐ 3 (extremely well)
    - ☐ 2 (fairly well)
    - ☐ 1 (not well)

5. After reading this article, how well do you think you could explain the difference between animals that use instinct and animals that really think?
    - ☐ 3 (extremely well)
    - ☐ 2 (fairly well)
    - ☐ 1 (not well)

Vocabulary Check

Look back at the work you did in the Vocabulary Builder. Then answer each question by circling the correct letter.

1. Alex the parrot can mimic the human voice. Which vocabulary word is a synonym of *mimic*?
    a. copy
    b. talk
    c. communicate

2. According to the article, many animals do things out of instinct. Which vocabulary word describes an instinct?
    a. talk
    b. group
    c. pattern

3. If you could add another pair of words to the clipboards in the Vocabulary Check, which pair would you add?
    a. *same* and *different*
    b. *hammers* and *nails*
    c. *twigs* and *sticks*

4. Which of the following is *not* a form of communication?
    a. a bird's song
    b. a human's sneeze
    c. a bee's dance

5. Which vocabulary word best describes animals that live together in a group?
    a. colony
    b. pattern
    c. complicated

Add the numbers that you just checked to get your Personal Checklist score. Fill in your score here. Then turn to page 217 and transfer your score onto Graph 1.

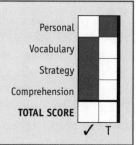

Check your answers with your teacher. Give yourself 1 point for each correct answer, and fill in your Vocabulary score here. Then turn to page 217 and transfer your score onto Graph 1.

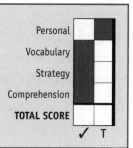

Strategy Check

Review the outline that you completed in the Strategy Follow-up. Then answer these questions:

1. Which of these sentences would be a main idea in the section called "Tool Time"?
   a. People eat with forks and knives.
   b. Some animals besides humans use tools.
   c. One chimp might notice some nuts.

2. Which of these sentences would *not* be a supporting detail under the main idea "Some animals live in groups"?
   a. Ants live in colonies made up of many, many ants.
   b. Wolves live and work in groups too.
   c. Wolves can make plans and change their behavior.

3. Which of these sentences would be a main idea in the section called "Animal Talk"?
   a. Many animals communicate with sounds, odors, colors, and "body language."
   b. Birds sing songs that say "This is *my* place!"
   c. Like any parrot, Alex can mimic the human voice.

4. Which of these sentences would be a supporting detail under the section called "Animal Talk"?
   a. Honey bees do a dance that "tells" other bees where to find food.
   b. Birds sing songs that say "This is *my* place!"
   c. Both of the above sentences would be supporting details.

5. Why do some scientists think that apes can think?
   a. Scientists have been able to teach them sign language.
   b. Apes can make up their own sentences in sign language.
   c. Like parrots, they can mimic the human voice.

Comprehension Check

Review the article if necessary. Then answer these questions:

1. In what way are some animals like robots?
   a. They have mechanical parts.
   b. They do what they do automatically.
   c. They mimic other animals' voices.

2. What have scientists learned from studying the size of animals' brains?
   a. The animals with the smallest brains are always the smartest.
   b. The animals with the largest brains are always the smartest.
   c. The animals with the largest brains are not always the smartest.

3. Which of these statements is true?
   a. A dog is thinking when it learns to "shake hands" for a treat.
   b. A sheepdog is thinking when it "outsmarts" a sheep.
   c. A beaver is thinking when it dams a stream with sticks and mud.

4. What is one behavior that scientists watch for as a clue that an animal is thinking?
   a. how the animal communicates
   a. what the animal looks like
   c. how well the animal dances

5. Which sentence best summarizes the conclusion, or ending, of this article?
   a. Scientists agree that all animals think like humans.
   b. Scientists agree that only humans can think.
   c. Many scientists agree that some animals can think.

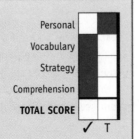

Check your answers with your teacher. Give yourself 1 point for each correct answer, and fill in your Strategy score here. Then turn to page 217 and transfer your score onto Graph 1.

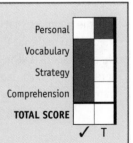

Check your answers with your teacher. Give yourself 1 point for each correct answer, and fill in your Comprehension score here. Then turn to page 217 and transfer your score onto Graph 1.

Extending

Choose one or more of these activities:

OBSERVE ANIMAL COMMUNICATION

Find a place where you can observe animals communicating, such as a park or a zoo. Observe as many animals as possible, and notice what they do. If you can, make a video or an audiotape of the animals. Do they communicate by using sounds, odors, "body language," or a combination? Take notes on what you observe, and share them with the class. Also share your tape if you made one.

DO MORE RESEARCH ON ANIMAL INTELLIGENCE

Using the resources listed on this page and ones you locate yourself, find out more about if and how animals think. If you take the poll described in the next activity, you might share some of your findings with the people you are polling in order to help them form their opinions. If you don't take the poll, you might share your findings in an oral or written report, or during a debate or a panel discussion.

TAKE A POLL

What if scientists could prove that certain animals think? Should humans stop eating meat? Should they stop using animal products in things such as clothing and cosmetics? Or should we increase our research into animal intelligence to determine which animals, if any, are smart enough to deserve special treatment? Interview a dozen or more classmates to discover their views on these questions. Create a poster to report your findings. Include charts, if possible, to indicate the most popular ideas.

Resources

Books

Facklam, Margery. *What Does the Crow Know? The Mysteries of Animal Intelligence.* Sierra Club Books for Children, 1994.

Freedman, Russell, and James E. Morriss. *How Animals Learn.* Holiday House, 1969.

Pascoe, Elaine. *Animal Intelligence: Why Is This Dolphin Smiling?* Blackbirch Press, 1998.

Patent, Dorothy Hinshaw. *How Smart Are Animals?* Harcourt, 1990.

Web Site

http://www.pbs.org/wnet/nature/animalmind/resources.html This Web site provides various features and links related to the animal mind.

Videos

Instinct and Learning. New Dimension Media, 1996.

The Private Lives of Dolphins. Nova. WBBH Boston Video, 1997.

Talking with the Animals. Time-Life Video, 1997.

Concha

Building Background

In "Concha," Mary Helen Ponce describes the games and other pastimes that she enjoyed when she was a child. What games or activities did you enjoy when you were a child? List details about them on the chart below. Then get together with a group of classmates, and discuss what you wrote. How do everyone's activities compare?

Game or Activity	When Played	Where Played	Number of Players	Why it Was Fun

avispas

donde habia hormigas

lodo

los pirules

mangera

para divertirnos

ya vamonos

Vocabulary Builder

1. The words and phrases in the margin are in Spanish. They are in italics because they are not part of the English language. If you don't speak Spanish, you can figure out the words by using context. **Context** is the information surrounding a word or phrase that helps you understand its meaning.

2. The following sentences are from "Concha." Underline the context clues that help you understand each italicized word or phrase.

3. Save your work. You will refer to it again in the Vocabulary Check.

   a. There were no set rules on how to get rid of *avispas*. We hit out at them, and tried to scare them off but the yellow jackets were fierce!

   b. We always knew where ants could be found, *donde habia hormigas*.

   c. The best remedy for insect bites was *lodo*. We applied mud to all bug stings to stop the swelling.

   d. We then collected berries from *los pirules*, the pepper trees that lined our driveway.

e. "Come on you guys, let's get her to the *mangera*," Beto cried. . . . "Come on, let's take her to the faucet."

f. My younger brother Joey and I were left alone to find ways *para divertirnos*, to keep ourselves busy.

g. "Let's go," interrupted Beto in his soft voice. "*Ya vamonos.*"

Strategy Builder

How to Read an Autobiographical Sketch

*   An **autobiography** is the story of a real person's life, written by that person. An **autobiographical sketch** is the story of a brief part of a real person's life.

*   An autobiographical sketch is always written in the **first-person point of view**. That means that the narrator tells his or her own story using the words *I, me, my,* and *mine*.

*   Most often, an autobiographical sketch follows the organizational pattern of sequence as the author recalls a series of events in chronological, or time, order. Sometimes, however, an autobiographical sketch follows the pattern of **description**. In such a case, an author describes a person, a thing, or an idea rather than a series of events. In "Concha," for example, the author describes her favorite childhood games and a girl named Concha.

*   To keep track of the details in a description, you can use a **concept map**. The example below shows the details that one author used to describe his childhood neighborhood.

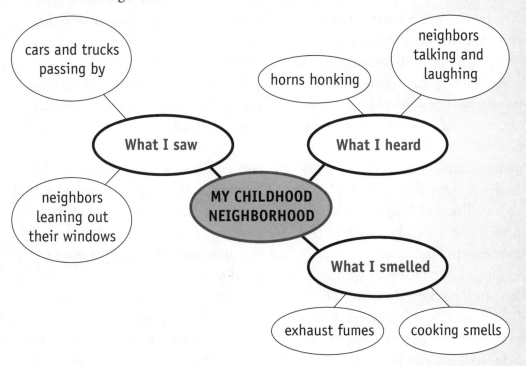

Concha

by Mary Helen Ponce

The author of this autobiographical sketch has many memories of days spent with her childhood friends. As you begin this selection, apply the strategies you just learned. Pay attention to the different games and pastimes the author describes and the details she includes about each one.

While growing up in the small barrio of Pacoima my younger brother Joey and I were left alone to find ways *para divertirnos*, to keep ourselves busy—and out of our mother's way. One way in which we whiled away long summer days was by making peashooters. These were made from a hollow reed which we first cleaned with a piece of wire. We then collected berries from *los pirules*, the pepper trees that lined our driveway. Once we amassed enough dry berries we put them in our mouths and spat them out at each other through the pea shooter.

The berries had a terrible taste—they were even said to be poison! I was most careful not to swallow them. We selected only the hard, firm peas. The soft ones, we knew, would get mushy, crumble in our mouths and force us to gag—and lose a fight. During an important battle a short pause could spell defeat. Oftentimes while playing with Joey I watched closely. When he appeared to gag I dashed back to the pepper tree to load up on ammunition. I pelted him without mercy until he begged me to stop.

"No more. *Ya no*," Joey cried as he bent over to spit berries. "No more!"

"Ha, ha I got you now." I spat berries at Joey until, exhausted, we called a truce and slumped onto a wooden bench.

In fall our game came to a halt—the trees dried up; the berries fell to the ground. This was a sign for us to begin other games.

Our games were seasonal. During early spring we made whistles from the long blades of grass that grew in the open field behind our house. In winter we made dams, forts and canals from the soft mud that was our street. We tied burnt matchsticks together with string. These were our men. We positioned them along the forts (camouflaged with small branches). We also played kick the can, but our most challenging game was playing with red ants.

The ants were of the common variety: red, round and treacherous. They invaded our yard and the *llano* every summer. We always knew where ants could be found, *donde habia hormigas*. We liked to build mud and grass forts smack in the middle of ant territory. The ants were the enemy, the matchstickmen the heroes, or good guys.

Playing with ants was a real challenge! While placing our men in battle positions we timed it so as not to get bitten. We delighted in beating the ants at their own game.

Sometimes we got really brave and picked up ants with a stick, then twirled the stick around until the ants got dizzy-drunk (or so we thought)—and fell to the ground. We made ridges of dirt and pushed the ants inside, covered them with dirt and made bets as to how long it would take them to dig their way out.

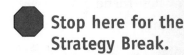 **Stop here for the Strategy Break.**

Strategy Break

If you were to make a concept map of details that describe the author's childhood games and pastimes, your map might look like this:

As you continue reading, pay attention to the details that the author uses to describe Concha. At the end of this selection, you will you will use some of those details to create a concept map about her.

Go on reading.

Concha, my best friend and neighbor, was quite timid at school. She avoided all rough games such as kickball and Red Rover. When it came to playing with ants, however, Concha held first place for bravery. She could stand with her feet atop an anthill for the longest time! We stood trembling as ants crawled up our shoes, then quickly stomped our feet to scare them off. But Concha never lost her nerve.

One time we decided to have an ant contest. The prize was a candy bar—a Sugar Daddy sucker. We first found an anthill, lined up, then took turns standing beside the anthill while the juicy red ants climbed over our shoes. We dared not move—but when the first ant moved towards our ankles we stomped away, our Oxfords making swirls of dust that allowed us to retreat to the sidelines. But not Concha. She remained in place as big red ants crept up her shoes. One, five, ten! We stood and counted, holding our breath as the ants continued to climb. Fifteen, twenty! Twenty ants were crawling over Concha!

"*Ujule*, she sure ain't scared," cried Mundo in a hushed voice. "*No le tiene miedo a las hormigas.*"

"Uhhhhh," answered Beto, his eyes wide.

". . . I mean for a girl," added Mundo as he poked Beto in the ribs. We knew Beto liked Concha—and always came to her rescue.

We stood and counted ants. We were so caught up in this feat that we failed to notice the twenty-first ant that climbed up the back of Concha's sock . . . and bit her!

"*Ay, ay, ay,*" screeched Concha.

"Gosh, she's gonna die," cried an alarmed Virgie as she helped stomp out ants. "She's gonna die!"

"She's too stupid to die," laughed Mundo, busy brushing ants off his feet. "She's too stupid."

"But sometimes people die when ants bite them," insisted Virgie, her face pale. "They gets real sick."

"The ants will probably die," Mundo snickered, holding his stomach and laughing loudly. "Ah, ha, ha."

"Gosh you're mean," said a shocked Virgie, hands on hips. "You are so mean."

"Yeah, but I ain't stupid."

"Come on you guys, let's get her to the ***mangera***," Beto cried as he reached out to Concha who by now had decided she would live. "Come on, let's take her to the faucet."

We held Concha by the waist as she hobbled to the water faucet. Her cries were now mere whimpers as no grownup had come out to investigate. From experience we knew that if a first cry did not bring someone to our aid we should stop crying—or go home.

We helped Concha to the faucet, turned it on and began to mix water with dirt. We knew the best remedy for insect bites was ***lodo***. We applied mud to all bug stings to stop the swelling. Mud was especially good for wasp stings, the yellow jackets we so feared—and from which we ran away at top speed. Whenever bees came close we stood still until they flew away, but there were no set rules on how to get rid of *avispas*. We hit out at them, and tried to scare them off but the yellow jackets were fierce! In desperation we flung dirt at them, screamed and ran home.

Not long after the ant incident Concha decided she was not about to run when a huge wasp broke up our game of jacks. She stood still, so still the wasp remained on her dark head for what seemed like hours. We stood and watched, thinking perhaps the wasp had mistaken Concha's curly hair for a bush! We watched—and waited.

"*Ujule*, she sure is brave," exclaimed Virgie as she sucked on a popsicle. "She sure is brave."

"She's stupid," grunted Mundo, trying to be indifferent. "She's just a big show-off who thinks she's so big."

"So are you," began Virgie, backing off. "So are you."

"Yeah? Ya wanna make something outta it?"

"Let's go," interrupted Beto in his soft voice. "*Ya vamonos.*" He smiled at Concha—who smiled back.

In time the wasp flew away. Concha immediately began to brag about how a "real big wasp" sat on her hair for hours. She never mentioned the ant contest—nor the twenty-first ant that led her to *el lodo*. ●

Strategy Follow-up

Now work by yourself or with a partner to complete the following concept map for Concha.
The categories have been filled in for you.

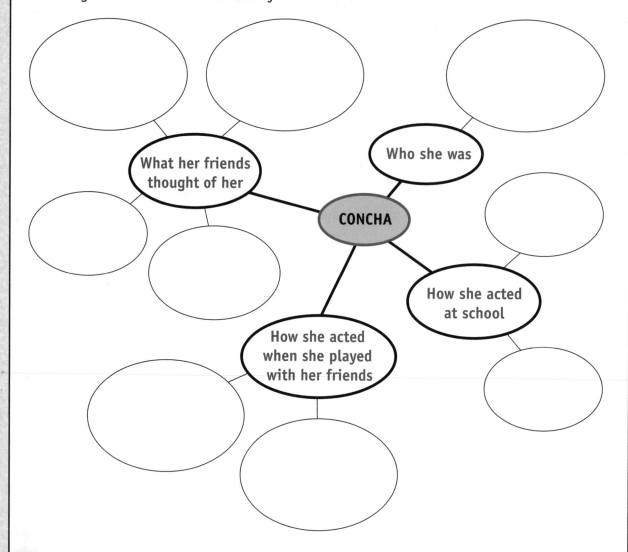

✓Personal Checklist

Read each question and put a check (✓) in the correct box.

1. In Building Background, how well were you able to complete the chart with details about your favorite childhood games and pastimes?
   - ☐ 3 (extremely well)
   - ☐ 2 (fairly well)
   - ☐ 1 (not well)

2. How well were you able to use context clues to figure out the meanings of the vocabulary words?
   - ☐ 3 (extremely well)
   - ☐ 2 (fairly well)
   - ☐ 1 (not well)

3. In the Strategy Follow-up, how well were you able to complete the concept map about Concha?
   - ☐ 3 (extremely well)
   - ☐ 2 (fairly well)
   - ☐ 1 (not well)

4. How well could you explain why some children admired Concha?
   - ☐ 3 (extremely well)
   - ☐ 2 (fairly well)
   - ☐ 1 (not well)

5. How well do you understand why Concha never mentioned the 21st ant that led her to *el lodo* (the mud)?
   - ☐ 3 (extremely well)
   - ☐ 2 (fairly well)
   - ☐ 1 (not well)

Vocabulary Check

Look back at the work you did in the Vocabulary Builder. Then answer each question by circling the correct letter.

1. Which of the following is the Spanish word for *mud*?
   a. *avispas*
   b. *pirules*
   c. *lodo*

2. When Beto suggests that they take Concha to the *mangera*, where does he want to take her?
   a. to the mud hole
   b. to the barrio
   c. to the faucet

3. Which activity might people be most likely to do *para divertirnos*?
   a. go to a funeral
   b. play cards
   c. take a science test

4. Which expression would you use if you wanted to go somewhere with your friend?
   a. *ya vamonos*
   b. *donde habia hormigas*
   c. *para divertirnos*

5. Which of these words names animals that can fly?
   a. *avispas*
   b. *hormigas*
   c. *pirules*

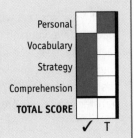

Add the numbers that you just checked to get your Personal Checklist score. Fill in your score here. Then turn to page 217 and transfer your score onto Graph 1.

Personal
Vocabulary
Strategy
Comprehension
TOTAL SCORE
✓ T

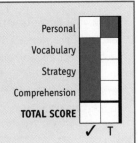

Check your answers with your teacher. Give yourself 1 point for each correct answer, and fill in your Vocabulary score here. Then turn to page 217 and transfer your score onto Graph 1.

Personal
Vocabulary
Strategy
Comprehension
TOTAL SCORE
✓ T

Strategy Check

Review the concept map that you completed in the Strategy Follow-up. Also review the selection if necessary. Then answer these questions:

1. What relationship did the author have to Concha?
   a. Concha was the author's distant cousin.
   b. Concha was the author's best friend and neighbor.
   c. Concha was the author's younger sister.

2. How did Concha act when she was at school?
   a. She was brave and played rough games.
   b. She was very outgoing and talkative.
   c. She was timid and avoided rough games.

3. How did Concha act when she was playing with her friends?
   a. She was timid and avoided rough games.
   b. She was brave, especially when playing with ants.
   c. She always lost her nerve when playing games.

4. Why do you think Mundo said Concha was stupid and a big show-off?
   a. He probably was jealous of Concha's bravery.
   b. He didn't like Concha and wanted her to leave.
   c. He probably was trying to become better friends.

5. Which sentence illustrates how Concha acted when the wasp landed on her head?
   a. "*Ujule*, she sure is brave."
   b. "*Ay, ay, ay*" screeched Concha.
   c. Her cries were now mere whimpers.

Comprehension Check

Review the selection if necessary. Then answer these questions:

1. From what did the children make peashooters?
   a. branches from pepper trees
   b. plastic straws from the cafeteria
   c. hollow reeds cleaned with wire

2. Why were the children careful not to swallow pepper berries?
   a. They had a terrible taste.
   b. They were said to be poisonous.
   c. Both of the above are correct.

3. What does the narrator say was the children's most challenging game?
   a. kick the can
   b. playing with red ants
   c. making forts and dams in the mud

4. Why did Concha finally cry out on the day of the ant contest?
   a. One ant gave her a painful bite.
   b. She was tired of people watching her.
   c. She was tired of Mundo teasing her.

5. How did Concha show that she liked Beto?
   a. She cried harder when he tried to help her.
   b. She smiled back at him when he was leaving.
   c. She let the ant bite her instead of Beto.

Check your answers with your teacher. Give yourself 1 point for each correct answer, and fill in your Strategy score here. Then turn to page 217 and transfer your score onto Graph 1.

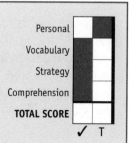

Check your answers with your teacher. Give yourself 1 point for each correct answer, and fill in your Comprehension score here. Then turn to page 217 and transfer your score onto Graph 1.

Extending

Choose one or more of these activities:

CONDUCT A SURVEY

Work with a small group, and ask people of all ages which games they remember playing as children. See if certain games are mentioned by people of every age level. Notice if certain games come up only in particular age groups. After you have finished your survey, create a graph or chart to show the results. Discuss it with the rest of the class.

CREATE A "CHILDHOOD MEMORIES" BULLETIN BOARD

Work together with other students to make a bulletin-board display depicting your own childhood pastimes. Include photos or drawn pictures of yourselves as children, involved in pastimes that you remember as enjoyable. If you conducted the survey described in the activity above, you might include that in your display also. After you are finished, everyone should explain how to play the games that their pictures show.

READ PONCE'S ENTIRE AUTOBIOGRAPHY

"Concha" is an excerpt from Mary Helen Ponce's book *Hoyt Street: An Autobiography*. Use the information in the resources to locate the book, and read it by yourself or with a few classmates. When you have finished, discuss the book. Which episodes did you enjoy reading about most? In what ways is Ponce's life story similar to and different from your own?

Resources

Books

Ponce, Mary Helen. *Hoyt Street: An Autobiography.* University of New Mexico Press, 1993.

Santiago, Esmeralda, and Joie Davidow, eds. *Las Christmas: Favorite Latino Authors Share Their Holiday Memories.* Vintage, 1999.

Web Site

http://www.amazon.com/exec/obidos/show-interview/ p-m-oncearyhelen/103-3526601-8315028
On this Web page, read an interview of Mary Helen Ponce where she discusses how she started writing in grammar school.

LESSON 5 *from* Taking Sides

We all would like to be happy and contented all of the time. However, no one's life is perfect. No one escapes the bad times—the times when we are sad, worried, nervous, or upset. Although we all experience the same uncomfortable feelings, each one of us reacts to them a little differently.

Think about the most important people in your life, for example, your family members and your friends. Picture how each one deals with strong negative emotions. Then complete the chart below. In the first column, record the names of the three people you know best. Then write a phrase or a sentence to describe how each one deals with sorrow, nervousness, and anger.

Showing Emotions			
Person	Sorrow	Nervousness	Anger
1.			
2.			
3.			

chuckled

hobbled

mouthed off

muttered

shivered

shuffled

thumped

wolfed down

Vocabulary Builder

1. As you recall from Lesson 3, **synonyms** are words with the same or similar meanings. Knowing a word's synonym can help you learn and remember the word.

2. Each boldfaced word or phrase below describes an action. One of the words or phrases that follows it is a synonym of the action. Underline that synonym.

3. If you don't know any of the words or phrases, find them in the selection and use context to figure them out. If using context doesn't help, look them up in a dictionary.

chuckled	laughed quietly	sobbed
hobbled	leaped	limped
mouthed off	spoke sarcastically	said respectfully
muttered	mumbled	shouted

shivered	stood steady	shook
shuffled	dragged one's feet	skipped very quickly
thumped	praised	pounded
wolfed down	nibbled slowly	ate quickly

4. Save your work. You will use it again in the Vocabulary Check.

Strategy Builder

Drawing Conclusions About Characters

- A **conclusion** is a decision that you reach after thinking about certain facts or information. When you read a story, you often draw conclusions based on information that the author gives you about the characters, the setting, or particular events.

- You can draw conclusions about the **characters** in a story by paying attention to their words, thoughts, feelings, and actions. These **clues** help you understand the characters better. They also help you understand why the characters do what they do.

- Read the following paragraph about a character named Gina. Then look at the **character map** below the paragraph. It shows the conclusions that one student drew about Gina, and why.

Gina woke up early this morning, even before the alarm rang. She smiled when she saw the sunlight streaming through her window and immediately hopped out of bed. She dressed in shorts and a T-shirt and then ate a quick breakfast. After putting her swimsuit, her suntan lotion, and a towel into a colorful bag, she said goodbye to her mother. Then she waited on the front porch, looking up the street excitedly.

CLUE:
Gina wakes up before her alarm even rings and hops out of bed quickly.
Conclusion:
She is excited about what is going to happen that day.

CLUE:
She smiles when she sees sunshine, and she dresses in shorts and a T-shirt.
Conclusion:
She's planning to do something casual outdoors.

CHARACTER: Gina

CLUE:
She packs a swimsuit, suntan lotion, and a towel.
Conclusion:
She'll probably spend the day at the beach or a pool.

CLUE:
She waits on the front porch and looks up the street.
Conclusion:
She is looking for the person who will be going with her to the beach or pool.

from Taking Sides

by Gary Soto

As you read this chapter from the book *Taking Sides,* apply the strategies that you just learned. Look for clues that the author provides to help you draw conclusions about Lincoln.

Many changes have taken place in Lincoln's life lately. Lincoln is doing his best to hold himself together, but will he be successful?

Lincoln woke to Flaco scratching the front door. His mother was in the bathroom using the hair dryer.

"Mom," Lincoln hollered sleepily. "Flaco wants in."

Flaco scratched and whined as the hair dryer wailed. Lincoln thought he heard eggs clacking in a pot of boiling water.

He lay in bed, eyes closed. It was Friday. There would be no basketball practice today. He wiggled his toe. It still hurt. His wrist was tender, and his shoulder pained him. He yawned and rolled onto his side.

As he lay in bed he thought of the gym at his old school; three banners from the championship years 1967, 1970, and 1977 hung near the rafters, faded and dusty with neglect. Those years were before his time, before anyone's time. It seemed so long ago.

He thought about Monica. Was she getting up from bed? Was she combing her hair in front of the bathroom mirror? Was she at the breakfast table, dabbing a piece of tortilla into yellow egg yolks? He wondered if she spoke in Spanish or English to her parents. Lately, he and his mother had started using English, even at home. Lincoln's Spanish was getting worse and worse.

When he heard his mother call, he rolled onto his stomach and pushed himself up quickly, letting his blankets slip onto the floor. He **shivered** and said, *"Ay, hace mucho frio,"* and pulled on a sweater, backward, over his pajama top. He felt the label tickle his chin, but he didn't bother to fix it.

He **shuffled** to the kitchen, where his mom, pink from showering, was putting bread into the toaster. He was right: soft-boiled eggs and toast with a smear of jam.

"I'm gonna let Flaco in," he said as he passed her and went into the living room.

Flaco's nose was pressed to the window, and when he saw Lincoln he barked loudly.

"Ya, perrito," Lincoln called, hurrying over the cold floor.

Flaco nudged his body through the door and, without even glancing up at Lincoln, **hobbled** to his bowl.

At the breakfast table, his mother said that Roy, her boyfriend, would be coming over that night. The three of them might go out for dinner.

"Do I have to?" Lincoln asked. He didn't like Roy, who was shorter than his mother. He drove a baby-blue BMW—a girl's color, Lincoln thought—and was, like Mr. Schulman, pudgy and pale. Lincoln figured he couldn't run around the block without stopping to pinch the pain in his side. Some man.

"It'd be nice," his mother said. "He likes you."

Lincoln chewed his toast but didn't say anything. For a second he thought of his father, but when he couldn't picture what he looked like he thought of the creaking rafters of his old gym—those three banners, limp and faded and nearly forgotten.

Without thinking, Lincoln asked, "What's Dad doing? We never hear from him."

His mother chewed slowly and, after clearing her throat, said, "He's still in Los Angeles. He's still a parole board officer."

"What's that?"

"You know. He works for the police department. He checks up on criminals when they get out of prison. It's a hard job."

"Do I look like him?"

His mother smiled and touched his hair. "You're just like him. Strong."

Lincoln didn't want to think about his father, and he didn't want to think about Roy. He cracked open his geography book, and once again it fell open to the page of the camel driver with the broken teeth and lined face. It was a hard life for him, too, and for everybody who worked under the sun.

"I have to hurry," Lincoln said, taking his plate to the sink.

"Then you'll come with us?" she asked.

"We might have late practice," he lied. There never was practice on Friday. Coach Yesutis belonged to a bowling league, and Friday was their night to play.

He could feel his mother staring at him as he walked to his bedroom. He dressed quickly, combed his hair and brushed his teeth, and was out the door before his mother could kiss him. He barely heard her say, "Have fun at school."

Lincoln caught up with James, and since they were early they stopped at the 7-Eleven for an apple pie, which they tore in half and **wolfed down**. They licked their fingers, and James said, "Man, that was good."

They walked in silence. Then Lincoln asked, "What does your dad do?"

"He's a surveyor."

"A surveyor?" Lincoln asked, surprised. He had expected to hear "a doctor" or "a lawyer." Everyone in Sycamore seemed to have a fancy job.

"Yeah, that's his racket. He's one of those guys you see standing in an orange vest by the freeway." James picked up a rock and hurled it at a sparrow on a telephone wire. "Mom's the one who makes the big bucks. She has an import store in Burlingame. Some of the stuff is from Mexico."

Lincoln kicked a pile of leaves and tried to remember if he had seen her store. His uncle Raymond lived in Burlingame, and Lincoln had spent a week there after his father and mother had gotten their divorce.

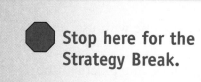

Stop here for the Strategy Break.

Strategy Break

If you were to create a character map for Lincoln based on what you have learned about him so far, it might look like this:

CLUE:
Lincoln wakes up thinking about basketball; his toe, wrist, and shoulder are sore from playing hard.

Conclusion:
He is an enthusiastic basketball player.

CLUE:
He calls to his mother to let the dog in and then rolls over; he stays in bed as long as possible.

Conclusion:
He doesn't like to get out of bed in the morning.

CHARACTER: Lincoln

CLUE:
He doesn't like Roy, and right after his mom mentions Roy, Lincoln talks about his father.

Conclusion:
He wishes his mother and father didn't get divorced.

CLUE:
Lincoln tells her he might have late practice, and he leaves before she can kiss him goodbye.

Conclusion:
He seems upset with his mother.

As you continue reading, keep looking for clues that the author gives about Lincoln and the other characters. At the end of this selection, you will create a character map of your own.

**Go on reading to see
what happens.**

They got to school a few minutes
before the tardy bell rang. Mr.
Kimball, his hair messy from a wind
that was hauling in dark storm clouds,
was waiting with his tardy slips.

"Not today, Mr. Kimball," James
mouthed off.

"But I'll get you," Mr. Kimball
answered back. He **chuckled** under
his breath.

Lincoln and James smiled as they
hurried past him to first period.
Lincoln couldn't concentrate on
algebra. Basketball was on his mind.
He closed his eyes and faces flashed
before him—his ex-girlfriend, Vicky;
Monica Torres; Roy in his baby-blue
BMW; his mother; Coach Yesutis
yelling on the sidelines. An image of
Vicky, snapping a mouthful of Juicy
Fruit gum, asked with a sneer, "What
side ya on?"

"Mendoza, answer this problem,"
Mr. Green called out, and Vicky's
image burst like a soap bubble. He
was pointing to a problem on the
board.

Lincoln looked up, startled. "Ah,
well, it's—ah, let me see, it's—
whatever you say."

A few students turned to look at
him. Durkins, the forward on the
second-string team, grinned at him.
He wouldn't have known the answer
either.

Mr. Green wet his lips and, behind
the glint of thick glasses, stared at
him, hard. Lincoln, feeling like an
idiot, looked down at his hands
folded on his desk, which was scarred
with the initials "C.O." Lincoln
traced his fingers over the letters, sorry
that he couldn't answer Mr. Green.

Rain was coming down hard by the
time the bell rang and algebra class let
out. Lincoln shouldered his backpack.
As he passed the teacher he **muttered**,
"I'm sorry." Mr. Green, shuffling a
batch of papers, said, "Your grades are
slipping. What's wrong?"

"Nothin'."

"Are you sure?"

"I'll try harder," Lincoln said, and
turned away. Then he turned back to
say, "This school's different," and left
without explaining what he meant.

In spite of his hurt toe, he ran to
his history class, where he learned that
chickens came to Egypt from India.

Man, that was a long walk, Lincoln
thought. He smiled as he pictured
hordes of white-throated chickens
clucking over sand dunes and taking
boats up the Nile to Alexandria.

"Were they chickens like today's
chickens?" Andy, the A-plus-in-
everything-but-P.E. student, asked.
His pen was poised and ready for
Mrs. Wade, the teacher, to answer.

"No one knows," she replied.

That's a good answer, Lincoln
thought. It seems like we can't
remember last week. How are we
gonna remember way back then?

By lunch period, the rain had
stopped and a slice of blue showed
above the school. Lincoln ate his
lunch standing under a tree. He bit
three times into a bruised apple and

pitched it into the trash can—two points, he thought—then went looking for Monica Torres. He wanted to see her, to talk with her. His heart **thumped** like a basketball bouncing down stairs.

"What am I gonna say to her?" he muttered to himself. He looked in the cafeteria, but she wasn't there amid the din of forks dropping and students laughing and yelling. He walked between the lockers. He went into the gym, where three girls were huddled together talking. But she wasn't there. Finally, he found her in the library, writing in what he figured was her journal for English.

He walked up to her and said, "Hi."

"Oh, hello, Lincoln," she replied. "Where's James?"

"I don't know," he answered, pulling out a chair and sitting down. The librarian looked his way, and he gave her a nod. "Eating lunch, I guess." He peeked at her journal and asked, "Whatta you writin'?"

She closed her journal and after a moment of silence said, "Oh, just about last night."

"What happened last night?"

She turned over an eraser between her fingers and said she had had an argument with her father. "I told my dad that I wanted to quit aikido, but he got mad and said I was spoiled. He said that when he was a kid he worked in the fields—" She stopped suddenly.

"Yeah, I know the rap. My mom did her share of field work in the

Valley." He took the eraser away from her and squeezed it until his knuckles turned bone white. "Yeah, every Christmas when we go down to Fresno—that's where *mi familia* is— they talk about cardboard in their shoes. Blisters. Lawn-mowing jobs. It's boring."

"My dad's from Salinas. He used to cut broccoli and artichokes. I don't like broccoli, do you?"

"It's all right. Brussels sprouts are my problem."

"Brussels sprouts," Monica mused. "That's another one I can't stand."

Lincoln looked up at the clock on the wall. It was five minutes to one. I had better make my move, he thought to himself. His heart did it again.

"Monica, I was wondering, uh," Lincoln began, biting his lip. "I was thinking maybe we can . . . I don't know, maybe shoot some hoop this Saturday?"

"Saturday? I can't," she answered, smiling and stuffing her binder into her backpack. "I'm going somewhere."

The basketball in his heart went flat.

Then she added, "But how about Sunday? Late afternoon, maybe three o'clock?"

The basketball filled with air and went bumping down the stairs, out of control.

"Yeah!" he cried. "Sounds fine! Where?"

The librarian looked at him and pursed her lips.

Monica, slinging her backpack onto her shoulder, said, "Cornell

Elementary. That's where I slam and dunk."

"'Slam and dunk'—I like that." Lincoln couldn't believe his good fortune. She talks like a guy, but she's so cute, he thought.

Lincoln walked to class in a daze. After school he hurried home, nearly running in spite of his hurt toe and the weight of weekend homework on his shoulders. Not to mention worry about Roy. ●

Strategy Follow-up

Concentrate on what you learned about Lincoln in the second part of this selection, and complete the character map below. The clues have been provided for you. Use them to draw your own conclusions.

CLUE:
Lincoln can't concentrate on his schoolwork.
Conclusion:

CLUE:
He pictures clucking chickens walking over sand dunes and taking boats up the Nile.
Conclusion:

CHARACTER: Lincoln

CLUE:
His heart thumps when he looks for Monica Torres at lunch.
Conclusion:

CLUE:
He nearly runs home after setting up a basketball date with Monica.

Conclusion:

✓Personal Checklist

Read each question and put a check (✓) in the correct box.

1. In Building Background, how well were you able to use what you wrote on the chart to help you understand Lincoln's feelings in this selection?
   - ☐ 3 (extremely well)
   - ☐ 2 (fairly well)
   - ☐ 1 (not well)

2. How many synonyms did you correctly identify in the Vocabulary Builder?
   - ☐ 3 (6–8 synonyms)
   - ☐ 2 (3–5 synonyms)
   - ☐ 1 (0–2 synonyms)

3. How well were you able to complete the character map in the Strategy Follow-up?
   - ☐ 3 (extremely well)
   - ☐ 2 (fairly well)
   - ☐ 1 (not well)

4. How well do you think you could describe Lincoln based on the clues that the author provides?
   - ☐ 3 (extremely well)
   - ☐ 2 (fairly well)
   - ☐ 1 (not well)

5. How well do you understand why Lincoln can't concentrate on his schoolwork?
   - ☐ 3 (extremely well)
   - ☐ 2 (fairly well)
   - ☐ 1 (not well)

Vocabulary Check

Look back at the work you did in the Vocabulary Builder. Then answer each question by circling the correct letter.

1. What would cause a person to shiver?
   - a. sitting on the beach on a very hot day
   - b. wearing a thin coat on a very cold day
   - c. sitting near a toasty fireplace

2. What usually happens to children who mouth off to their parents?
   - a. Their parents scold or punish them.
   - b. Their parents laugh at them.
   - c. Their parents try to imitate them.

3. If you saw someone hobbling, what would he or she be doing?
   - a. running
   - b. limping
   - c. skipping

4. Which word or phrase is a synonym of *ate very quickly*?
   - a. mouthed off
   - b. thumped
   - c. wolfed down

5. Which of these people is a good example of someone who shuffles?
   - a. a person in a hurry to get somewhere
   - b. an athlete who is training for a race
   - c. a child walking in shoes that are too large

Add the numbers that you just checked to get your Personal Checklist score. Fill in your score here. Then turn to page 217 and transfer your score onto Graph 1.

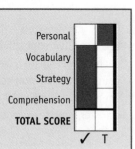

Check your answers with your teacher. Give yourself 1 point for each correct answer, and fill in your Vocabulary score here. Then turn to page 217 and transfer your score onto Graph 1.

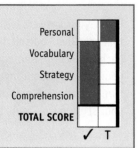

Strategy Check

Review the character map that you completed in the Strategy Follow-up. Also review the selection if necessary. Then answer the following questions:

1. Why do you think Lincoln can't concentrate on his schoolwork?

   a. He doesn't understand the assignments.

   b. He has many other things on his mind.

   c. He is in pain from his basketball injuries.

2. Lincoln pictures clucking chickens walking over sand dunes and taking boats up the Nile. What does this clue help you conclude about him?

   a. In spite of everything, he still has a sense of humor.

   b. He wishes he could travel up the Nile.

   c. His pain medication is making him hallucinate.

3. Why does Lincoln's heart thump as he looks for Monica at lunch?

   a. He has a heart ailment.

   b. He is nervous about seeing her.

   c. He was doing strenuous exercises.

4. Lincoln feels like running home after Monica says she will play basketball with him. What does this clue help you conclude?

   a. He doesn't like Monica and is trying to get away from her.

   b. He is late for dinner.

   c. He is extremely happy.

5. Taking all the clues about Lincoln into consideration, which conclusion about him would you say is most accurate?

   a. Lincoln is unhappy right now.

   b. Lincoln is comfortable right now.

   c. Lincoln is spoiled and doesn't care about others.

Comprehension Check

Review the selection if necessary. Then answer these questions:

1. How does Lincoln feel about his mother's boyfriend?

   a. He doesn't like Roy very much.

   b. He is glad his mother is seeing Roy.

   c. He thinks Roy is mean.

2. What does Lincoln's father do for a living?

   a. He is a surveyor.

   b. He runs an import store.

   c. He is a parole board officer.

3. How do you know that Lincoln used to be a better student?

   a. He is able to picture chickens walking to Alexandria.

   b. His teacher tells him that his grades are slipping.

   c. He is tardy for school fairly often.

4. For whom does Lincoln look after lunch?

   a. his friend James

   b. Monica Torres

   c. his ex-girlfriend, Vicky

5. How do you think Monica feels about Lincoln?

   a. She dislikes him but is willing to play basketball with him.

   b. She thinks he is a fairly decent basketball player.

   c. She is interested in getting to know him better.

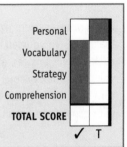

Check your answers with your teacher. Give yourself 1 point for each correct answer, and fill in your Strategy score here. Then turn to page 217 and transfer your score onto Graph 1.

Personal / Vocabulary / Strategy / Comprehension / TOTAL SCORE ✓ T

Check your answers with your teacher. Give yourself 1 point for each correct answer, and fill in your Comprehension score here. Then turn to page 217 and transfer your score onto Graph 1.

Personal / Vocabulary / Strategy / Comprehension / TOTAL SCORE ✓ T

Extending

Choose one or more of these activities:

MAKE A STORYBOARD

When directors are working on a movie, they often make storyboards to help them picture the events in the story. On a storyboard, important scenes are depicted and arranged in time order on a large bulletin board. Decide what the important scenes in this story are. Draw sketches of the scenes, including details about the people in each scene, as well as the location. Arrange the sketches in time order on a large board. See if others can tell what is happening in each scene.

WRITE A MINI-PLAY

Alone or with one other student, transform this chapter from *Taking Sides* into a play. Write lines for a narrator who will explain what Lincoln is thinking and feeling. The narrator's lines can come straight from the story. Also write lines in play form for the various characters, as in this example:

Lincoln: (*hollering sleepily*) Mom! Flaco wants in.

Take the characters' lines directly from the story too. Then, if possible, ask some friends to help you perform your play. Practice it a few times, and then present it to the rest of the class.

READ OTHER WORKS BY GARY SOTO

Choose one of the books by Gary Soto that is listed on this page, and report on it to the class. You can give your report orally or in writing. If you'd like, read aloud or mention some of your favorite passages, and explain why they appeal to you.

Resources

Books

Soto, Gary. *Baseball in April and Other Stories.* Harcourt, 2000.

———. *Local News.* Harcourt, 2003.

———. *Neighborhood Odes.* Harcourt, 1992.

———. *Pacific Crossing.* Harcourt, 2003.

———. *Petty Crimes.* Harcourt, 1998.

———. *Taking Sides.* Harcourt, 2003.

Web Site

http://www.garysoto.com
This is Gary Soto's official Web site.

Learning New Words

Synonyms

A synonym is a word that means the same thing—or close to the same thing—as another word. For example, the author of "Do Animals Think?" uses the words *mimic* and *copy* to describe what Alex the parrot can do: He can mimic, or copy, the human voice.

Draw a line from each word in Column 1 to its synonym in Column 2.

COLUMN 1	COLUMN 2
excited	ponder
think	shop
remember	thrilled
store	rest
relax	recall

Antonyms

An antonym is a word that means the opposite of another word. For example, in "Alex, the Talking Parrot," you read that Alex learned to identify which objects are bigger and smaller or the same and different. The words *bigger* and *smaller* are antonyms, or opposites. So are the words *same* and *different.*

Draw a line from each word in Column 1 to its antonym in Column 2.

COLUMN 1	COLUMN 2
whisper	darkness
filthy	spotless
daylight	rivals
laughter	holler
teammates	tears

Multiple-Meaning Words

As you know, a single word can have more than one meaning. For example, the word *pattern* can mean "design" or "model for something to be made" or "instinct." To figure out which meaning of *pattern* an author is using, you have to use context—the information surrounding a word or situation that helps you understand it.

When you read "Do Animals Think" you used context to figure out that the meaning of *pattern* that the author was using was "instinct."

Now use context to figure out the correct meaning of each underlined word. Circle the letter of the correct meaning.

1. Fashion magazines are always a good <u>barometer</u> of the most current clothing trends.

    a. something that indicates changes

    b. tool for measuring air pressure

2. Since children <u>communicate</u> chicken pox very easily, it's a good idea to have them vaccinated against the disease.

    a. exchange spoken or written information

    b. transfer or pass along

3. The reporter needed to gather <u>hard</u> facts in order to write an accurate account of the crime.

    a. solid and firm to the touch

    b. true and meaningful

4. A <u>colony</u> of popular artists just bought the most expensive building in the city.

    a. people with the same occupation, who live as a group

    b. organisms of the same species, living or growing together

5. Maria <u>thumped</u> the honeydew melon with her finger to see how ripe it was.

    a. struck or knocked on

    b. beat violently

VOCABULARY

From Lesson 1
- barometer

From Lesson 3
- colony
- communicate
- hard
- know
- pattern

From Lesson 5
- thumped

Faces in Sports: Jackie Joyner-Kersee

Building Background

Most of us enjoy sports. They offer us a chance to test ourselves, learn new skills, and have fun. Your favorite sport may be different from someone else's. You might like to play baseball, while your friend might enjoy tennis. No matter which sport you play, you develop particular physical and mental skills as you participate in it.

Choose two sports that you like to play or watch. On the chart below, identify the physical and mental abilities that a person needs in order to be successful in each one. When you have finished, compare your chart with those of some classmates. Which skills and abilities are listed most often?

	Physical abilities needed	Mental abilities needed
Sport #1:		
Sport #2:		

athletes

champion

commitment

energy

medalist

medals

records

strength

Vocabulary Builder

1. Words that are all related to a particular topic are called **specialized vocabulary**. The specialized vocabulary words in the margin are all related to the topic of the Olympics.

2. Use the words to fill in the word map on page 59. You will need to add your own verbs to answer the question, "What do the participants try to do?"

3. Save your work. You will refer to it again in the Vocabulary Check.

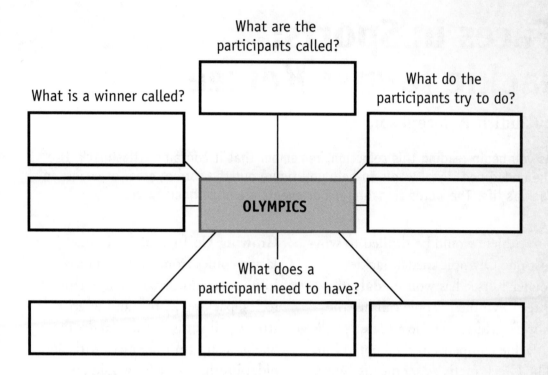

Strategy Builder

How to Read a Biography

- The selection you are about to read is a brief biography of the life of Jackie Joyner-Kersee. A **biography** is the story of a real person's life, written by someone else.

- Like all biographies, Jackie's life story is written in the **third-person point of view**. That means that the author describes Jackie and her life using the words *she, her,* and *hers.*

- The events in most biographies are organized in chronological order, or **sequence**. There are times, however, when events are told out of sequence. In such cases, the author uses a **flashback** to tell about an important event (or events) that happened earlier in a person's life. Then the author goes back and relates the events that led up to that important event.

- When you read a biography that contains a flashback, it is more important than ever to use **signal words** to help keep the sequence of events straight. Some signal words—such as *then, next,* and *a short time later*—help you link one smaller event to the next in a person's life. However, signal words such as *at age thirteen* or *in 1992* help you see the sequence of the major events.

- Even though the flashback events in this selection are told out of sequence, you still can record the major events in Jackie's life on a **time line**. The Strategy Break and Strategy Follow-up will show you how to do it.

Faces in Sports: Jackie Joyner-Kersee

by Judith P. Josephson

As you begin reading this selection, remember that it contains a flashback. Use the underlined signal words to help you figure out the correct order of events in Jackie's life. The words signaling major events are underlined twice.

Any athlete would be thrilled to win just one Olympic medal. Jackie Joyner-Kersee has won **medals** in three Olympics! People call her the world's greatest female athlete.

Jackie competes in the heptathlon. The Greek prefix *hepta* means "seven." In the heptathlon, **athletes** compete in seven different events: the 100-meter hurdles, the shot put, the high jump, the 200-meter run, the long jump, the javelin throw, and the 800-meter run. The person who wins the most points in all seven events wins.

Jackie Joyner-Kersee doesn't know the meaning of the word "limit." She feels that the only person who can stop her is herself. That's probably why she has set four world **records**, holds Olympic and world heptathlon titles, and has earned the five highest scores for the heptathlon ever (more than 7,000 points each). At the 1984 Olympics in Los Angeles, Jackie Joyner-Kersee won the silver medal in the heptathlon. In 1988 in Seoul, South Korea, she won gold medals in the heptathlon and the long jump. And at the Barcelona, Spain, Olympics in 1992, she won her second gold medal in the heptathlon.

Growing Up in East St. Louis

Jackie comes from East St. Louis, Illinois, an industrial town where factories, packing plants, and weed-strewn rail yards dot the landscape. She grew up running races with her older brother Al, who would also become an Olympic gold **medalist**. When Jackie was born on March 3, 1962, her grandmother suggested she be named Jacqueline after Jacqueline Kennedy, the wife of the then-president of the United States. Her grandmother thought that Jackie Joyner—like Jacqueline Kennedy—would amount to something, too.

The Joyner family was poor. Often they had to sleep in the kitchen because the stove was the only source of heat in the house. Jackie remembers times when she had to wear the same clothes two days in a row, and keep her shoes until they fell apart. But she thinks her childhood helped make her tough.

At the age of nine, Jackie enrolled in a special community track program and discovered running. Jackie wasn't the fastest and best runner. But she tried hard, struggling along with the other kids. Suddenly, at age thirteen, she began to do well. She sold penny candies to kids at school so she'd have enough money to travel with her track club.

Jackie's parents, Al and Mary, were strict. They pushed their kids to do well in school, stay out of trouble, and reach for the stars. They supported Jackie's **commitment** to sports. The training and competing helped her release **energy** and emotions. If Jackie was in a bad mood, she let off steam by running or doing something else physical.

<u>At Lincoln High School</u>, Jackie was a star basketball player, and she played volleyball and long jumped. Like many other athletes at Lincoln, she was good enough to win a college scholarship. <u>When Jackie graduated</u>, she headed to the University of California at Los Angeles (UCLA).

 Stop here for the Strategy Break.

Strategy Break

If you were to stop and arrange the main events in this biography so far, your time line might look like the one below. Notice that even though the selection starts with a flashback, the time line starts with the day that Jackie was born and goes in sequence from there.

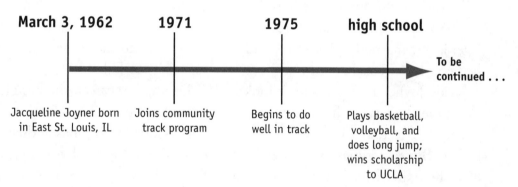

As you continue reading, keep paying attention to the major events and the words that signal when they happened. At the end of this selection, you will complete Jackie's time line.

Go on reading.

A Tough Hurdle to Clear

At UCLA, Jackie continued to work hard on her studies and her sports. She was a starter for the Bruins basketball team all four years. She also competed in track, the long jump, and the heptathlon, setting college, state, and national records.

Not long after Jackie started college, she faced a hurdle that was hard to clear. Her mother died suddenly of meningitis, an infection in the brain and spinal cord. One person who helped Jackie during this tough time was a UCLA track coach, Bob Kersee. He, too, had lost his mother at a young age, so he knew how Jackie felt. Jackie and Bob became friends. In 1986, after she graduated from college, Jackie married Bob Kersee, and he became her coach.

Jackie Joyner-Kersee makes it look easy to hurl a javelin, jump almost twenty-five feet, and leap over a hurdle. But sometimes, no matter how hard she trains, bad things happen in a race. Jackie knows what it feels like to twist an ankle, or to fall hard and lie sprawled in pain in the sand. In 1991 at the World Championships, she was on her way to setting another heptathlon world record in the 200-meter race when she pulled a hamstring muscle and could not finish.

Jackie also suffers from asthma, a condition that sometimes makes it hard for her to breathe. She runs anyway, but must take medicine and has to be sure to drink enough water after a race to clear her system.

What Is Jackie Like?

Jackie is tough on the track, and doesn't always let people know what she's feeling, but there's another side to her. Friends say she's strong on the outside, but soft on the inside—a warm, funny, generous, and genuinely nice person.

Fred Thompson, a coach for the 1988 women's Olympic track team, said, "I don't know a person in this world who has a negative thing to say about Jackie. . . . She's a lady. And it's not just on her lips—she goes out there and does things."

What's Important to Jackie

Besides athletics, what's important to Jackie are kids. She knows kids look up to her, and she feels it's her duty as an Olympic **champion** to give something back to the community, and especially to kids.

During her career, she has given motivational talks at schools and spoken to kids in hospitals and churches. Over the past several years, Jackie has donated money to help reopen the Mary Brown Community Center in East St. Louis, where she first learned to run. She cares about doing something to fight poverty and homelessness.

"I like kids to get to know me," Jackie says. "Sure, I've achieved a lot, but the thing is to let them see that everyone is raw material. I want to be a good statement of possibilities."

No matter where her athletic career leads her, Jackie Joyner-Kersee will be remembered for her tremendous **strength** and ability and for the heptathlon. Many years ago, another multi-sport athlete, Babe Didrikson Zaharias, was called the best female athlete of the twentieth century. Like Babe, Jackie will be thought of as the best of the best. ●

Strategy Follow-up

Now complete Jackie's time line. Use a separate sheet of paper if you need more room to write. Remember that for three of the years listed, you will have to look back at the beginning of the selection.

college	1984	1986	1988	1991	1992

✓Personal Checklist

Read each question and put a check (✓) in the correct box.

1. How well do you understand the information presented in this article?
   - ☐ 3 (extremely well)
   - ☐ 2 (fairly well)
   - ☐ 1 (not well)

2. After reading this selection, how well would you be able to describe Jackie Joyner-Kersee's achievements?
   - ☐ 3 (extremely well)
   - ☐ 2 (fairly well)
   - ☐ 1 (not well)

3. In Building Background, how well were you able to identify the physical and mental abilities that a person needs in order to be successful in your two chosen sports?
   - ☐ 3 (extremely well)
   - ☐ 2 (fairly well)
   - ☐ 1 (not well)

4. How well were you able to complete the word map in the Vocabulary Builder?
   - ☐ 3 (extremely well)
   - ☐ 2 (fairly well)
   - ☐ 1 (not well)

5. How well were you able to complete the time line in the Strategy Follow-up?
   - ☐ 3 (extremely well)
   - ☐ 2 (fairly well)
   - ☐ 1 (not well)

Vocabulary Check

Look back at the work you did in the Vocabulary Builder. Then answer each question by circling the correct letter.

1. The selection says that Jackie's parents supported her commitment to sports. What is a *commitment* in this context?
   a. a pledge to perform
   b. being sent to prison
   c. a transferring of information

2. How many events are in a heptathlon?
   a. five
   b. six
   c. seven

3. What does the word *records* mean in the context of this selection?
   a. official accounts that are written and kept
   b. the best score, speed, etc., ever attained so far
   c. thin, flat discs onto which music is copied

4. What do Olympic athletes receive after they win events?
   a. trophies
   b. medals
   c. ribbons

5. Which phrase describes a medalist?
   a. person who trades medals
   b. person who makes medals
   c. person who wins medals

Add the numbers that you just checked to get your Personal Checklist score. Fill in your score here. Then turn to page 217 and transfer your score onto Graph 1.

Check your answers with your teacher. Give yourself 1 point for each correct answer, and fill in your Vocabulary score here. Then turn to page 217 and transfer your score onto Graph 1.

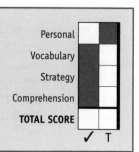

Strategy Check

Review the time line that you completed in the Strategy Follow-up. Also review the rest of the selection if necessary. Then answer the following questions:

1. Which of these dates on the time line was mentioned out of sequence in the selection?
   a. 1986
   b. 1991
   c. 1992

2. When did Jackie lose her mother to meningitis?
   a. when Jackie was in college
   b. in 1984
   c. in 1991

3. What happened to Jackie in 1986?
   a. She won an Olympic silver medal.
   b. She married Bob Kersee.
   c. She had to drop out of the World Championships.

4. Which of these events occurred first?
   a. Jackie won an Olympic silver medal.
   b. Jackie attended UCLA.
   c. Jackie won her first Olympic gold medal.

5. Which of the following is *not* an example of signal words?
   a. at Lincoln High School
   b. on March, 3, 1962
   c. at the age of nine

Comprehension Check

Review the selection if necessary. Then answer these questions:

1. In which Olympics did Jackie win medals?
   a. Munich, Los Angeles, and Seoul
   b. Los Angeles, Seoul, and Barcelona
   c. Los Angeles, Barcelona, and St. Louis

2. Why does Jackie think that her childhood of poverty was good?
   a. It was the reason she got a scholarship to UCLA.
   b. It was the only reason she took up sports.
   c. It made her tough and able to face life.

3. What condition does Jackie have that sometimes makes it hard for her to breathe?
   a. sinusitis
   b. allergies
   c. asthma

4. How does Jackie give something back to the community?
   a. She donates money and gives talks to children.
   b. She sets athletic records so others can try to break them.
   c. She gives away the Olympic medals that she wins.

5. According to the article, in what way is Jackie Joyner-Kersee like Babe Didrikson Zaharias?
   a. Both are multi-sport athletes who are called the best of their time.
   b. Both are Olympic heptathlon champions.
   c. Both have two last names.

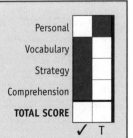

Check your answers with your teacher. Give yourself 1 point for each correct answer, and fill in your Strategy score here. Then turn to page 217 and transfer your score onto Graph 1.

Personal
Vocabulary
Strategy
Comprehension
TOTAL SCORE
✓ T

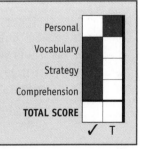

Check your answers with your teacher. Give yourself 1 point for each correct answer, and fill in your Comprehension score here. Then turn to page 217 and transfer your score onto Graph 1.

Personal
Vocabulary
Strategy
Comprehension
TOTAL SCORE
✓ T

Extending

Choose one or more of these activities:

INTERVIEW A COACH

Interview one of the coaches at your school. Before you do the interview, list a few questions that you would like him or her to answer. For example, you might ask which skills and abilities are most essential for the sport he or she coaches. Or you might ask for his or her opinion about the qualities that make a successful athlete. During the interview, if it's all right with the coach, tape record the questions and answers, or else take notes on the answers you get. After the interview, gather your notes and write a short question-and-answer article to share with other students.

WRITE A BRIEF BIOGRAPHY OF ANOTHER OLYMPIC ATHLETE

Choose another Olympic athlete, and write a brief biography of his or her life. You can use the resources on this page if you need help getting started. Find out about the athlete's childhood, athletic achievements, and everyday life. Then assemble what you have learned and write a short biography. Before you begin writing, you might want to use a time line to help you order the most important events from the athlete's life.

READ ABOUT JACKIE JOYNER-KERSEE IN HER OWN WORDS

In this lesson you read about Jackie Joyner-Kersee from someone else's point of view. To get Jackie's own point of view, read or listen to her autobiography, which is listed in the resources on this page. Compare what Judith P. Josephson says in this selection to what Jackie says about herself. How are the accounts alike and different?

Resources

Books

Davis, Michael D. *Black American Women in Olympic Track and Field: A Complete Illustrated Reference.* McFarland, 1992.

Greenspan, Bud. *100 Greatest Moments in Olympic History.* General Publishing Group, 1995.

Joyner-Kersee, Jackie, with Sonja Steptoe. *A Kind of Grace: The Autobiography of the World's Greatest Female Athlete.* Warner, 1997.

Wise, Michael T., Christina Bankes, Jane Laing, and Mary Sutherland, eds. *Chronical of the Olympics, 1896–2000.* DK Publishing, 1996.

Web Sites

http://www.usatf.org/athletes/bios/oldBios/1997/jjk.shtml
This is the Jackie Joyner-Kersee page of the official Web site of USA Track and Field.

http://www.usoc.org
On this Web site of the U.S. Olympic Committee, click on the "Athletes" and then "Bios" to read brief biographies of Olympic athletes.

Audio Recording

Joyner-Kersee, with Sonja Steptoe. *A Kind of Grace.* Time Warner AudioBooks, 1997.

Video/DVD

100 Years of Olympic Glory. Turner Home Entertainment, 1996.

Building Background

The short story you are about to read is set in a Native American community in the Northwestern United States. To the people in the story, dancing is not merely a social activity. It is also a way of passing on a tribe's tradition and preserving the identity of the tribe. Through dance, modern tribespeople feel connected to each other and to past members of the tribe. They believe that the spirits of ancestors who once performed the same steps might still be watching and sharing in the enjoyment of the dance.

The people of this tribe, like many other Native Americans, have had a tradition called the *vision seek*, or *vision quest*. This is a period during which a person, usually a young man, goes off alone for several weeks and tries to get in touch with supernatural forces. The vision seek is successful if the seeker goes into a trance, or dreamlike condition, and sees something magical or supernatural that can serve as a guide for future actions.

As you read "Dancer," look for other details about the customs and beliefs of this group of Native Americans. They will add to your understanding of the story.

ferocious

powwow

preening

reservation

sociopathic

Vocabulary Builder

1. The words in the margin are all from the short story "Dancer." Choose the best word to complete each of the following sentences, and write it in the blank.

   a. Another word for *extremely fierce* is _____.

   b. A _____ is an area set aside for a certain group of people to live on.

   c. A _____ is a conference or gathering of Native Americans.

   d. A person who is moving proudly, as if showing off, is _____.

   e. A person who has deep personal problems that make him or her unable to get along with others is _____.

2. As you read the story, look for these words and decide whether you have used them correctly. If necessary, change your answers.

3. Save your work. You will use it again in the Vocabulary Check.

Strategy Builder

Drawing Conclusions About Characters

- As you learned in Lesson 5, a **conclusion** is a decision that you reach after thinking about certain facts or information. When you read a story, you can draw conclusions about the **characters** based on what they say, do, think, and feel. You also can draw conclusions about a particular character based on what other characters say *about* him or her.

- In many stories, the characters change in some way. These characters are called **dynamic characters**. Other characters stay the same throughout a story. They are called **static characters**. As you read the paragraph below, see if you can draw any conclusions about Anita based on what she says, does, thinks, and feels. Is she a static or a dynamic character? Why?

> When a new girl moved in next door, Anita knew that she wasn't going to like her. After all, Erin dressed in odd clothes and didn't talk much. She never looked anyone in the eye and never joined Anita and her friends at lunch. Even though Anita's mom became friendly with Erin's mom, Anita decided to avoid Erin.
>
> One day, Anita forgot her house key and was locked out. She remembered that her mom had given a key to Erin's mom, so she knocked on Erin's door. Erin answered the door and let Anita in. As Erin handed Anita a soda, Anita noticed that Erin was listening to CD of her favorite musical group. The girls began talking and realized their tastes in music were very similar. Anita stayed at Erin's all afternoon, talking and listening to music.
>
> From then on, Anita stopped at Erin's every morning, and they walked to school together.

- Did you conclude that Anita is a dynamic character? If you wanted to track the changes in her character, you could record them on a **character wheel** like the one below. The conclusions that one reader drew about Anita are in *italics*.

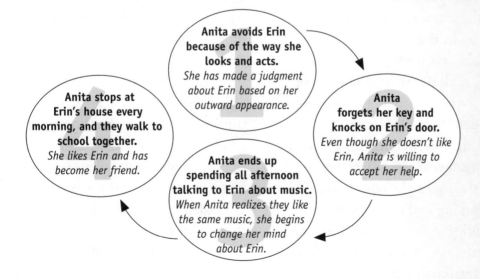

Dancer

by Vickie Sears

As you read the first part of this short story, notice what Clarissa says, does, thinks, and feels—and what the narrator says about her. What conclusions can you draw about Clarissa?

Tell you just how it was with her. Took her to a dance not long after she come to live with us. Smartest thing I ever done. Seems like some old Eaglespirit woman saw her living down here and came back just to be with Clarissa.

Five years old she was when she come to us. Some foster kids come with lots of stuff, but she came with everything she had in a paper bag. Some dresses that was too short. A pair of pants barely holding a crotch. A pile of ratty underwear and one new nightgown. Mine was her third foster home in as many months. The agency folks said she was *so-cio-path-ic*. I don't know nothing from that. She just seemed like she was all full up with anger and scaredness like lots of the kids who come to me. Only she was a real loner. Not trusting nobody. But she ran just like any other kid, was quiet when needed. Smiled at all the right times. If you could get her to smile, that is. Didn't talk much, though.

Had these **ferocious** dreams, too. Real screamer dreams they were. Shake the soul right out of you. She'd be screaming and crying with her little body wriggling on the bed, her hair all matted up on her woody-colored face. One time I got her to tell me what she was seeing, and she told me

how she was being chased by a man with a long knife what he was going to kill her with and nobody could hear her calling out for help. She didn't talk too much about them, but they was all bad like that one. Seemed the most fierce dreams I ever remember anybody ever having outside of a vision seek. They said her tribe was Assiniboin, but they weren't for certain. What was for sure was that she was a fine dark-eyed girl just meant for someone to scoop up for loving.

Took her to her first dance in September, like I said, not long after she came. It wasn't like I thought it would be a good thing to do. It was just that we was all going. Me, my own kids, some nieces and nephews and the other children who was living with us. The **powwow** was just part of what we done all the time. Every month. More often in the summer. But this was the regular first Friday night of the school year. We'd all gather up and go to the school. I was thinking on leaving her home with a sitter cause she'd tried to kill one of the cats a couple days before. We'd had us a big talk and she was grounded, but, well, it seemed like she ought to be with us.

Harold, that's my oldest boy, he and the other kids was mad with her, but he decided to show her around anyhow. At the school he went through the gym telling people, "This here's my sister, Clarissa." Wasn't no fuss or anything. She was just another one of the kids. When they was done meeting folks, he put her on one of the bleachers near the drum and went to join the men. He was in that place where his voice cracks but was real proud to be drumming. Held his hand up to his ear even, some of the time. Anyhow, Clarissa was sitting there, not all that interested in the dance or drum, when Molly Graybull come out in her button dress. Her arms was all stretched out, and she was slipping around, **preening** on them spindles of legs that get skinnier with every year. She was well into her seventies, and I might as well admit, Molly had won herself a fair share of dance contests. So it wasn't no surprise how a little girl could get so fixated on Molly. Clarissa watched her move around-around-around. Then all the rest of the dancers after Molly. She sure took in a good eyeful. Fancy dance. Owl dance. Circle dance. Even a hoop dancer was visiting that night. Everything weaving all slow, then fast. Around-around until that child couldn't see nothing else. Seemed like she was struck silent in the night, too. Never had no dreams at all. Well, not the hollering kind anyways.

Next day she was more quiet than usual only I could see she was looking at her picture book and tapping the old one-two, one-two. Tapping her toes on the rug with the inside of her head going around and around. As quiet as she could be, she was.

 Stop here for the Strategy Break.

Strategy Break

What conclusions can you draw about Clarissa so far? Do you see a change in her? If you were to begin a character wheel for her, it might look like this:

Clarissa is on her third foster home and has been labeled sociopathic. *Her problems must make her very hard to live with.*

She seems angry and scared. She's a loner, and she has terrible dreams. *Something really bad must have happened to her to make her act that way.*

After she goes to her first dance, she stops having violent dreams. *Something about dancing makes her feel better.*

The next day she is much quieter, and she is tapping her toes. *She seems calmer, and she's thinking a lot about the dance.*

As you continue reading, keep drawing conclusions about Clarissa. At the end of the story, you will finish her character wheel. Does she continue to change?

Go on reading to see what happens.

A few days went on before she asks me, "When's there gonna be another dance?"

I tell her in three weeks. She just smiles and goes on outside, waiting on the older kids to come home from school.

The very next day she asks if she can listen to some singing. I give her the tape recorder and some of Joe Washington from up to the Lummi **reservation** and the Kicking Woman Singers. Clarissa, she takes them tapes and runs out back behind the chicken shed, staying out all afternoon. I wasn't worried none, though, cause I could hear the music the whole time. Matter of fact, it like to make me sick of them same songs come the end of three weeks. But that kid, she didn't get into no kind of mischief. Almost abnormal how good she was. Worried me some to see her so caught up but it seemed good too. The angry part of her slowed down so's she wasn't hitting the animals or chopping on herself with sticks like she was doing when she first come. She wasn't laughing much either, but she started playing with the other kids when they come home. Seemed like everybody was working hard to be better with each other.

Come March, Clarissa asks, "Can I dance?"

For sure, the best time for teaching is when a kid wants to listen, so we stood side to side with me doing some steps. She followed along fine. I put on a tape and started moving faster,

and Clarissa just kept up all natural. I could tell she'd been practicing lots. She was doing real good.

Comes the next powwow, which was outside on the track field, I braided Clarissa's hair. Did her up with some ermine and bead ties, then give her a purse to carry. It was all beaded with a rose and leaves. Used to be my aunt's. She held it right next to her side with her chin real high. She joined in a Circle dance. I could see she was watching her feet a little and looking how others do their steps, but mostly she was doing wonderful. When Molly Graybull showed up beside her, Clarissa took to a seat and stared. She didn't dance again that night, but I could see there was dreaming coming into her eyes. I saw that fire that said to practice. And she did. I heard her every day in her room. Finally bought her her very own tape recorder so's the rest of us could listen to music too.

Some months passed on. All the kids was getting bigger. Clarissa, she went into the first grade. Harvey went off to community college up in Seattle, and that left me with Ronnie being the oldest at home. Clarissa was keeping herself busy all the time going over to Molly Graybull's. She was coming home with Spider Woman stories and trickster tales. One night she speaks up at supper and says, right clear and loud, "I'm an Assiniboin." Clear as it can be, she says it again. Don't nobody have to say nothing to something that proud said.

Next day I started working on a wing dress for Clarissa. She was going to be needing one for sure real soon.

Comes the first school year pow-wow and everyone was putting on their best. I called for Clarissa to come to my room. I told her, "I think it's time you have something special for yourself." Then I held up the green satin and saw her eyes full up with glitter. She didn't say nothing. Only kisses me and runs off to her room.

Just as we're all getting out of the car, Clarissa whispered to me, "I'm gonna dance with Molly Graybull." I put my hand on her shoulder to say, "You just listen to your spirit. That's where your music is."

We all danced an Owl dance, a Friendship dance, and a couple of Circle dances. Things was feeling real warm and good, and then it was time for the women's traditional. Clarissa joined the circle. She opened her arms to something nobody but her seemed to hear. That's when I saw that old Eagle woman come down and slide right inside of Clarissa, scooping up that child. There Clarissa was, full up with music. All full with that old, old spirit, letting herself dance through Clarissa's feet. Then Molly Graybull come dancing alongside Clarissa, and they was both the same age. ●

Strategy Follow-up

Work with a partner to complete this activity. On a large sheet of paper, copy the character wheel below. Then fill in circles 5–9 with information from the second part of the story.

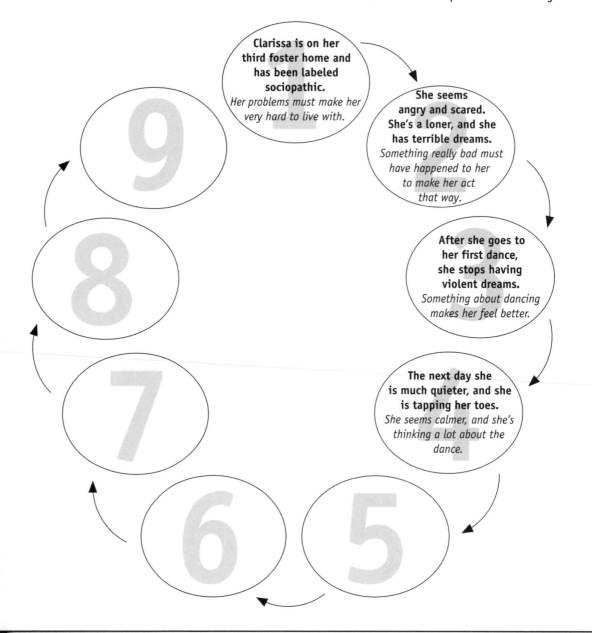

Clarissa is on her third foster home and has been labeled sociopathic.
Her problems must make her very hard to live with.

She seems angry and scared. She's a loner, and she has terrible dreams.
Something really bad must have happened to her to make her act that way.

After she goes to her first dance, she stops having violent dreams.
Something about dancing makes her feel better.

The next day she is much quieter, and she is tapping her toes.
She seems calmer, and she's thinking a lot about the dance.

✓Personal Checklist

Read each question and put a check (✓) in the correct box.

1. How well do you understand what the narrator means when she says "Then Molly Graybull come dancing alongside Clarissa, and they was both the same age"?
    - ☐ 3 (extremely well)
    - ☐ 2 (fairly well)
    - ☐ 1 (not well)

2. How well were you able to use the information in Building Background to help you understand what happens in this story?
    - ☐ 3 (extremely well)
    - ☐ 2 (fairly well)
    - ☐ 1 (not well)

3. How well were you able to complete the sentences in the Vocabulary Builder?
    - ☐ 3 (extremely well)
    - ☐ 2 (fairly well)
    - ☐ 1 (not well)

4. How well were you able to complete the character wheel in the Strategy Follow-up?
    - ☐ 3 (extremely well)
    - ☐ 2 (fairly well)
    - ☐ 1 (not well)

5. Now that you've read the story, how well would you be able to explain what dancing means to Clarissa?
    - ☐ 3 (extremely well)
    - ☐ 2 (fairly well)
    - ☐ 1 (not well)

Vocabulary Check

Look back at the work you did in the Vocabulary Builder. Then answer each question by circling the correct letter.

1. Which of these things might best be described as ferocious?
    a. a sleeping puppy
    b. winds in a hurricane
    c. a frightened child

2. Which meaning of the word *reservation* does this story use?
    a. land set aside by the government as a living area for Native Americans
    b. a doubt or uncertainty about a statement or an agreement
    c. an arrangement by which something is set aside in advance

3. If someone is preening, how does that person feel about himself or herself?
    a. The person is very proud of himself or herself.
    b. The person is very ashamed of himself or herself.
    c. The person is very embarrassed about himself or herself.

4. Which of these activities is *not* likely to happen at a powwow?
    a. ceremonial dancing
    b. speechmaking
    c. research on possible life on Mars

5. Which word best describes someone who is sociopathic?
    a. outgoing
    b. antisocial
    c. pathetic

Add the numbers that you just checked to get your Personal Checklist score. Fill in your score here. Then turn to page 217 and transfer your score onto Graph 1.

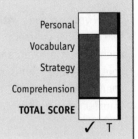

Check your answers with your teacher. Give yourself 1 point for each correct answer, and fill in your Vocabulary score here. Then turn to page 217 and transfer your score onto Graph 1.

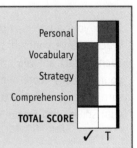

Strategy Check

Review the character wheel that you completed in the Strategy Follow-up. Also review the selection if necessary. Then answer these questions:

1. At what point in the story does the narrator notice the first inkling of change in Clarissa?
   a. After Clarissa has her first bad dream.
   b. After Clarissa tries to kill the cat.
   c. After Clarissa goes to her first dance.

2. During the three weeks that Clarissa listens to music, she doesn't get into any mischief. What does this help you conclude?
   a. The music is helping her feel less angry.
   b. The music is making her more sleepy.
   c. The music is making her depressed.

3. What does Clarissa do that lets you know how important dancing is to her?
   a. She learns from Molly and practices every day.
   b. She preens in front of the mirror as she dances.
   c. She watches Molly dance every day.

4. What does Clarissa say that helps you know she's starting to take pride in her heritage?
   a. "When's there gonna be another dance?"
   b. "Can I dance?"
   c. "I'm an Assiniboin."

5. Clarissa is a dynamic character. What is the difference between a dynamic character and a static character?
   a. Static characters change, while dynamic characters stay the same.
   b. Dynamic characters change, while static characters stay the same.
   c. Dynamic characters are always more important than static characters.

Comprehension Check

Review the story if necessary. Then answer these questions:

1. How old is Clarissa when she goes to live with the narrator?
   a. three years old
   b. five years old
   c. seven years old

2. How often are dances held on the reservation?
   a. about once a year
   b. about twice a year
   c. about once a month

3. What does the narrator say that indicates that Clarissa is beginning to change?
   a. "Almost abnormal how good she was."
   b. "Five years old she was when she come to us."
   c. "The agency folks said she was *so-cio-path-ic*."

4. What clue helps you know that the narrator understands how important dancing is to Clarissa?
   a. She buys Clarissa her very own tape recorder.
   b. She makes Clarissa a wing dress for the dances.
   c. Both of the above answers are correct.

5. What does the speaker mean when she says, "Then Molly Graybull come dancing alongside Clarissa, and they was both the same age"?
   a. Clarissa looks as old Molly Graybull at that very moment.
   b. Molly turns into a child, and she and Clarissa are the same age for a while.
   c. Clarissa is filled with an old spirit, which makes her seem as old and wise as Molly.

Check your answers with your teacher. Give yourself 1 point for each correct answer, and fill in your Strategy score here. Then turn to page 217 and transfer your score onto Graph 1.

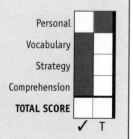

Check your answers with your teacher. Give yourself 1 point for each correct answer, and fill in your Comprehension score here. Then turn to page 217 and transfer your score onto Graph 1.

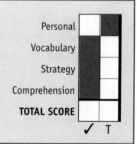

Extending

Choose one or more of these activities:

RESEARCH CURRENT NATIVE AMERICAN LIFE

Do all Native American tribes have powwows with dances? What is housing like on different reservations? How many reservations have their own schools? What are different tribes doing to keep their traditions alive and their members connected? With one or two partners, research at least two different tribes, preferably in different parts of North America. Put together a multimedia presentation that includes such things as recorded singing or instrumental music; drawings, photographs, or a video showing tribal dancers in costume; and either a written or oral report about what you learned.

LEARN A FOLK DANCE

Native Americans are not the only Americans who have traditional dances. Immigrants from Europe, Africa, Asia, and other parts of the world have also brought their dances to this country. Find a way to learn a folk dance of an ethnic group in your city. If you can't find a person to teach you the dance, learn from a tape or written directions. (For a start, check out the resources listed on this page.) Then teach the dance to your class, or to a small group that will demonstrate for the rest of the class. If possible, find out whether the dance has some special meaning or is performed only on special occasions. Share that information with your classmates.

Resources

Books

Bernstein, Diane Morris. *We Dance Because We Can: People of the Powwow.* Longstreet Press, 1996.

Hunt, W. Ben. *The Complete Book of Indian Crafts and Lore.* Goldencraft, 1974.

Fletcher, Alice C. *Indian Games and Dances with Native Songs: Arranged from American Indian Ceremonials and Sports.* University of Nebraska Press, 1994.

Web Sites

http://members.aol.com/ladyscribe/indig/index.htm
This Web site provides links to information on Native American life.

http://www.geocities.com/Heartland/3382/l_links.html
This Web page contains international and ethnic folk dance links. Click on "Dance Descriptions" and look for instructions on dances from around the world.

http://www.powwows.com/dance/
This Web page has information on Native American powwows and dance styles.

Videos/DVDs

The American Indian Dance Theatre: Finding the Circle. Dance in America. Thirteen/WNET, 1989.

Into the Circle: An Introduction to Native American Powwows. Film Ideas, 1992.

Powwow. Schlessinger Video Productions, 1996.

LESSON ❽

chamber

draw

gobbled

mad

retire

sap

show

well

The Faithful Sister

Building Background

There is an old saying that states, "Things aren't always what they seem." What is your opinion of this saying? Do you agree or disagree with it? On the lines below, give an example that supports your opinion. Then predict whether the characters in "The Faithful Sister" would agree or disagree with the saying.

_____

_____

_____

_____

_____

CLIPBOARD

chamber
_____
_____

draw
_____
_____

gobbled
_____
_____

Vocabulary Builder

1. A **multiple-meaning word** has more than one meaning. For example, the word *faithful* can mean "devoted" or it can mean "true," as in a film adaptation that is faithful, or true, to the book upon which it is based.

2. On the clipboards, write two short definitions for each word. Use dictionary if you need help. Then predict which meaning the author will use in "The Faithful Sister."

3. As you read the story, decide which meaning the author uses, and put an asterisk (*) next to that meaning on the clipboard.

4. Save your work. You will refer to it again in the Vocabulary Check.

CLIPBOARD

mad
retire
_____

sap
_____

show
well
_____

Strategy Builder

Identifying Causes and Effects in a Story

- In many fictional stories, events are connected by time order. One event happens, and then another, and then another. In other stories, however, events are connected by **cause and effect**. One event will cause another event to happen, which will cause another event, and so on. The causes and effects in a story are often all related. Like the falling dominoes on this page, a single event can cause a chain reaction of more causes and effects.

- To find cause-and-effect relationships while you read, keep asking yourself, "What happened?" and "Why did it happen?" Doing this will help you understand what has happened so far. It also will help you predict what might happen next.

- As you read the following paragraphs, look for the chain of causes and effects.

> When Jessica's friends took up smoking in high school, Jessica did too. The habit became such a normal part of her life that she didn't even notice when it became a necessary part—an addiction. In time, she was smoking a pack of cigarettes a day.
>
> Her addiction became so bad that at work, she had to go outside almost every hour to light up. Her clothes smelled so strongly of smoke that a co-worker in the next cubicle sprayed disinfectant several times a day to try to cover up.
>
> As embarrassed as she was at the office, Jessica couldn't stop smoking. Then last spring she thought she had a cough due to a lingering cold. She went for a checkup and learned that she has bronchitis due to smoking. Now Jessica is making a real effort to break her smoking habit.

- If you wanted to track the causes and effects in the paragraphs above, you could put them on a **cause-and-effect chain**. It might look like this:

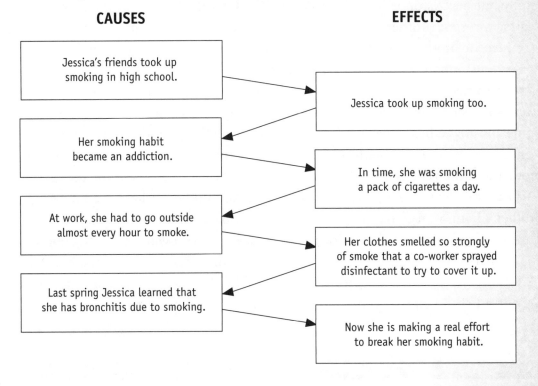

CAUSES

EFFECTS

Jessica's friends took up smoking in high school.

Jessica took up smoking too.

Her smoking habit became an addiction.

In time, she was smoking a pack of cigarettes a day.

At work, she had to go outside almost every hour to smoke.

Her clothes smelled so strongly of smoke that a co-worker sprayed disinfectant to try to cover it up.

Last spring Jessica learned that she has bronchitis due to smoking.

Now she is making a real effort to break her smoking habit.

The Faithful Sister

by Madhur Jaffrey

As you read the first part of this story, apply the strategies that you just learned. To find the causes and effects, keep asking yourself, "What happened?" and "Why did it happen?"

There once was a family with a single child—a shy girl who longed for a baby brother to play with. But it was not to be until she was fifteen years old, when her mother gave birth to a boy and at the same time announced to her daughter that it was high time she was married. While the marriage was being arranged and prepared for, the girl spent most of her time with the new baby.

Unfortunately, she was with her brother for only a year. Then she was married off to a man who lived quite far away.

The brother grew up knowing that he *had* a sister, but not knowing his sister at all.

The sister gradually had her own family but never stopped missing her dearest, sweetest brother.

When the brother was about to get married, he announced to his parents, "I want to make sure that my sister attends my wedding. I will go to her home and invite her in person."

The sister was so delighted to see her brother that she begged him to stay.

"I cannot stay for long," said the brother. "I am soon to be married and came only to invite you. Why don't you return with me?"

"Oh my dearest, sweetest brother, of course I shall come to your wedding, but I will not leave for a few days. Stay for a while and eat and rest. I will cook you rice puddings and breads and sweets and also some extra food for you to take on your journey back home."

The sister made all kinds of sweets for her brother to eat on his return trip. She tied them in a green cloth bundle and gave them to him.

After the brother had left, one of her children came to her and said, "Mother, may I have some sweets?" The sister picked up a sweet that she had not packed and broke it in two. She threw half of it to her dog—who promptly **gobbled** it up—and was just about to pop the other half into the mouth of her youngest child when the dog rolled over and died.

She quickly examined all the pots, pans, and grinding stones in her kitchen and discovered to her horror that a poisonous snake had got into the bag of grain and that she had accidentally ground it when she was preparing her sweets.

She began to cry, "Oh my dearest, sweetest brother. What have I done? What have I done? If you eat the sweets I gave you, you will die like my dog."

She then rushed out of the house to find her brother. She ran and ran and finally found him sleeping under a mango tree beside the road. She began shaking him. "Wake up. Wake up. Don't die."

The brother sat up. "What on earth are you saying? I am not dying."

"Dearest, sweetest brother," said the sister, "I accidentally ground a snake in the grain when I was making the sweets. Please forgive me. Why don't you come with me now, and I will

make some fresh sweets for your journey."

"I would return with you," said the brother, "but my marriage day is drawing near, and I cannot delay. However, instead of returning home, why don't you come along with me?"

 Stop here for the Strategy Break.

Strategy Break

If you were to create a cause-and-effect chain for this story so far, it might look like this:

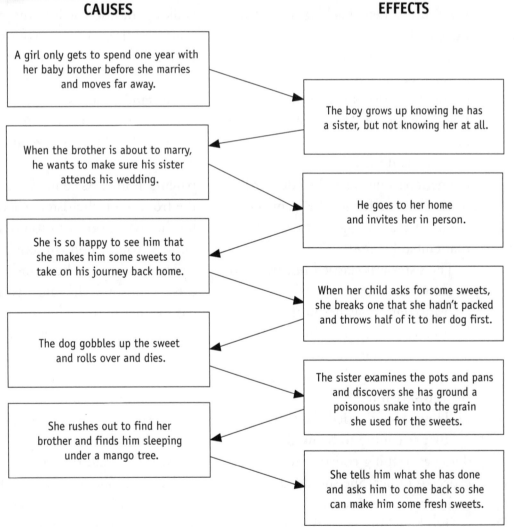

CAUSES

- A girl only gets to spend one year with her baby brother before she marries and moves far away.
- When the brother is about to marry, he wants to make sure his sister attends his wedding.
- She is so happy to see him that she makes him some sweets to take on his journey back home.
- The dog gobbles up the sweet and rolls over and dies.
- She rushes out to find her brother and finds him sleeping under a mango tree.

EFFECTS

- The boy grows up knowing he has a sister, but not knowing her at all.
- He goes to her home and invites her in person.
- When her child asks for some sweets, she breaks one that she hadn't packed and throws half of it to her dog first.
- The sister examines the pots and pans and discovers she has ground a poisonous snake into the grain she used for the sweets.
- She tells him what she has done and asks him to come back so she can make him some fresh sweets.

As you continue reading, keep looking for causes and effects. At the end of this story you will create a cause-and-effect chain of your own.

Go on reading to see what happens.

The sister agreed and, with just the clothes on her back, set off with her brother. The two of them continued on their long journey. Soon they came to a **well**. The sister wanted a drink of water, so the brother said, "You go ahead to the well and **draw** some water. I'll just rest here on this embankment."

When the sister got to the well, she noticed that there was an old stonecutter there, hacking away at a huge rock.

The sister smiled at him sympathetically, offering him a drink of the water that she had drawn. She said, "That is very hard work you are doing."

"Yes," said the old stonecutter, "sometimes one is fated to do hard work. Fate is strange," he went on. "Look at that young man resting on that embankment."

The sister was startled but tried not to **show** it.

"Fate, right now, has nothing good in store for him. He is doomed to die. There is only one way in which he can be saved. If he has a loving sister, she can save him."

"How? How?" cried the sister.

"By pretending to be **mad** and by doing everything contrary to what is expected of her. She should also curse and swear at her brother."

"For how long must the sister do this?"

"Until his fate changes. And that will only happen after the young

man's bride has been in his house for a day."

The sister then ran toward her brother crying out, "You idiot, you fool, you lout, you son of an owl!"

The brother could not believe his ears. "What is the matter with you? Until an hour ago, I was your 'dearest, sweetest brother,' and now you are calling me all kinds of names. You must have gone mad."

"I may be mad," yelled the sister, "but you are a cowardly she-monkey. Come on, come on, let's keep walking, or else you'll never get to your wedding to marry your stupid bride."

The brother just could not understand what had happened to his sister. He thought it best to be quiet. They walked like this, he quiet, she cursing and rude, all the way to their parents' home. As soon as they entered the front door, the sister yelled at her brother, "You **sap**, you son of a donkey, you pigeon without a tail."

The mother put her hands to her ears. "Oh, son," she said, "your sister has lost her senses. She comes to the wedding in an old, worn-out sari, cursing like a maniac. It would have been best if you had not brought her with you. She is going to ruin this entire wedding. What will all our guests think?"

"Mother," said the son, "I don't understand. She was fine . . . for a while. Then I don't know what happened. She just lost her senses when we were halfway here."

The day of the wedding came. Just as the groom was about to have his wedding crown placed on his head, his sister began screaming, "Wait. Wait, you numskulls." So saying, she began to prod the crown with a needle, and suddenly, a thin viper wriggled out of it.

Everyone gasped and said, "His sister may be mad, but at least she has done him some good."

When the brother mounted the wedding horse that would follow the wedding procession to the bride's house, the sister began yelling again, "Get my rotten brother off that horse. I want to ride it."

She made such a fuss that the family thought the best way to keep her quiet would be to let her ride. The "mad" sister got on the horse, and just as she was leaving the house, the gateway collapsed on her, slightly hurting her. All the family and guests came running.

"She may be mad," they said, "but she has done some good."

The brother then went off with his wedding procession to marry his bride, and all the women of the household waited, as is the custom, in their home.

When the son came back with his bride and was just about to **retire** to the bridal **chamber**, the sister began screaming again, "I want to sleep in that bed. Get my brother and sister-in-law out of here. I must sleep in that flower-decorated bed."

Again, the family decided to let her have her way. As soon as the sister lay down on the bridal bed, a large scorpion crawled out of it.

The next day, the mother said to her son, "Your sister is completely mad. Why bother to give her that nice gold sari we bought for her as a wedding favor? We will just give her a torn, old sari. She won't even know the difference."

A whole day had passed since the new bride had come home. The sister now spoke out in her normal, sober voice, "No, you will not give me the torn, old sari. I deserve the gold sari for all I have been through. An old, wise stonecutter on the way here told me that my brother's stars were crossed and that the only way I could save his life was by cursing him, by being mad, and by being contrary. I have done all that—and suffered the abuse you have heaped on me. Now I will leave with my gold sari. Don't forget:

With my love
I have saved a mother's son
A sister's brother
And a bride's groom

No, I am not mad. Good-bye to you all!" ●

Strategy Follow-up

Work with a partner or a small group to create a cause-and-effect chain for the second part of "The Faithful Sister." To help identify the causes and effects, keep asking each other, "What happened?" and "Why did it happen?"

✓Personal Checklist

Read each question and put a check (✓) in the correct box.

1. How well do you understand why the sister acts as she does in the second part of this story?
   - ☐ 3 (extremely well)
   - ☐ 2 (fairly well)
   - ☐ 1 (not well)

2. In Building Background, how well were you able to give an example to support your opinion of the saying, "Things aren't always what they seem"?
   - ☐ 3 (extremely well)
   - ☐ 2 (fairly well)
   - ☐ 1 (not well)

3. How well could you use this story to explain the saying, "Things aren't always what they seem"?
   - ☐ 3 (extremely well)
   - ☐ 2 (fairly well)
   - ☐ 1 (not well)

4. How well were you able to complete the activity in the Vocabulary Builder?
   - ☐ 3 (extremely well)
   - ☐ 2 (fairly well)
   - ☐ 1 (not well)

5. In the Strategy Follow-up, how well were you able to help your partner or group create a cause-and-effect chain for the second part of this story?
   - ☐ 3 (extremely well)
   - ☐ 2 (fairly well)
   - ☐ 1 (not well)

Vocabulary Check

Look back at the work you did in the Vocabulary Builder. Then answer each question by circling the correct letter.

1. Which meaning of *chamber* is used in this story?
   a. part of a gun that holds the ammunition
   b. group of lawmakers, such as the Senate
   c. room in a house, such as a bedroom

2. The boy tells his sister that she must have gone mad. What does *gone mad* mean in this context?
   a. became insane
   b. gotten very angry
   c. gotten very happy

3. Which word would you use to tell someone that you're going to go to bed?
   a. retire
   b. draw
   c. sap

4. Which meaning of *draw* is used in this story?
   a. end a contest in which neither side wins
   b. take something out, such as water from a well
   c. make a picture with a pen or pencil

5. The sister's dog gobbled up the sweet and then rolled over and died. What does *gobbled* mean in this context?
   a. made sounds like a turkey
   b. made gagging sounds
   c. ate quickly and greedily

Add the numbers that you just checked to get your Personal Checklist score. Fill in your score here. Then turn to page 217 and transfer your score onto Graph 1.

Check your answers with your teacher. Give yourself 1 point for each correct answer, and fill in your Vocabulary score here. Then turn to page 217 and transfer your score onto Graph 1.

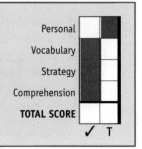

Strategy Check

Review the cause-and-effect chain that you helped create in the Strategy Follow-up. Then answer the following questions:

1. When the stonecutter tells the sister how to save her brother, what is the effect?
   a. She runs toward her brother and calls him names.
   b. She runs toward her brother and gives him a hug.
   c. She runs toward her brother and tells him not to die.

2. What does the sister's sudden change in behavior cause the brother to do?
   a. wake up and tell her he's not dying
   b. tell her she must have gone mad
   c. hug her back very tightly

3. What happens when the sister prods her brother's wedding crown with a needle?
   a. A scorpion crawls out of it.
   b. A gateway collapses on her.
   c. A snake wriggles out of it.

4. What causes the mother to tell her son to give his sister a torn, old sari instead of the gold one they bought for her?
   a. She thinks the sister won't know the difference anyway.
   b. She thinks the sister will just ruin the gold one anyway.
   c. She decides she wants to keep the gold sari for herself.

5. What is the final effect of all the sister's "mad" behavior?
   a. Her family asks her to leave the wedding.
   b. She ends up saving her brother's life.
   c. Her family rewards her with a gold sari.

Comprehension Check

Review the story if necessary. Then answer these questions:

1. How long does the sister live with her brother before she marries and moves away?
   a. one year
   b. three years
   c. five years

2. Why does the brother go to his sister's house?
   a. to invite her to his wedding
   b. to get some sweets from her
   c. to bring her a gold sari

3. Why do you think the author might have decided to have the sister give a piece of the sweet to her dog before she gives it to her child?
   a. Feeding your dog first is a tradition in the sister's culture.
   b. She probably was giving the dog the burned part of the sweet.
   c. The author probably doesn't want to have the child die.

4. The sister wears a sari in this story. From this clue, where can you conclude the story takes place?
   a. Italy
   b. China
   c. India

5. Why does the sister agree to go to her brother's home with just the clothes on her back?
   a. She wants her brother to give her a new gold sari to wear.
   b. Her brother's marriage day is nearing, and he can't delay.
   c. She is wearing the sari that she had planned to wear to the wedding.

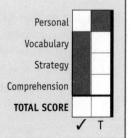

Check your answers with your teacher. Give yourself 1 point for each correct answer, and fill in your Strategy score here. Then turn to page 217 and transfer your score onto Graph 1.

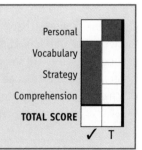

Check your answers with your teacher. Give yourself 1 point for each correct answer, and fill in your Comprehension score here. Then turn to page 217 and transfer your score onto Graph 1.

Extending

Choose one or more of these activities:

RESEARCH WEDDING CUSTOMS

In this story, you read about some of the traditional wedding customs that are practiced in India. Research traditional wedding customs practiced in other countries or cultures, and then answer as many of these questions as possible:

- Are special foods made for the event? Do they have special meaning?
- Do the bride and groom wear special clothes? Does any part of their clothing have special meaning?
- Where are the ceremonies held—at the woman's home, the man's home, a church or other building, outside? Are different parts of the ceremonies held in different places?

Report your findings in an oral or written report. Or if you'd like, ask some classmates to help you stage a mock wedding ceremony.

DRAMATIZE "THE FAITHFUL SISTER"

Work with a group of students to perform "The Faithful Sister" as a play. Reread the story, and decide how many characters will be in the play. (Don't forget to include a narrator and the dog.) If you can, create simple props and costumes. Practice acting out the play until everyone feels comfortable, and then perform it for your class or for a group of younger students.

READ OTHER TALES FROM INDIA

Use the resources listed on this page to locate other tales from India. Read or listen to several tales, and then decide which one is your favorite. Prepare a brief oral or written report on the tale. Be sure to explain why you chose it.

Resources

Books

Jaffrey, Madhur. *Seasons of Splendour: Tales, Myths and Legends of India*. Antheneum, 1989.

Ramanujan, A. K., ed. *Folktales from India: A Selection of Oral Tales from Twenty-two Languages*. Pantheon Books, 1994.

Spagnoli, Cathy. *Asian Tales and Tellers*. August House Publishers, 1998.

Web Sites

http://ark.cdlib.org/ark:/13030/ft067n99wt/
There is Web site includes more than 75 oral tales from India.

http://www.ultimatewedding.com/articles/
index.php?action=section&sec=24
Use links on this Web site to explore various wedding customs, including those of the Irish, Jewish, African American, and interfaith communities.

Audio Recording

Tales from India. Spoken Arts, 1983.

A Retrieved Reformation

anguish

assiduously

eminent

novelties

resumed

retribution

rogue-catchers

virtuous

CLIPBOARD

anguish

_____

assiduously

_____

eminent

_____

novelties

_____

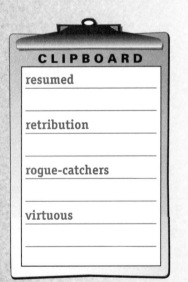

CLIPBOARD

resumed

_____

retribution

_____

rogue-catchers

_____

virtuous

_____

Building Background

O. Henry (1862–1910) is the pen name of William Sydney Porter, one of the most popular short-story writers who ever lived. When Porter was 20, he moved from his hometown of Greensboro, North Carolina, to Texas to work as a ranch hand. Quite unlike the other cowboys, Porter carried a dictionary and a poetry book in his pockets while he worked.

After his stint as a cowboy, Porter worked in a bank and wrote short stories and sketches. When funds disappeared from the bank, Porter was accused of stealing them. Rather than stand trial for the crime (for which he probably would have been found not guilty), Porter escaped to Honduras, Central America. When he returned two years later to visit his dying wife, Porter was arrested and jailed for three years. While in jail, he published about 20 stories under several different pen names, including O. Henry.

When Porter was released from prison, he moved to New York City, a place that fascinated and delighted him. It was the setting for many of his nearly 300 short stories. Some of O. Henry's finest stories are collected in _The Four Million, The Voice of the City,_ and _Hearts of the West._ O. Henry's stories are known for their surprise endings.

Vocabulary Builder

1. The words in the margin are all from "A Retrieved Reformation." On the clip-boards write a meaning for each word. If a word has more than one meaning, predict how the word might be used in the story and use that meaning.

2. Then use the vocabulary words and the title to help you predict what might happen in this story. Write your predictions on a separate sheet of paper. Use as many vocabulary words as possible.

3. Save your work. You will refer to it again in the Vocabulary Check.

Strategy Builder

Making Predictions While Reading

- When you read a story, you continually make predictions about what will happen next. As you know, a **prediction** is a guess that you make, based on information or clues that the author provides. Those clues, called **context clues**, help set the scene and help you understand what's happening. They also help you predict what might be coming next.

- As you read "A Retrieved Reformation," you will pause twice to make predictions. At Strategy Break #1 you will write your predictions. You will also write which clues helped you make your predictions.

- At Strategy Break #2 you will check your earlier predictions. Then you will make more predictions, and you will tell which clues helped you make them.

- After you finish reading, you will see if any of your predictions match what actually happened in the story.

A Retrieved Reformation

by O. Henry

As you read this story, see if you can use the clues that the author provides to help you make predictions.

A guard came to the prison shoeshop, where Jimmy Valentine was **assiduously** stitching uppers, and escorted him to the front office. There the warden handed Jimmy his pardon, which had been signed that morning. Jimmy took it in a tired kind of way. He had served nearly ten months of a four-year sentence. He had expected to stay about three months, at the longest.

"Now, Valentine," said the warden, "you'll go out in the morning. Brace up, and make a man of yourself. You're not a bad fellow at heart. Stop cracking safes, and go straight."

"Me?" said Jimmy, in surprise. "Why, I never cracked a safe in my life."

"Oh, no," laughed the warden. "Of course not. Let's see now. How was it you happened to get sent up on that Springfield job? Was it simply a case of a mean old jury that had it in for you? It's always that way with you innocent victims."

"Me?" said Jimmy, still looking **virtuous**. "Why, Warden, I never was in Springfield in my life!"

"Take him back, Cronin," smiled the warden, "and fix him with out-going clothes. Unlock him at seven in the morning. Better think over my advice, Valentine."

At a quarter past seven on the next morning Jimmy stood in the warden's outer office. He had on a suit of poorly fitting, ready-made clothes and a pair of the stiff, squeaky shoes that the state furnishes to its discharged guests.

The clerk handed him a railroad ticket and a five-dollar bill. The warden slapped him on the back and shook hands, and Mr. James Valentine, Number 9762, walked out into the sunshine.

Disregarding the song of the birds, the waving green trees, and the smell of the flowers, Jimmy headed straight for a restaurant. There he tasted the first sweet joys of liberty in the shape of a broiled chicken and a piece of apple pie. From there he proceeded leisurely to the depot. He tossed a quarter into the hat of a blind man sitting by the door, and then boarded his train. Three hours later found him in a little town near the state line. He went to a café and shook hands with his old pal, Mike, who was standing alone behind the counter.

"Great to see you, Jimmy," said Mike. "Feeling all right?"

"Fine," said Jimmy. "Got my key?"

He got his key and went upstairs, unlocking the door of a room at the rear. Everything was just as he had left it. There on the floor was still Ben Price's collar button that had been torn from that well-known and **eminent** detective's shirt when he had overpowered Jimmy to arrest him.

Pulling out from the wall a folding bed, Jimmy slid back a panel in the wall and dragged out a dust-covered suitcase. He opened this and gazed fondly at the finest set of burglar's tools in the East. It was a complete set, made of specially tempered steel, the latest designs in drills, punches, braces, clamps, and bits, with two or three **novelties** invented by Jimmy himself, in which he took pride. Over nine hundred dollars they had cost him to have made—at a place where they make such things for the profession.

In half an hour Jimmy went downstairs and through the café. He was now dressed in tasteful and well-fitting clothes and carried his dusted and cleaned suitcase in his hand.

"Going on a job?" asked Mike, genially.

"Me?" said Jimmy, in a puzzled tone. "I don't understand. I'm representing the New York Amalgamated Short Snap Biscuit Cracker and Frazzled Wheat Company."

With that, both men burst out into laughter.

 Stop here for Strategy Break #1

Strategy Break #1

1. What do you predict will happen next? _____

_____

2. Why do you think so? _____

_____

3. What clues from the story helped you make your prediction(s)?_____

_____

_____

 Go on reading to see what happens.

A week after the release of Valentine, 9762, there was a neat job of safe burglary done in Richmond, Indiana, with no clue to the culprit. Eight hundred dollars was taken. Two weeks after that, a patented, new and improved burglar-proof safe in Logansport was opened like a cheese to the tune of fifteen hundred dollars. That began to interest the **rogue-catchers** greatly. Then an old-fashioned bank safe in

Jefferson City was cracked, yielding up an amount of five thousand dollars. The losses were high enough now to be brought to the attention of Ben Price. By comparing notes on the burglaries, a remarkable similarity in methods was noticed. Ben Price investigated the scenes of the robberies and was heard to remark:

"That's Dandy Jim Valentine's autograph. He's **resumed** business. Look at that combination lock—ripped out as easy as pulling up a radish in wet weather. He's got the only clamps that can do it. And look how clean those tumblers were punched out! Jimmy never has to drill more than one hole. Yes, I guess I want Mr. Valentine, all right. He'll do a nice long stay in prison this time."

Ben Price knew Jimmy's habits. He had learned them while working up the Springfield case. Quick getaways, no partners, a taste for good society— all of these had helped Mr. Valentine to become noted as a successful dodger of punishment and **retribution**. Word got out that Ben Price had taken up Valentine's trail, and other people with burglarproof safes felt a bit more at ease.

One afternoon Jimmy Valentine and his suitcase climbed out of a railroad car in the little town of Elmore, Arkansas. Jimmy, looking like an athletic young senior just home from college, made his way down the sidewalk toward the hotel.

A young woman crossed the street, passed him at the corner, and entered a door over which was the sign "The Elmore Bank." Jimmy Valentine looked into her eyes, forgot what he was, and became another man. She lowered her eyes and blushed slightly. Young men of Jimmy's style and looks were scarce in Elmore.

Jimmy collared a boy who was loafing on the steps of the bank as though he were one of the stockholders, and began to ask him questions about the town, feeding him dimes at intervals. By and by the young woman came out, taking pains not to look at the young man with the suitcase, and went on her way.

"Isn't that Miss Polly Simpson?" asked Jimmy, innocently.

"Naw," said the boy. "She's Annabel Adams. Her pa owns this bank. What'd you come to Elmore for? Is that a gold watch chain? I'm going to get a bulldog. Got any more dimes?"

Jimmy went to Planters' Hotel, registered as Ralph D. Spencer, and rented a room. He leaned on the desk and declared his plans to the clerk. He said he had come to Elmore to look for a location to go into business. How was the shoe business, now, in the town? He had thought of the shoe business. Was there a need?

The clerk was impressed with Jimmy's clothes and manner. He thought of himself as a fancy dresser but, upon seeing Jimmy, realized his own shortcomings.

"Yes," he said, "there ought to be a good opportunity in the shoe line. There isn't a real shoe store in town. The general stores handle them all. Business in that line would probably be quite good."

While trying to figure out how Jimmy knotted his tie, the clerk

LESSON 9: A RETRIEVED REFORMATION 93

cordially hoped that Mr. Spencer would decide to locate in Elmore. He would find it a pleasant town to live in, and the people very sociable.

Mr. Spencer thought he would stop over in the town a few days and look over the situation. No, the clerk needn't call for the bellhop. He would carry up his suitcase himself; it was rather heavy.

And so Mr. Ralph Spencer arose from Jimmy Valentine's ashes—ashes left by the flame of a sudden and transforming attack of love. He became a completely changed man, remained in Elmore, and prospered. He opened a shoe store and developed a thriving trade.

Socially he was also a success and made many friends. And he accomplished the wish of his heart. He met Miss Annabel Adams, and became more and more captivated by her charms.

At the end of a year the situation of Mr. Ralph Spencer was this: He had won the respect of the community, his shoe store was flourishing, and he and Annabel were engaged to be married in two weeks. Mr. Adams, the highly respected country banker, liked Spencer, and Annabel's pride in him almost equaled her affection.

One day Jimmy sat down in his room and wrote this letter, which he mailed to the safe address of one of his old friends in St. Louis:

Dear Old Pal:

I want you to be at Sullivan's place in Little Rock, next Wednesday night, at nine o'clock. I want you to wind up some little matters for me. And, also, I want to make you a present of my kit of tools. I know you'll be glad to get them—you couldn't duplicate the lot for a thousand dollars. Say, Billy, I've quit the old business—a year ago. I've got a nice store. I'm making an honest living, and I'm going to marry the finest woman on earth two weeks from now. It's the only life, Billy—the straight one. I wouldn't touch a dollar of another person's money now for a million. After I get married, I'm going to sell out and go West, where there won't be so much danger of having old scores brought up against me. I tell you, Billy, she's an angel. She believes in me; and I wouldn't do another crooked thing for the whole world. Be sure to be at Sully's, for I must see you. I'll bring along the tools with me.

Your old friend,
Jimmy

On the Monday night after Jimmy wrote this letter, Ben Price slipped into Elmore without drawing any attention to himself. He lounged around town in his quiet way until he found out just what he wanted to know. From the drugstore across the street from Spencer's shoe store, he got a good look at Ralph D. Spencer.

"Going to marry the banker's daughter, are you, Jimmy?" said Ben to himself softly. "Well, I don't know!"

The next morning Jimmy had breakfast at the Adamses'. He said he was going to Little Rock that day to order his wedding suit and to buy something nice for Annabel. That would be the first time he had left town since he came to Elmore. It had been more than a year now since those last professional "jobs," and he thought he could safely venture out.

After breakfast quite a family party went down together. There were Mr. Adams, Annabel and Jimmy, and Annabel's married sister with her two little girls, aged five and nine. They went by the hotel where Jimmy still stayed, and he ran up to his room and got his suitcase. Then they went on to the bank. There stood Jimmy's carriage and Dolph Gibson, who was going to drive him over to the railroad station.

All went past the high, carved oak railings into the banking room— Jimmy included, for Mr. Adams' future son-in-law was welcome anywhere. The clerks were pleased to be greeted by the good-looking, agreeable man who was going to marry Annabel. Jimmy set his suitcase down. Annabel, whose heart was bubbling with happiness and high spirits, put on Jimmy's hat and picked up the suitcase. But she put it down at once.

"My, Ralph," she said, "how heavy it is! Feels like it was filled with gold bricks."

"Lot of nickel-plated shoehorns in there that I'm going to return," said Jimmy coolly. "Thought I'd save shipping charges by taking them down myself. I'm getting awfully economical."

The Elmore Bank had just put in a new safe and vault. Mr. Adams was very proud of it and insisted on an inspection by everyone. The vault was a small one, but it had a new patented door. It fastened with three solid steel bolts thrown simultaneously with a single handle, and it had a time lock. Mr. Adams, beaming, explained its workings to Mr. Spencer, who showed a polite interest, but seemed a bit confused by it all. The two children, May and Agatha, were delighted by the shining metal and funny clock and knobs.

While they were thus involved, Ben Price dropped in and leaned on his elbow, looking casually inside between the railings. He told the teller that he didn't want anything; he was just waiting for a man he knew.

Suddenly there were loud screams and a commotion. Without being perceived by the elders, May, the nine-year-old girl, in a spirit of play, had shut Agatha in the vault. She had then dropped the bolts and turned the knob of the combination lock as she had seen Mr. Adams do.

The old banker sprang to the handle and tugged at it for a moment. "The door can't be opened," he groaned. "The clock hasn't been wound nor the combination set."

Mr. Adams raised his trembling hands. "Everyone be very quiet for a moment," he said. "Agatha!" he called as loudly as he could. "Listen to me." During the following silence they could just hear the faint sound of a child shrieking wildly in terror from within the dark vault.

"Agatha!" wailed the mother. "She'll die of fright! Open the door! Break it open! Can't anyone do something?"

"There isn't a man nearer than Little Rock who can open that door," said Mr. Adams, in a shaky voice.

"Spencer, what shall we do? That child—she can't stand it very long in there. There isn't enough air, and, besides, she may go into convulsions from fright."

Agatha's mother, frantic now, beat the door of the vault with her hands. Somebody wildly suggested dynamite.

Annabel turned to Jimmy, her large eyes full of **anguish**, but not yet of despair.

"Can't you do something, Ralph— *try*, won't you?"

 Stop here for Strategy Break #2.

Strategy Break #2

1. Do your earlier predictions match what happened? _____ Why or why not? _____

_____

_____

2. What do you predict will happen next? _____

_____

3. Why do you think so? _____

_____

4. What clues from the story helped you make your prediction(s)? _____

_____

_____

➡ Go on reading to see what happens.

He looked at her for what seemed a long moment. There was a funny, soft smile on his lips and in his keen eyes.

"Annabel," he said, "give me that rose you are wearing, will you?"

Hardly believing that she heard him right, she unpinned the bud from her dress, and placed it in his hand. Jimmy stuffed it into his vest pocket, threw off his coat, and rolled up his shirt sleeves. With that act Ralph D.

Spencer passed away, and Jimmy Valentine took his place.

"Get away from the door, all of you!" he commanded.

He set his suitcase on the floor, and opened it out flat. From that time on he did not seem to be conscious of the presence of anyone else. He carefully laid out the shining, strange tools, swiftly and in order, whistling softly to himself as he always did when at work. In a deep silence without moving, the others watched him as though under a spell.

In a minute, Jimmy's pet drill was biting smoothly into the steel door. In ten minutes—breaking his own record—he threw back the bolts and opened the door.

Agatha, nearly unconscious, but still breathing, was safe on the floor.

Jimmy Valentine put on his coat, and walked beyond the railing toward the front door. As he went he thought he heard a faraway voice call, "Ralph!" But he never hesitated.

At the door a big man stood in his way.

"Hello, Ben!" said Jimmy, still with his strange smile. "Got around at last, have you? Well, let's go. I don't know that it makes much difference now."

And then Ben Price acted rather strangely.

"Guess you're mistaken, Mr. Spencer," he said. "Don't believe I recognize you. Your carriage is waiting for you, isn't it?"

And Ben Price turned and strolled down the street. ●

Strategy Follow-up

Go back and look at the predictions that you wrote in this lesson. Do any of them match what actually happened in this story? Why or why not?

_____

_____

_____

_____

_____

_____

_____

_____

_____

_____

_____

_____

✓Personal Checklist

Read each question and put a check (✓) in the correct box.

1. How well do you understand what happened in this story?
   - ☐ 3 (extremely well)
   - ☐ 2 (fairly well)
   - ☐ 1 (not well)

2. How well do you understand this story's surprise ending?
   - ☐ 3 (extremely well)
   - ☐ 2 (fairly well)
   - ☐ 1 (not well)

3. When you wrote your prediction in the Vocabulary Builder, how many vocabulary words were you able to use?
   - ☐ 3 (7–8 words)
   - ☐ 2 (4–6 words)
   - ☐ 1 (0–3 words)

4. How well were you able to predict what might happen next in this story?
   - ☐ 3 (extremely well)
   - ☐ 2 (fairly well)
   - ☐ 1 (not well)

5. How well would you be able to explain the title of this story?
   - ☐ 3 (extremely well)
   - ☐ 2 (fairly well)
   - ☐ 1 (not well)

Vocabulary Check

Look back at the work you did in the Vocabulary Builder. Then answer each question by circling the correct letter.

1. What does a rogue-catcher do?
   a. tracks down stray dogs and brings them to the pound
   b. tracks down criminals and arrests them
   c. tracks down defective plants and uproots them

2. Which of the following best describes doing something assiduously?
   a. construction workers putting up a building
   b. children watching cartoons on a Saturday afternoon
   c. lying on the beach on a summer day

3. Where might you be most likely to find novelty items?
   a. in a store full of one-of-a-kind gifts
   b. in an expensive jewelry store
   c. in a store that sells building supplies

4. Which of these people would *not* be considered virtuous?
   a. a judge
   b. a police officer
   c. a convicted criminal

5. At the end of this story, it appears that Ralph Spencer will resume his life as Jimmy Valentine. What does this mean?
   a. Ralph Spencer will summarize his life as Jimmy Valentine.
   b. Ralph Spencer will stop his life as Jimmy Valentine.
   c. Ralph Spencer will live his life as Jimmy Valentine again.

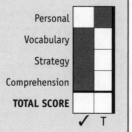

Add the numbers that you just checked to get your Personal Checklist score. Fill in your score here. Then turn to page 217 and transfer your score onto Graph 1.

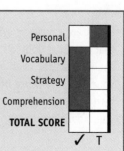

Check your answers with your teacher. Give yourself 1 point for each correct answer, and fill in your Vocabulary score here. Then turn to page 217 and transfer your score onto Graph 1.

Strategy Check

Review the predictions that you wrote and review the story. Then answer the following questions:

1. Which clue would have best supported your prediction that Ben Price would catch Jimmy Valentine?

    a. Ben Price knew Jimmy's habits.

    b. A week after Valentine's release, there was a neat burglary with no clue to the culprit.

    c. Valentine was a successful dodger of punishment.

2. Which prediction would *not* have fit the story at Strategy Break #1?

    a. Ben Price will track down Jimmy Valentine.

    b. Ben Price will turn out to be the real burglar.

    c. Ben Price will not catch Jimmy Valentine.

3. Which clue might indicate that Ralph Spencer's business in Elmore would be successful?

    a. He worked for the New York Amalgamated Short Snap Biscuit Cracker and Frazzled Wheat Company.

    b. He carries lots of money in his suitcase.

    c. He worked in the prison shoeshop, and he knows how shoes are made.

4. Which clue would *not* have supported the prediction that Ralph would crack the safe?

    a. Look at that combination lock—ripped out.

    b. "That child—she can't stand it very long in there. There isn't enough air."

    c. "The door can't be opened. The clock hasn't been wound nor the combination set."

5. If you thought that Ben Price was going to arrest Jimmy at the end of the story, which clue would *not* have supported your prediction?

    a. "I want Mr. Valentine, all right."

    b. And then Ben Price acted rather strangely.

    c. A big man stood in Jimmy Valentine's way.

Comprehension Check

Review the story if necessary. Then answer these questions:

1. At the beginning of this story, why is Jimmy Valentine in prison?

    a. He is there to sell shoes to the inmates.

    b. He is there to speak with the warden.

    c. He is serving time for cracking a bank safe.

2. Why do you think Jimmy heads straight for a restaurant when he gets out of prison?

    a. He is tired of prison food and wants something else.

    b. The prison didn't feed him the night before he left.

    c. His safe-cracking tools are at the restaurant.

3. What does Jimmy keep in the suitcase that he carries around with him?

    a. all of his money

    b. his burglar's tools

    c. the only clothing he owns

4. What causes Jimmy Valentine to become a completely changed man?

    a. the threat of being caught again

    b. his love for Annabel Adams

    c. both of the above

5. Why do you think that Ben Price doesn't arrest Jimmy at the end of the story?

    a. He lets Jimmy off for saving Agatha's life.

    b. He can see that Jimmy has turned his life around.

    c. Both of the above are possible reasons.

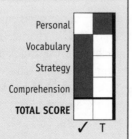

Check your answers with your teacher. Give yourself 1 point for each correct answer, and fill in your Strategy score here. Then turn to page 217 and transfer your score onto Graph 1.

Personal
Vocabulary
Strategy
Comprehension
TOTAL SCORE

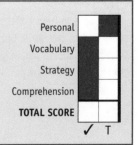

Check your answers with your teacher. Give yourself 1 point for each correct answer, and fill in your Comprehension score here. Then turn to page 217 and transfer your score onto Graph 1.

Personal
Vocabulary
Strategy
Comprehension
TOTAL SCORE

Extending

Choose one or both of these activities:

READ MORE SHORT STORIES BY O. HENRY

Locate other short stories by O. Henry, and read or listen to several of them. (See the resources listed on this page for where to find some of them.) Either orally or in writing, discuss your stories with the rest of the class. If other students have read or heard any of O. Henry's stories, you might hold a panel discussion to compare your favorites.

WRITE YOUR OWN STORY WITH A SURPRISE ENDING

Examine the surprise endings of a few of O. Henry's stories. How does he create the element of surprise? What makes the endings work? By yourself or with a partner, write a short story with a surprise ending. When you have finished, ask a few classmates to listen as you read the story aloud. Stop once or twice while reading, and ask your classmates to make predictions. When you have finished the story, discuss everyone's predictions. Did anyone predict the surprise ending?

Resources

Books

Henry, O. *41 Stories by O. Henry.* Signet, 1991.

———. *The Best Short Stories of O. Henry.* Modern Library, 1994.

———. *The Ransom of Red Chief and Other Stories.* Running Press, 1989.

Henry, O. and Lisbeth Zwenger, ill. *The Gift of the Magi.* Aladdin Picture Books. Aladdin, 1997.

Web Site

http://www.unityspot.com/arthurs/ohenry.html
This Web site offers a collection of short stories by O. Henry.

Audio Recordings

Henry, O. *Audio Drama 101, Volume I: O. Henry.* Lend a Hand Society, 1998.

———. *The Ransom of Red Chief.* Listening Library, 1995.

LESSON ⑩ The Printer's Apprentice

Building Background

Imagine you are celebrating your 12th birthday. After you blow out the candles on your cake and everyone has a piece, your parents say, "Tomorrow you will begin your new job and move out." If you were a boy in the 1700s or early 1800s, you wouldn't have been too surprised by such news. Twelve years old was about the right age for a young person to begin learning a trade.

The informational article you are about to read tells how one group of teenagers learned their important trade—printing books and newspapers. On the lines below, write five questions that you would like this article to answer. Your questions might be about being an apprentice, about the trade of printing, or about what life was like for boys in that time period. As you read the article, see if you can find answers to any of your questions.

_____

_____

_____

_____

_____

apprentice

contract

craftsman

foreman

lever

press

recruiters

Vocabulary Builder

1. The words in the margin are all specialized vocabulary words from "The Printer's Apprentice." As you know, **specialized vocabulary** words are all related to a particular topic. For example, the specialized vocabulary words in Lesson 6 are all related to the Olympics. In this lesson, they are all related to the trade of printing.

2. Match each specialized vocabulary word in Column 1 to its definition in Column 2. Use a dictionary if you need help.

3. Save your work. You will refer to it again in the Vocabulary Check.

apprentice	machine for printing reading materials
contract	person skilled in a trade
craftsman	people who get others to join their group
foreman	bar that is pulled, lifted, or pushed down
lever	person learning a trade; student
press	person in charge of a group of workers
recruiters	written agreement

Strategy Builder

Summarizing Nonfiction

- As you know, **nonfiction** is writing that gives readers facts and information about different topics. Types of nonfiction that you have read in this book so far include informational articles, autobiographies, and biographies. Other types of nonfiction include directions and recipes for how to do or make things, persuasive essays, newspaper and magazine articles, and your history textbook.

- In Lesson 2 you learned that every piece of nonfiction follows a particular organizational pattern. The article you are about to read follows the pattern of **description**. The article describes what life was like for young boys who became printer's apprentices in the 18th and early 19th centuries.

- As most nonfiction does, this article gives you a lot of information at once. To keep the information straight and remember it better, it helps to stop from time to time to summarize what you have read. When you **summarize** a portion of text, you list or retell the most important ideas in your own words.

- To refresh your memory, read the following summary for the first part of "Alex, the Talking Parrot." Notice that it summarizes a few pages of text in only one paragraph by stating just the article's main ideas and leaving out unnecessary details.

Teaching Alex to speak and understand wasn't easy at first. Dr. Irene Pepperberg had to teach the parrot one word at a time. It took Alex many weeks to learn his first word, but after that, it became easier. Irene spent so much time getting Alex to talk because she's interested in discovering how smart animals are and how their brains work. Teaching Alex to speak words that he understands has allowed Irene to ask questions and Alex to answer. By talking with Alex, Irene can find out what sorts of things his brain can do. She now knows that parrots are much smarter than scientists used to think.

The Printer's Apprentice

by Linda Roberts

As you read the first part of this informational article, think about how you might summarize it. Jot down your ideas on a separate sheet of paper. When you get to the Strategy Break, you will have a chance to compare your summary with the sample provided.

In the 1700s and early 1800s most boys left school at the age of twelve or fourteen. It was time to learn a trade. So a boy would look for work as an **apprentice** to a master **craftsman**. In return for the work, a master would teach the boy his craft. In time, the boy hoped to become a master craftsman himself.

To see what kind of work he was suited for, a boy and his father might visit the carpenter, the weaver, or the blacksmith. But more and more people were learning to read, and newspapers and books were selling fast. So a would-be apprentice and his father often chose the printer.

If the printer was willing, he and the father signed a **contract**. It promised that the boy would work for the printer, usually for seven years, and the printer would teach him the "art and mystery of printing." The boy promised not to tell anyone the secrets of how printing was done. Then he moved in with his master. He ate at his master's table, slept in his house or in the shop with the other apprentices, and was given clothes to wear.

Although he might have been glad to leave school, the boy soon found that life wasn't easy for apprentices during their first year. They had to do the chores that no one else wanted. They got up early in the morning to make the fire, fetch water, and sweep the floor. They had to do the master's bidding day and night. If the master was a cruel man, the apprentices could be beaten for idleness, and they weren't allowed to talk back or leave.

The food or clothes might not be all that they had hoped for, either. When he was twelve, Mark Twain, who later wrote *Tom Sawyer* and *Huckleberry Finn,* was apprenticed to a printer named Ament. To save money, Ament gave Twain his own old clothes to wear. Twain wrote, "I was only about half as big as Ament, consequently his shirts gave me the uncomfortable sense of living in a circus tent, and I had to turn up his pants to my ears to make them short enough."

But hard work and rough treatment couldn't keep apprentices from having fun. In the evening, they played the accordion and sang. They played chess and perhaps cards in secret, since a strict master might believe that cards were sinful. Apprentices were even known to sneak out at night to roam the streets or visit taverns.

Sometimes they played tricks on each other. One shy country boy named Horace Greeley had his blond hair inked black by the other apprentices. But they must not have discouraged him too badly. He kept working at the printer's craft, learning how to edit and publish a newspaper. Later he became the most famous newspaper editor of his time.

 Stop here for the Strategy Break.

Strategy Break

Did you jot down your summary as you read? If you did, see if it looks anything like this:

During the 18th and early 19th centuries, most boys became apprentices between ages 12 and 14. Since books were becoming more popular, many boys apprenticed to printers. Most apprenticeships lasted seven years, during which time the boy moved in with his master and learned "the art and mystery of printing."

An apprentice's first year wasn't easy. He had to work day and night, doing whatever his master wanted. If his master was mean, he might beat the apprentice, and there wasn't anything the boy could do about it, least of all talk back or leave.

Some printers didn't give their apprentices the proper food or clothing. For example, Mark Twain had to wear his master's old clothes, even though his master was twice his size.

In spite of all these hardships, apprentices still managed to have fun. In the evenings, they sang, played games, and even sneaked out to taverns. They also played tricks on each other, such as inking Horace Greeley's blond hair black.

Go on reading.

After a year or so of drudgery, an apprentice was finally allowed to learn printing. He began with setting type. He might start with a handwritten article to be printed in the newspaper. With the article in front of him, the apprentice copied each sentence in type. He took the letters, one by one, from the case where they were kept, and inserted them onto a slotted stick that he held. This was especially tricky since he had to set all the letters backward so they would come out the correct way when they were printed.

P's and q's looked much the same, especially backward. They could easily be mixed up, which may have given rise to the expression still heard today, "Mind your p's and q's!"

The apprentice set several lines of type on his stick, then put them aside and set several more. The shop **fore-man** put all the lines together into a heavy metal form that could print several small pages. When all of these pages were printed, the apprentice put the type back in the case. With enough practice, he could set type quickly without looking.

Apprentices also learned to put fresh ink on the metal printing forms by beating them with inked leather balls tied to the ends of long wooden sticks. They made the ink themselves by boiling lampblack, or soot, with other ingredients in a large vat. This could take as long as twenty-four hours, and the mixture had to be watched and stirred constantly.

When the apprentice got older, he learned to work the wooden **press** that printed the sheets of paper. This was hard work and took strong arms. Some boys never grew big enough. A pressman had to pull a **lever** twice for each sheet, over and over, until all the sheets were printed, while a younger apprentice fed each sheet of paper onto the form and removed it after it was printed.

Sometimes it was hard to keep working day in and day out at the same job, especially if exciting things were happening elsewhere. When the guns of the American Revolution started to fire, many apprentices ran away and joined the army. Naval **recruiters** walked the streets and sang:

All you that have bad masters,
And cannot get your due;
Come, come, my brave boys,
And join with our ship's crew.

Some ran away even before the Revolution. Benjamin Franklin was apprenticed at twelve to his older brother James, who was a printer. They quarreled often. Although Ben admitted that he was "saucy and provoking" to James, he grew tired of his brother's blows and decided he had learned enough about printing. At seventeen, he secretly took a ship out of Boston and found his way to Philadelphia, where he set up his own print shop. In time he became the colony's most celebrated printer, publisher, and writer.

As the years went on, other apprentices seemed to catch Ben's independent spirit. By the 1850s boys no longer wanted to serve a master. They were eager to earn wages and make their own way, and since free public high schools were opening their doors, many stayed in school. Besides, by then great mechanical presses had appeared in large printing houses, producing many thousands of pages in one hour, and the printer's apprentices became a thing of the past.

But they had served their country well. The spirit of independence that raced through the colonies in the late 1700s and that finally led to a new nation was spread by newspapers, pamphlets, and books. And all of these were printed in the little shops by boys who set the type, stirred the ink, and dreamed of the day they could pass on the "art and mystery of printing" to apprentices of their own. ●

Strategy Follow-up

First, go back and read the questions that you wrote in Building Background. Did you find the answers to any of them as you read this article? If so, which ones?

Next, on a separate sheet of paper, summarize the second part "the Printer's Apprentice." Use your own words. Be sure to list only the most important ideas and skip unnecessary details.

✓ Personal Checklist

Read each question and put a check (✓) in the correct box.

1. In Building Background, how well were you able to list five questions that you hoped this article would answer?
   - ☐ 3 (extremely well)
   - ☐ 2 (fairly well)
   - ☐ 1 (not well)

2. How well were you able to find answers in the article to some or all of your questions?
   - ☐ 3 (extremely well)
   - ☐ 2 (fairly well)
   - ☐ 1 (not well)

3. In the Vocabulary Builder, how well were you able to match the specialized vocabulary words and their definitions?
   - ☐ 3 (extremely well)
   - ☐ 2 (fairly well)
   - ☐ 1 (not well)

4. In the Strategy Follow-up, how well were you able to summarize the second part of this article?
   - ☐ 3 (extremely well)
   - ☐ 2 (fairly well)
   - ☐ 1 (not well)

5. Now that you've read this article, how well would you be able to explain the experiences of many printers' apprentices?
   - ☐ 3 (extremely well)
   - ☐ 2 (fairly well)
   - ☐ 1 (not well)

Vocabulary Check

Look back at the work you did in the Vocabulary Builder. Then answer each question by circling the correct letter.

1. In which of these sentences is *press* used as a verb?
   a. In the 1700s, as today, the press is accused of sensationalism.
   b. To get ink on the stamp, press it firmly onto the inkpad.
   c. If the paper is too soft, it will tear in the press.

2. Which pair of words best completes the sentence *A new _____ has very little skill, while a _____ has great skill?*
   a. apprentice, craftsman
   b. foreman, craftsman
   c. apprentice, recruiter

3. Which phrase best describes a foreman?
   a. person who is skilled in a trade
   b. person who gets others to join his or her group
   c. person in charge of a group of workers

4. Which of these sentences uses the word *contract* in the same way that the article does?
   a. If a rabid animal bites you, you may contract rabies.
   b. Bars made of steel contract in very cold temperatures.
   c. Mr. and Mrs. Clement just signed a contract to buy a home.

5. Which of the following is *not* an example of a modern-day recruiter?
   a. someone who tries to get people to become printers' apprentices
   b. someone who tries to get people to join the armed forces
   c. someone who tries to get people to fill certain job openings

Add the numbers that you just checked to get your Personal Checklist score. Fill in your score here. Then turn to page 217 and transfer your score onto Graph 1.

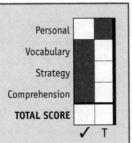

Check your answers with your teacher. Give yourself 1 point for each correct answer, and fill in your Vocabulary score here. Then turn to page 217 and transfer your score onto Graph 1.

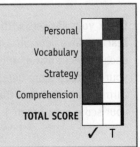

Strategy Check

Review the summary that you wrote in the Strategy Follow-up. Also review the article if necessary. Then answer these questions:

1. Which sentence best summarizes what a young boy did during the first year of his apprenticeship?
   a. He had to make the ink by boiling lampblack.
   b. He had to do the chores that no one else wanted.
   c. He worked the wooden press that printed the paper.

2. Which word from the article best summarizes what a young boy did during the first year of his apprenticeship?
   a. drudgery
   b. mystery
   c. easy

3. Which sentence best summarizes what a boy did during the second year of his apprenticeship?
   a. He had to do his master's bidding day and night.
   b. The boy was finally allowed to learn printing.
   c. He learned to work the wooden printing press.

4. What is an unnecessary detail that you should *not* have included in your summary of the second part of this article?
   a. Ben Franklin was "saucy and provoking."
   b. Many apprentices ran away and joined the army.
   c. Both of the above are unnecessary details.

5. Why did printers' apprentices become a thing of the past?
   a. Mechanical presses printed many thousands of pages an hour.
   b. Boys wanted to make their own money rather than serve masters.
   c. Both of the above answers are correct.

Comprehension Check

Review the article if necessary. Then answer these questions:

1. For how long did an apprentice usually work for a master printer?
   a. three years
   b. five years
   c. seven years

2. What promise did an apprentice have to make when he began working for a printer?
   a. not to tell anyone the secrets of printing
   b. not to play tricks on his master
   c. not to run away from his master

3. Why was setting type onto a slotted stick especially tricky?
   a. The lines of type had to be placed in a metal form.
   b. The letters had to be set backwards.
   c. In those days, all the letters looked the same.

4. Which of today's expressions might have come about as a result of setting type?
   a. "Keep your eye on the ball!"
   b. "Act your age!"
   c. "Mind your p's and q's!"

5. According to the article, what did Mark Twain, Horace Greeley, and Benjamin Franklin have in common?
   a. They all ran away from their masters.
   b. All three were apprenticed to printers.
   c. Other apprentices played tricks on all three of them.

Check your answers with your teacher. Give yourself 1 point for each correct answer, and fill in your Strategy score here. Then turn to page 217 and transfer your score onto Graph 1.

Personal / Vocabulary / Strategy / Comprehension / TOTAL SCORE ✓ T

Check your answers with your teacher. Give yourself 1 point for each correct answer, and fill in your Comprehension score here. Then turn to page 217 and transfer your score onto Graph 1.

Personal / Vocabulary / Strategy / Comprehension / TOTAL SCORE ✓ T

Extending

Choose one or both of these activities:

CREATE A DIARY

How do you suppose you would take to the life of a printer's apprentice? Keeping in mind the details from the article, imagine your first week as an apprentice. Write diary entries for each day of the week.

SPEAK FOR FAMOUS PRINTERS

"The Printer's Apprentice" mentions three famous printers' apprentices: Benjamin Franklin, Mark Twain, and Horace Greeley. Choose one of these men and do research on him, both in books and on the World Wide Web. Take notes on what you discover. Then use your notes to develop a short speech that your chosen subject might deliver as the opening speaker at a Career Day at your school. If possible, deliver your speech to your class.

Resources

Books

Burch, Joann Johansen. *Fine Print: A Story About Johann Gutenberg.* Carolrhoda Books, 1992.

Krensky, Stephen. *Breaking into Print: Before and After the Invention of the Printing Press.* Little, Brown, 1996.

Steffens, Bradley. *Printing Press: Ideas into Type.* Encyclopedia of Discovery and Invention. Lucent Books, 1990.

Web Sites

http://sln.fi.edu/tfi/preview/benpreview.html
Click on "Begin Your Tour" on the Web site of the Franklin Institute Science Museum to learn about the life of Ben Franklin. Click "printer" to see a photo of Franklin's press and to read his wise sayings.

http://www.harcourtschool.com/activity/biographies/greeley/
Read a brief biography of Horace Greeley on this Web site.

http://www.nytimes.com/specials/presses
This Web site takes you on a tour showing how the *New York Times* is printed.

http://www.twainquotes.com/Apprenticeship.html
On this Web page, read a quote from Mark Twain about being a printer's apprentice and see a photograph of young Twain as an apprentice.

Video/DVD

Gutenberg: The Birth of Printing. Barr Films, 1990.

Learning New Words

Compound Words

A compound word is made up of two words put together. In Lesson 10 you read that a young boy would leave his home at around 12 or 14 years of age to become an apprentice to a craftsman. *Craftsman* is the name given to a *man* (or woman) who is very skilled in a particular *craft* or trade.

Fill in each blank with a compound word by combining a word from Row 1 with a word from Row 2.

Row 1: sports   late   night   space   golden
Row 2: comer   port   rod   wear   stick

1. place where rockets can take off = _____

2. police officer's club = _____

3. person who arrived tardy or recently = _____

4. plant with small yellow flowers = _____

5. informal or outdoor clothing = _____

Suffixes

A suffix is a word part that is added to the end of a root word. When you add a suffix, you often change the root word's meaning and function. For example, the suffix *-ful* means "full of," so the root word *fear* changes from a noun to an adjective meaning "full of fear."

-ic

The suffix *-ic* changes a noun into an adjective. Some meanings for this suffix are "of or having to do with" or "having the nature of" or "made up of." In "Dancer," the adoption agency calls Clarissa *sociopathic*. A sociopathic person has the nature of a sociopath, or an antisocial person.

Write the word that describes each person below.

1. having to do with calories   _____

2. having the nature of a hero   _____

3. having to do with anemia   _____

4. having to do with photography   _____

Multiple-Meaning Words

As you know, the same word can have more than one meaning. For example, the word *draw* can mean "make a picture" or "take something out of" or "pull or drag." To figure out which meaning of *draw* an author is using, you have to use context—the information surrounding a word or situation that helps you understand it.

When you read "The Faithful Sister" you used context to figure out that the meaning of *draw* that the author was using was "take something out of," as in drawing water from a well.

Now use context to figure out the correct meaning of each underlined word. Circle the letter of the correct meaning.

1. My little sister likes to <u>draw</u> horses.

   a. take something out of

   b. sketch

2. Mike's father plans to <u>retire</u> from his job in seven years.

   a. leave or give up

   b. go back or retreat

3. My brother is so <u>mad</u> about the Chicago Bears that he goes to every home game they play.

   a. wildly enthusiastic

   b. extremely angry

4. If you want to eat at the most popular restaurant, you need a <u>reservation</u>.

   a. land set aside for Native Americans to live on

   b. time set aside in advance

5. At the party, we listened to <u>records</u> and danced all night long.

   a. thin, flat discs on which music is recorded

   b. histories of people's offenses and crimes

VOCABULARY

From Lesson 6
• records

From Lesson 7
• reservation

From Lesson 8
• chamber
• draw
• gobbled
• mad
• retire
• sap
• show
• well

From Lesson 10
• contract
• press

LESSON 11 Duffy's Jacket

Building Background

Why do authors write? The answer to that question depends on many things. For example, if authors write to explain facts and information about things, their purpose is to **inform**. If authors write to give their opinion about something, and try convince others to share that opinion, their purpose is to **persuade**. If they write to describe how they feel about an experience—such watching as a beautiful sunset or riding on a crowded bus—their purpose is to **express**. If they want to make readers smile, laugh, or be surprised, their purpose is to **entertain**. As you will see, the author's purpose for writing "Duffy's Jacket" is to entertain.

When writing to entertain, good writers choose their words carefully to set the right **mood**, or feeling, that they want readers to get from the story. Think, for example, of the feeling you would get if an author described a red object as *blood red*. How would you feel if that same object was described as *candy-apple red*?

As you read "Duffy's Jacket," watch for changes in the mood. How does the author use words to make you smile or shiver?

clomping

fumigating

heebie-jeebies

lurking

sabotage

sentinel

tick

turnip

Vocabulary Builder

1. The words in the margin are from "Duffy's Jacket." Before you begin reading this short story, see how many of the words you can match with their meanings.

feeling of uneasiness	_____
walking clumsily and heavily	_____
plant that's eaten as a vegetable	_____
hiding and waiting for someone	_____
insect that attaches to the skin	_____
cause to fail	_____
one that keeps guard	_____
using smoke to kill insects	_____

2. As you read the story, watch for these words. Change your answers if necessary.

3. Then save your work. You will refer to it again in the Vocabulary Check.

Strategy Builder

Making Predictions While Reading a Story

- While you read most stories, you probably try to **predict**, or guess, what will happen next. Almost like a detective, you piece together clues that the author gives, and you use them to make your predictions.

- The clues that the author gives are called context clues. **Context** is the information that comes before or after a word or a situation to help you figure it out. For example, read the following paragraphs. See if you can use the context clues to figure out what is happening and to predict what might happen next.

A ballerina, a police officer, a clown, and a vampire were sitting around a table. "Please pass that luscious slab of meat, would you please?" said the vampire.

"Why certainly. Please feast to your heart's content," said the officer. "I'll take some of those blood-red beets, if you don't mind."

"I just love red. It's my favorite color," said the vampire while passing the beets.

"Oh, it's mine too," said the clown, "especially for noses and cheeks." Everyone at the table laughed.

"From now on, let's do this every October thirty-first!" said the ballerina. Suddenly there was a knock on the door . . .

- Can you predict who might be at the door? You can if you use context clues. By the end of these paragraphs, you probably figured out that the setting of this story is a Halloween dinner-party, and that the characters are all in costume. The strongest clue is the ballerina's speech, particularly the words *every October thirty-first*. Without this clue, you might not be able to make an appropriate prediction about what might happen next. Now that you know that it's Halloween, however, you can use that information to predict that the person at the door will most likely be a trick-or-treater.

Duffy's Jacket

by Bruce Coville

As you read this short story, keep the author's purpose in mind. Also look for context clues to help you predict what might happen next.

If my cousin Duffy had the brains of a **turnip** it never would have happened. But as far as I'm concerned, Duffy makes a turnip look bright. My mother disagrees. According to her, Duffy is actually very bright. She claims the reason he's so scatter-brained is that he's too busy being brilliant inside his own head to remember everyday things. Maybe. But hanging around with Duffy means you spend a lot of time saying, "Your glasses, Duffy," or "Your coat, Duffy," or—well, you get the idea: a lot of three-word sentences that start with "Your," end with "Duffy," and have words like *book, radio, wallet,* or whatever it is he's just put down and left behind, stuck in the middle.

Me, I think turnips are brighter.

But since Duffy's my cousin, and since my mother and her sister are both single parents, we tend to do a lot of things together—like camping, which is how we got into the mess I want to tell you about.

Personally, I thought camping was a big mistake. But since Mom and Aunt Elise are raising the three of us—me, Duffy, and my little sister, Marie—on their own, they're convinced they have to do man-stuff with us every once in a while. I think they read some book that said me and Duffy would come out weird if they don't. You can take

him camping all you want. It ain't gonna make Duffy normal.

Anyway, the fact that our mothers were getting wound up to do something fatherly, combined with the fact that Aunt Elise's boss had a friend who had a friend who said we could use his cabin, added up to the five of us bouncing along this horrible dirt road late one Friday in October.

It was late because we had lost an hour going back to get Duffy's suitcase. I suppose it wasn't actually Duffy's fault. No one remembered to say, "Your suitcase, Duffy," so he couldn't really have been expected to remember it.

"Oh, Elise," cried my mother, as we got deeper into the woods. "Aren't the leaves beautiful?"

That's why it doesn't make sense for them to try to do man-stuff with us. If it had been our fathers, they would have been drinking beer and burping and maybe telling dirty stories instead of talking about the leaves. So why try to fake it?

Anyway, we get to this cabin, which is about eighteen million miles from nowhere, and to my surprise, it's not a cabin at all. It's a house. A big house.

"Oh, my," said my mother as we pulled into the driveway.

"Isn't it great?" chirped Aunt Elise. "It's almost a hundred years old, back from the time when they used to build big hunting lodges up here. It's the only one in the area still standing. Horace said he hasn't been able to get up here in some time. That's why he was glad to let us use it. He said it would be good to have someone go in and air the place out."

Leave it to Aunt Elise. This place didn't need airing out—it needed **fumigating**. I never saw so many spiderwebs in my life. From the sounds we heard coming from the walls, the mice seemed to have made it a population center. We found a total of two working lightbulbs: one in the kitchen, and one in the dining room, which was paneled with dark wood and had a big stone fireplace at one end.

"Oh, my," said my mother again.

Duffy, who's allergic to about fifteen different things, started to sneeze.

"Isn't it charming?" asked Aunt Elise hopefully.

No one answered her.

Four hours later we had managed to get three bedrooms clean enough to sleep in without getting the **heebie-jeebies**—one for Mom and Aunt Elise, one for Marie, and one for me and Duffy. After a supper of beans and franks we hit the hay, which I think is what our mattresses were stuffed with. As I was drifting off, which took about thirty seconds, it occurred to me that four hours of housework wasn't all that much of a man-thing, something it might be useful to remember the next time Mom got one of these plans into her head.

Things looked better in the morning when we went outside and found a stream where we could go wading. ("Your sneakers, Duffy.")

Later we went back and started poking around the house, which really was enormous.

That was when things started getting a little spooky. In the room next to ours I found a message scrawled on the wall. BEWARE THE **SENTINEL**, it said in big black letters.

When I showed Mom and Aunt Elise they said it was just a joke and got mad at me for frightening Marie.

Marie wasn't the only one who was frightened.

We decided to go out for another walk. ("Your lunch, Duffy.") We went deep into the woods, following a faint trail that kept threatening to disappear but never actually faded away altogether. It was a hot day, even in the deep woods, and after a while we decided to take off our coats.

When we got back and Duffy didn't have his jacket, did they get mad at him? My mother actually had the nerve to say, "Why didn't you remind him? You know he forgets things like that."

What do I look like, a walking memo pad?

Anyway, I had other things on my mind—like the fact that I was convinced someone had been following us while we were in the woods.

I tried to tell my mother about it, but first she said I was being ridiculous, and then she accused me of trying to **sabotage** the trip.

So I shut up. But I was pretty nervous, especially when Mom and Aunt Elise announced that they were going into town—which was twenty miles away—to pick up some supplies (like lightbulbs).

"You kids will be fine on your own," said Mom cheerfully. "You can make popcorn and play Monopoly. And there's enough soda here for you to make yourselves sick on."

And with that they were gone.

 **Stop here for Strategy Break #1.**

Strategy Break #1

1. What do you predict will happen next? _____

_____

2. Why do you think so? _____

_____

3. What clues from the story helped you make your prediction(s)? _____

_____

_____

Go on reading to see what happens.

It got dark.

We played Monopoly.

They didn't come back. That didn't surprise me. Since Duffy and I were both fifteen they felt it was okay to leave us on our own, and Mom had warned us they might decide to have dinner at the little inn we had seen on the way up.

But I would have been happier if they had been there.

Especially when something started scratching on the door.

"What was that?" said Marie.

"What was what?" asked Duffy.

"That!" she said, and this time I heard it, too. My stomach rolled over, and the skin at the back of my neck started to prickle.

"Maybe it's the Sentinel!" I hissed.

"Andrew!" yelled Marie. "Mom told you not to say that."

"She said not to try to scare you," I said. "I'm not. *I'm* scared! I told you I heard something following us in the woods today."

Scratch, scratch.

"But you said it stopped," said Duffy. "So how would it know where we are now?"

"I don't know. I don't know what it is. Maybe it tracked us, like a blood-hound."

"Don't bloodhounds have to have something to give them a scent?" asked Marie. "Like a piece of clothing, or—"

We both looked at Duffy.

"Your jacket, Duffy!"

Duffy turned white.

"That's silly," he said after a moment.

"There's something at the door," I said frantically. "Maybe it's been **lurking** around all day, waiting for our mothers to leave. Maybe it's been waiting for years for someone to come back here."

Scratch, scratch.

"I don't believe it," said Duffy. "It's just the wind moving a branch. I'll prove it."

He got up and headed for the door. But he didn't open it. Instead he peeked through the window next to it. When he turned back, his eyes looked as big as the hard-boiled eggs we had eaten for supper.

"There's something out there!" he hissed. *"Something big!"*

"I told you," I cried. "Oh, I knew there was something there."

"Andrew, are you doing this just to scare me?" said Marie. "Because if you are—"

Scratch, scratch.

"Come on," I said, grabbing her by the hand. "Let's get out of here."

I started to lead her up the stairs.

"Not there!" said Duffy. "If we go up there, we'll be trapped."

"You're right," I said. "Let's go out the back way!"

The thought of going outside scared the daylights out of me. But at least out there we would have somewhere to run. Inside—well, who knew what might happen if the thing found us inside.

We went into the kitchen.

I heard the front door open.

"Let's get out of here!" I hissed.

We scooted out the back door. "What now?" I wondered, looking around frantically.

"The barn," whispered Duffy. "We can hide in the barn."

"Good idea," I said. Holding Marie by the hand, I led the way to the barn. But the door was held shut by a huge padlock.

The wind was blowing harder, but not hard enough to hide the sound of the back door of the house opening, and then slamming shut.

"Quick!" I whispered. "It knows we're out here. Let's sneak around front. It will never expect us to go back into the house."

Duffy and Marie followed me as I led them behind a hedge. I caught a glimpse of something heading toward the barn and swallowed nervously. It was big. Very big.

"I'm scared," whispered Marie.

"*Shhhh!*" I hissed. "We can't let it know where we are."

We slipped through the front door. We locked it, just like people always do in the movies, though what good that would do I couldn't figure, since if something really wanted to get at us, it would just break the window and come in.

"Upstairs," I whispered.

We tiptoed up the stairs. Once we were in our bedroom, I thought we were safe. Crawling over the floor, I raised my head just enough to peek out the window. My heart almost stopped. Standing in the moonlight was an enormous, manlike creature. It had a scrap of cloth in its hands. It was looking around—looking for us. I saw it lift its head and sniff the wind. To my horror, it started back toward the house.

"It's coming back!" I yelped, more frightened than ever.

"How does it know where we are?" asked Marie.

 Stop here for Strategy Break #2.

Strategy Break #2

1. What do you predict will happen next? _____
_____

2. Why do you think so? _____
_____

3. What clues from the story helped you make your prediction(s)? _____
_____
_____

Go on reading to see what happens.

I knew how. It had Duffy's jacket. It was tracking us down, like some giant bloodhound.

We huddled together in the middle of the room, trying to think of what to do.

A minute later we heard it.

Scratch, scratch.

None of us moved.

Scratch, scratch.

We stopped breathing, then jumped up in alarm at a terrible crashing sound.

The door was down.

We hunched back against the wall as heavy footsteps came **clomping** up the stairs.

I wondered what our mothers would think when they got back. Would they find our bodies? Or would there be nothing left of us at all?

Thump. Thump. Thump.

It was getting closer.

Thump. Thump. Thump.

It was outside the door.

Knock, knock.

"Don't answer!" hissed Duffy.

Like I said, he doesn't have the brains of a turnip.

It didn't matter. The door wasn't locked. It came swinging open. In the shaft of light I saw a huge figure. The Sentinel of the Woods! It had to be. I thought I was going to die.

The figure stepped into the room. Its head nearly touched the ceiling.

Marie squeezed against my side, tighter than a **tick** in a dog's ear.

The huge creature sniffed the air. It turned in our direction. Its eyes seemed to glow. Moonlight glittered on its fangs.

Slowly the Sentinel raised its arm. I could see Duffy's jacket dangling from its fingertips.

And then it spoke.

"You forgot your jacket, stupid."

It threw the jacket at Duffy, turned around, and stomped down the stairs.

Which is why, I suppose, no one has had to remind Duffy to remember his jacket, or his glasses, or his math book, for at least a year now.

After all, when you leave stuff lying around, you never can be sure just who might bring it back. ●

Strategy Follow-up

Now go back and look at the predictions that you wrote in this lesson. Do any of them match what actually happened in this story? Why or why not?

_____

_____

_____

_____

_____

_____

_____

_____

_____

_____

_____

_____

_____

_____

_____

_____

_____

✓Personal Checklist

Read each question and put a check (✓) in the correct box.

1. How well were you able to use the information in Building Background to help you understand the author's purpose for writing "Duffy's Jacket"?
   ☐ 3 (extremely well)
   ☐ 2 (fairly well)
   ☐ 1 (not well)

2. In the Vocabulary Builder, how many words were you able to match with their definitions?
   ☐ 3 (7–8 words)
   ☐ 2 (4–6 words)
   ☐ 1 (0–3 words)

3. How well were you able to use context clues to help you make predictions as you read?
   ☐ 3 (extremely well)
   ☐ 2 (fairly well)
   ☐ 1 (not well)

4. How well were you able to identify the changing moods in this story?
   ☐ 3 (extremely well)
   ☐ 2 (fairly well)
   ☐ 1 (not well)

5. How well do you understand why no one has to remind Duffy to remember his things anymore?
   ☐ 3 (extremely well)
   ☐ 2 (fairly well)
   ☐ 1 (not well)

Vocabulary Check

Look back at the work you did in the Vocabulary Builder. Then answer each question by circling the correct letter.

1. How would you make a room that is full of flies, mosquitoes, and spiders fit for use by humans?
   a. Sabotage the room.
   b. Fumigate the room.
   c. Clomp through the room.

2. If you were going away for a few days, who or what would you ask to keep an eye on your house?
   a. a turnip
   b. the heebie-jeebies
   c. a sentinel

3. Which meaning of *tick* is used in this story?
   a. insect that attaches to the skin
   b. clicking sound that a clock makes
   c. work well and efficiently

4. How would you typically use a turnip?
   a. You would wear it.
   b. You would invest it.
   c. You would eat it.

5. Think about the words *clomping* and *stomping*. Which of the following is true?
   a. They have similar sounds and similar meanings.
   b. They have similar sounds and opposite meanings.
   c. They have nothing in common.

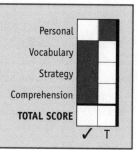

Add the numbers that you just checked to get your Personal Checklist score. Fill in your score here. Then turn to page 217 and transfer your score onto Graph 1.

Personal / Vocabulary / Strategy / Comprehension / TOTAL SCORE ✓ T

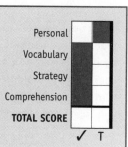

Check your answers with your teacher. Give yourself 1 point for each correct answer, and fill in your Vocabulary score here. Then turn to page 217 and transfer your score onto Graph 1.

Personal / Vocabulary / Strategy / Comprehension / TOTAL SCORE ✓ T

Strategy Check

Review what you wrote at each Strategy Break. Then answer these questions:

1. At Strategy Break #1, if you had predicted that something scary was going to happen, which clue would have best supported your prediction?
   a. "You kids will be fine on your own."
   b. I was convinced someone had been following us while we were in the woods.
   c. "There's enough soda here for you to make yourselves sick on."

2. Which clue helped you predict who or what the cousins' problem might involve?
   a. "You can make popcorn and play Monopoly."
   b. "There's enough soda here for you to make yourselves sick on."
   c. BEWARE THE SENTINEL, it said in big black letters.

3. At Strategy Break #2, how did you answer Marie's question?
   a. The creature knows where they are because Duffy dropped food all the way home.
   b. The scrap of cloth is Duffy's jacket, and the creature is using the scent to find him.
   c. The creature is following the scent of popcorn.

4. Which clue from the story helped you answer Marie's question?
   a. It was looking around—looking for us.
   b. "Don't bloodhounds have to have something to give them a scent?"
   c. "But you said it stopped. . . . how would it know where we are now?"

5. How do you know that the creature is polite?
   a. It scratches and knocks on the doors before it opens them.
   b. It is trying to return Duffy's jacket to him.
   c. Both of the above

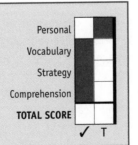

Check your answers with your teacher. Give yourself 1 point for each correct answer, and fill in your Strategy score here. Then turn to page 217 and transfer your score onto Graph 1.

Personal
Vocabulary
Strategy
Comprehension
TOTAL SCORE
✓ T

Comprehension Check

Review the story if necessary. Then answer these questions:

1. Why do you think the author calls this story "Duffy's Jacket"?
   a. because Duffy loses his jacket, and the travelers lose an hour going back to get it
   b. because Duffy wears it, and its color causes the Sentinel to lurk around the children
   c. because Duffy forgets it, and its scent helps the Sentinel find Duffy and return it

2. Why do you think the narrator keeps saying that Duffy doesn't have the brains of a turnip?
   a. to remind us that the situation they're in is all Duffy's fault
   b. to remind us that turnips are very intelligent
   c. to explain that Duffy is more intelligent than a turnip

3. Why are Duffy and his cousin on this trip?
   a. Their mothers heard about the beautiful leaves and wanted to see them.
   b. Their mothers want to punish their children by having the Sentinel scare them.
   c. Their mothers think they have to do man-stuff with them once in a while.

4. At what point does the mood begin to shift in this story?
   a. as the relatives are on their way to the cabin
   b. after the relatives clean the cabin for four hours
   c. when the narrator finds a message on the wall

5. What is the Sentinel trying to do?
   a. track the children down and eat them
   b. track the children down and return Duffy's jacket
   c. track the children down and play Monopoly with them

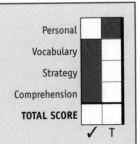

Check your answers with your teacher. Give yourself 1 point for each correct answer, and fill in your Comprehension score here. Then turn to page 217 and transfer your score onto Graph 1.

Personal
Vocabulary
Strategy
Comprehension
TOTAL SCORE
✓ T

Extending

Choose one or both of these activities:

SCARE AN AUDIENCE

Read one or more collections of scary stories, or listen to recordings of storytellers telling scary tales. (The ones listed on this page will give you a place to start.) Choose the story that you think is most frightening. Read or listen to it several times, and then tell it to a group of listeners. You don't have to memorize it word for word; just be sure to include the most important details and events. If you'd like, you can practice in front of a mirror and/or with a tape recorder until you feel comfortable with your words, the speed at which you speak them, and your expressions. Remember to make eye contact when you tell the story, and keep your purpose in mind: to scare the daylights out of your audience!

CONDUCT A SURVEY

Poll your family, classmates, and others on the subject of scary entertainment—tales told in short stories, books, movies, or TV programs. Ask each person to name or describe at least three scary stories that he or she can remember. Which story was the most frightening? Why? Which would the person most want to see, read, or hear a second time? Compare everyone's answers, and then report your findings in the form of a "Top Ten" list. Make sure your list includes the outstanding features that make each story scary.

WHERE DID THAT WORD COME FROM?

Do you ever wonder where and how certain words originated? For example, who first used the word *heebie-jeebies*? In what context was it used? Research *heebie-jeebies* and other interesting or scary words from this story. Find out their meanings and what language or country they came from. Are there other, related words that come from the same source? Make a chart of your findings and display it for the class.

Resources

Books

Coville, Bruce. *Oddly Enough*. Simon Pulse, 1997.

————, ed. *Bruce Coville's Book of Ghosts: Tales to Haunt You.* Apple, 1995.

————, ed. *Bruce Coville's Book of Monsters: Tales to Give You the Creeps.* Scholastic, 1995.

Web Sites

http://www.geocities.com/twobits_2/ghoststories.html
This Web site offers a collection of scary stories.

http://www.wordorigins.org/index.htm
Look up the origins of some 400 words and phrases on this Web site.

Audio Recordings

Coville, Bruce, ed. *Bruce Coville's Book of Monsters: Tales to Give You the Creeps.* Bantam Books-Audio, 2000.

Coville, Bruce, and William Dufris, narr. *Aliens Ate My Homework.* Bantam Books-Audio, 2000.

LESSON 12 The Mysterious
Mr. Lincoln

Building Background

Abraham Lincoln, Honest Abe, the Great Emancipator, "Father Abraham." If you
grew up in the United States—and even if you didn't—you probably already know
quite a bit about America's 16th president. Get together with a partner and share
what you know about Lincoln. Then fill in the first column of the K-W-L chart
below with at least five things that you know about him. Fill in the second column
with at least five things that you want to know about him. When you finish reading this selection, you will fill in the last column of the chart with things that you
learned about Lincoln.

Abraham Lincoln

| K
(What I Know) | W
(What I Want to Know) | L
(What I Learned) |
| --- | --- | --- |
| 1. | 1. | 1. |
| 2. | 2. | 2. |
| 3. | 3. | 3. |
| 4. | 4. | 4. |
| 5. | 5. | 5. |

ambitious

gawky

legendary

logical

preeminently

reticent

sensitive

Vocabulary Builder

1. All of the words in the margin are **descriptive words**. Some of the words may
be familiar to you. Find those words in the statements below. If a statement is
true, write a **T** on the line beside it. If a statement is false, write an **F** on the
line.

2. Then, as you read the selection, use context clues to figure out any of the
vocabulary words that you don't know. Write a **T** or an **F** next to the sentences
containing those words. Double-check your earlier work, too, and make any
necessary changes.

_____ a. An **ambitious** person is lazy and lacks motivation.

_____ b. A person who is **gawky** has the grace of a ballerina.

_____ c. A **legendary** person is well-known for his or her special
accomplishments.

_____ d.   An unreasonable idea that makes no sense is considered **logical**.

_____ e.   A person who is noticed above all others stands out **preeminently**.

_____ f.   A **reticent** person is quiet and shy.

_____ g.   A **sensitive** person doesn't care about the feelings of others.

3. Save your work. You will refer to it again in the Vocabulary Check.

Strategy Builder

Comparing Facts and Opinions While You Read

• As you learned earlier in this book, a **biography** is the story of a real person's life, as written by someone else. The selection you are about to read is a chapter from Russell Freedman's photobiography of Abraham Lincoln.

• Freedman's entire biography tells the story of Lincoln's life in chronological order, or sequence, from his birth to his death. You will only be reading the first chapter of the book, however, which is a description of Lincoln's appearance and personality.

• In order to describe who Lincoln was—and wasn't—the author combines the organizational patterns of **description** and **compare-contrast**: He describes Abraham Lincoln by separating the **opinions** that people had of him from the **facts** that exist about him.

• As you read this selection, you will learn to use a **comparison chart** to examine and compare those facts and opinions more easily.

The Mysterious Mr. Lincoln

by Russell Freedman

As you begin reading this selection, apply the strategies that you just learned. Look for how people's opinions of Lincoln compare to the real facts about him.

"If any personal description of me is thought desirable, it may be said, I am, in height, six feet, four inches, nearly; lean in flesh, weighing, on average, one hundred and eighty pounds; dark complexion, with coarse black hair and grey eyes—no other marks or brands recollected."

Abraham Lincoln wasn't the sort of man who could lose himself in a crowd. After all, he stood six feet four inches tall, and to top it off, he wore a high silk hat.

His height was mostly in his long bony legs. When he sat in a chair, he seemed no taller than anyone else. It was only when he stood up that he towered above other men.

At first glance, most people thought he was homely. Lincoln thought so too, referring once to his "poor, lean, lank face." As a young man he was **sensitive** about his **gawky** looks, but in time, he learned to laugh at himself. When a rival called him "two-faced" during a political debate, Lincoln replied: "I leave it to my audience. If I had another face, do you think I'd wear this one?"

According to those who knew him, Lincoln was a man of many faces. In repose, he often seemed sad and gloomy. But when he began to speak, his expression changed. "The dull, listless features dropped like a mask," said a Chicago newspaperman. "The eyes began to sparkle, the mouth to smile, the whole countenance was wreathed in animation, so that a stranger would have said, 'Why, this man, so angular and solemn a moment ago, is really handsome!'"

Lincoln was the most photographed man of his time, but his friends insisted that no photo ever did him justice. It's no wonder. Back then, cameras required long exposures. The person being photographed had to "freeze" as the seconds ticked by. If he blinked an eye, the picture would be blurred. That's why Lincoln looks so stiff and formal in his photos. We never see him laughing or joking.

Artists and writers tried to capture the "real" Lincoln that the camera missed, but something about the man always escaped them. His changeable features, his tones, gestures, and expressions, seemed to defy description.

Today it's hard to imagine Lincoln as he really was. And he never cared to reveal much about himself. In company he was witty and talkative, but he rarely betrayed his inner feelings.

According to William Herndon, his law partner, he was "the most secretive—**reticent**—shut-mouthed man that ever lived."

In his own time, Lincoln was never fully understood even by his closest friends. Since then, his life story has been told and retold so many times, he has become as much a legend as a flesh-and-blood human being. While the legend is based on truth, it is only partly true. And it hides the man behind it like a disguise.

The **legendary** Lincoln is known as Honest Abe, a humble man of the people who rose from a log cabin to the White House. There's no doubt that Lincoln was a poor boy who made good. And it's true that he carried his folksy manners and homespun speech to the White House with him. He said "howdy" to visitors and invited them to "stay a spell." He greeted diplomats while wearing carpet slippers, called his wife "mother" at receptions, and told bawdy jokes at cabinet meetings.

Lincoln may have seemed like a common man, but he wasn't. His friends agreed that he was one of the most **ambitious** people they had ever known. Lincoln struggled hard to rise above his log-cabin origins, and he was proud of his achievements. By the time he ran for president he was a wealthy man, earning a large income from his law practice and his many investments. As for the nickname Abe, he hated it. No one who knew him well ever called him Abe to his face. They addressed him as Lincoln or Mr. Lincoln.

 Stop here for the Strategy Break.

Strategy Break

If you were to create a comparison chart for the first part of this selection so far, it might look like this:

	Opinions	Facts
Lincoln's face	• Most people thought he was homely and often looked sad and gloomy. • Lincoln himself agreed.	• When he spoke, his features became animated and he looked handsome. Photos couldn't capture that or do him justice.
His behavior in company	• He was witty and talkative.	• His law partner called him "the most secretive . . . man that ever lived."
His image	• He was known as Honest Abe, a humble man of the people who rose from a log cabin to the White House. • He acted folksy at the White House and told jokes at Cabinet meetings.	• He wasn't common—he was very ambitious. • By the time he was president, he was a wealthy man with many investments. • He hated the name Abe; his friends never called him that.

 Go on reading.

Lincoln is often described as a sloppy dresser, careless about his appearance. In fact, he patronized the best tailor in Springfield, Illinois, buying two suits a year. That was at a time when many men lived, died, and were buried in the same suit.

It's true that Lincoln had little formal "eddication," as he would have pronounced it. Almost everything he "larned" he taught himself. All his life he said "thar" for *there*, "git" for *get*, "kin" for *can*. Even so, he became an eloquent public speaker who could hold a vast audience spellbound, and a great writer whose finest phrases still ring in our ears. He was known to sit up late into the night, discussing Shakespeare's plays with White House visitors.

He was certainly a humorous man, famous for his rollicking stories. But he was also moody and melancholy, tormented by long and frequent bouts of depression. Humor was his therapy. He relied on his yarns, a friend observed, to "whistle down sadness."

He had a cool, **logical** mind, trained in the courtroom, and a practical, commonsense approach to problems. Yet he was deeply superstitious, a believer in dreams, omens, and visions.

We admire Lincoln today as an American folk hero. During the Civil War, however, he was the most unpopular president the nation had ever known. His critics called him a tyrant, a hick, a stupid baboon who was unfit for his office. As commander in chief of the armed forces, he was denounced as a bungling amateur who meddled in military affairs he knew nothing about. But he also had his supporters. They praised him as a farsighted statesman, a military mastermind who engineered the Union victory.

Lincoln is best known as the Great Emancipator, the man who freed the slaves. Yet he did not enter the war with that idea in mind. "My paramount object in this struggle *is* to save the Union," he said in 1862, "and is *not* either to save or destroy slavery." As the war continued, Lincoln's attitude changed. Eventually he came to regard the conflict as a moral crusade to wipe out the sin of slavery.

No black leader was more critical of Lincoln than the fiery abolitionist writer and editor Frederick Douglass. Douglass had grown up as a slave. He had won his freedom by escaping to the North. Early in the war, impatient with Lincoln's cautious leadership, Douglass called him "**preeminently** the white man's president, entirely devoted to the welfare of white men." Later, Douglass changed his mind and came to admire Lincoln. Several years after the war, he said this about the sixteenth president:

"His greatest mission was to accomplish two things: first, to save his country from dismemberment and ruin; and, second, to free his country from the great crime of slavery. . . . taking him for all in all, measuring the tremendous magnitude of the work before him, considering the necessary means to ends, and surveying the end from the beginning, infinite wisdom has seldom sent any man into the world better fitted for his mission than Abraham Lincoln." ●

Strategy Follow-up

First, work with your partner to fill in the last column of the K-W-L chart on page 124. List at least five things that you learned about Abraham Lincoln while reading this selection.

Then, copy the comparison chart below onto a large sheet of paper. Work with your partner to fill in the empty columns with facts and opinions from the second part of the selection.

	Opinions	Facts
Lincoln's clothing and appearance		
His education		
What and how he thought		
His reputation		

✓Personal Checklist

Read each question and put a check (✓) in the correct box.

1. In Building Background, how well were you able to fill in the first two columns of the K-W-L chart?

   ☐ 3   (extremely well)
   ☐ 2   (fairly well)
   ☐ 1   (not well)

2. In the Vocabulary Builder, how many sentences were you able to correctly identify as true or false?

   ☐ 3   (6–7 sentences)
   ☐ 2   (3–5 sentences)
   ☐ 1   (0–2 sentences)

3. How well were you able to complete the comparison chart in the Strategy Follow-up?

   ☐ 3   (extremely well)
   ☐ 2   (fairly well)
   ☐ 1   (not well)

4. Now that you've read this selection, how well could you describe who Abraham Lincoln was—and was not?

   ☐ 3   (extremely well)
   ☐ 2   (fairly well)
   ☐ 1   (not well)

5. How well do you understand why this chapter of Freedman's book is called "The Mysterious Mr. Lincoln"?

   ☐ 3   (extremely well)
   ☐ 2   (fairly well)
   ☐ 1   (not well)

Vocabulary Check

Look back at the work you did in the Vocabulary Builder. Then answer each question by circling the correct letter.

1. Which word best describes a newborn colt's walk?

   a. gawky
   b. reticent
   c. preeminent

2. In which sentence is the word *ambitious* used correctly?

   a. Lincoln was so ambitious that even his close friends didn't know him well.
   b. Lincoln was an ambitious man who worked hard to achieve his goals.
   c. Lincoln was very ambitious because he believed in dreams and omens.

3. When Frederick Douglass called Lincoln "preeminently the white man's president," what did he mean?

   a. that Lincoln put the white man's needs above the needs of all others
   b. that Lincoln was the best white president the nation had ever had
   c. that Lincoln was first a president and then a white man

4. What does it mean when a story is legendary?

   a. It is based entirely on a true account.
   b. It is based on lies but is believed to be true.
   c. It is based on truth, but it is only partly true.

5. Which of these words means "quiet and reserved"?

   a. reticent
   b. ambitious
   c. sensitive

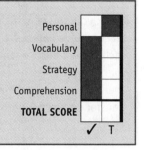

Add the numbers that you just checked to get your Personal Checklist score. Fill in your score here. Then turn to page 217 and transfer your score onto Graph 1.

Personal
Vocabulary
Strategy
Comprehension
TOTAL SCORE
✓ T

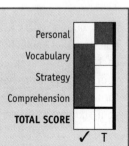

Check your answers with your teacher. Give yourself 1 point for each correct answer, and fill in your Vocabulary score here. Then turn to page 217 and transfer your score onto Graph 1.

Personal
Vocabulary
Strategy
Comprehension
TOTAL SCORE
✓ T

Strategy Check

Review the comparison chart you completed in the Strategy Follow-up. Also review the selection if necessary. Then answer the following questions:

1. How do people's opinions of Lincoln's clothing and appearance differ from the facts?

    a. He's often described as a careless dresser, but he went to the best tailor in Springfield.

    b. He's often described as a flawless dresser, but he was actually very untidy.

    c. He's often described as a careless dresser, and he was the sloppiest man in Springfield.

2. What is the difference between people's opinions of Lincoln's education and the facts about it?

    a. People said he taught himself almost everything he knew, but he actually went to college.

    b. People said he taught himself almost everything he knew, and this is true.

    c. People said he went to school, but he taught himself almost everything he knew.

3. Which fact from the selection backs up the opinion that Lincoln had a good sense of humor?

    a. He was known to discuss Shakespeare.

    b. He was famous for his playful stories.

    c. His finest phrases still ring in our ears.

4. Which fact supports the opinion that Lincoln had a cool, logical mind?

    a. He was trained that way in school.

    b. He learned to think in the White House.

    c. He learned to think that way in court.

5. Which fact states that Lincoln wasn't always viewed as the Great Emancipator?

    a. When he entered the Civil War, freeing the slaves was not his goal.

    b. His supporters praised him as a statesman.

    c. "His greatest mission was to . . . free his country from the great crime of slavery."

Comprehension Check

Review the selection if necessary. Then answer these questions:

1. Why do we never see Lincoln laughing or joking in photographs?

    a. He never laughed or joked.

    b. He hated to have his picture taken.

    c. He had to "freeze" for photos, so he looked stiff and formal.

2. Which of these habits made Lincoln appear to be a "man of the people"?

    a. He discussed Shakespeare with his guests.

    b. He greeted diplomats while wearing his slippers.

    c. He wore a high silk hat that made him look taller.

3. Which of these statements best summarizes the main idea of this selection?

    a. Lincoln has never been fully understood, and the tales about him often hide the truth.

    b. Lincoln was a quiet man who was also moody and melancholy.

    c. Lincoln is best known as the Great Emancipator, yet he didn't enter the war with that idea in mind.

4. The word pairs below are opposites. Which of these pairs does *not* describe Lincoln?

    a. logical/superstitious

    b. humorous/melancholy

    c. eloquent/tongue-tied

5. Why were jokes and humor so important to Lincoln?

    a. He used them to get out of his bouts of depression.

    b. He used them to make fun of his enemies.

    c. He used them to make people do what he wanted them to do.

Check your answers with your teacher. Give yourself 1 point for each correct answer, and fill in your Strategy score here. Then turn to page 217 and transfer your score onto Graph 1.

Personal
Vocabulary
Strategy
Comprehension
TOTAL SCORE
✓ T

Check your answers with your teacher. Give yourself 1 point for each correct answer, and fill in your Comprehension score here. Then turn to page 217 and transfer your score onto Graph 1.

Personal
Vocabulary
Strategy
Comprehension
TOTAL SCORE
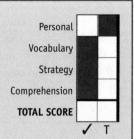
✓ T

Extending

Choose one or more of these activities:

STUDY ONE OF MR. LINCOLN'S SPEECHES

A few of Abraham Lincoln's speeches are short yet memorable. One such speech is the Gettysburg Address, which Lincoln delivered at the dedication of a cemetery. The other is the speech he delivered upon leaving his hometown of Springfield to begin his presidency in Washington, D.C. Find a copy of one of these speeches and read it carefully. Imagine how Lincoln felt when he wrote and delivered the speech, and what effect he wanted it to have on his listeners. Examine how he used words, both for their meanings and their sounds. Then write a paragraph or two that describes what you learned about Lincoln by reading his speech.

LEARN MORE ABOUT MR. LINCOLN

Work with a group to learn more about Abraham Lincoln. Then present your findings in a multimedia presentation. To begin your research, you might read *Lincoln: A Photobiography,* the book from which "The Mysterious Mr. Lincoln" was taken. For this and many other resources, see the listings on this page.

FIND MR. LINCOLN ON THE MAP

Use an atlas, an encyclopedia, a set of state maps, and/or a search engine on the Internet to research places named after Abraham Lincoln. Before you begin, choose one or more ways to present your findings so that as you come across data you will record what you need for your final report. Some of the ways you could present your findings are as follows:

- on a map of the United States, marked with stars for all the towns with *Lincoln* in the name
- in a booklet with a page about each of the towns named after Lincoln
- in a list with several categories such as cities and towns; rivers, mountains, and other natural features; and important buildings and monuments named after Lincoln

FIND MR. LINCOLN IN LITERATURE

Alone or with a team, find out how many plays, poems, short stories, and other literary works you can find about Abraham Lincoln. You might choose to read as many of them as you can, or you might simply list their titles in appropriate categories. Can you find a total of 25? of 50? of more than 50?

Resources

Books

Freedman, Russell. *Lincoln: A Photobiography.* Scott Foresman, 1989.

Sandak, Cass R. *The Lincolns.* First Families. Crestwood House, 1992.

Zall, P. M. *Abe Lincoln Laughing: Humorous Anecdotes from Original Sources By and About Abraham Lincoln.* University of Tennessee Press, 1995.

Web Sites

http://showcase.netins.net/web/creative/lincoln/speeches/speech.htm
This site contains the text of some of Lincoln's speeches, including his farewell speech in Springfield and the Gettysburg Address.

http://www.historyplace.com/lincoln
This Web site provides a time line of Lincoln's life and several historical photographs.

Audio Recordings

Donald, David Herbert, and James Naughtor, narr. *Lincoln.* Simon & Schuster Audio, 1995.

Perkins, Jack, narr. *Abraham Lincoln.* A & E Audiobooks, 1996.

Videos/DVDs

Abraham Lincoln: Preserving the Union. A & E Television Network, 1996.

Lincoln: A Photobiography Videorecording. Russell Freedman. McGraw-Hill Media, 1989.

The Story of the Amistad Africans

abolitionists

befriended

determination

freedom

illegal

jail cell

kidnapped

mutiny

supporters

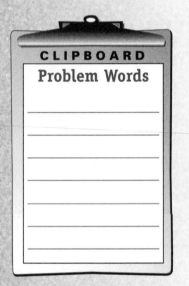

CLIPBOARD

Problem Words

CLIPBOARD

Solution Words

Building Background

Historical fiction tells made-up stories that are based on historical facts. The historical-fiction selection that you are about to read describes the experiences of a real group of people known as the Amistad Africans. The Amistad Africans were kidnapped from their homeland of Sierra Leone, West Africa, and were sold into slavery in Cuba. From Cuba they were then transported to Connecticut.

They traveled under the worst possible conditions, from a land where it never snows to a place where it is cold and snowy almost half the year. To more fully understand the hardships they faced on their journey, find a world map or globe and trace a rough route from Sierra Leone to Cuba to the United States. As you trace the route, keep in mind that in the late 1830s, crossing the Atlantic usually took about two months.

Vocabulary Builder

1. Before you begin "The Story of the Amistad Africans," read the vocabulary words in the margin. All of the words have to do with the problem in this selection and the solutions that people tried in order to solve it.

2. Think about what all of the words mean. If you don't know any of the words, look them up in a dictionary. Then decide if they would best describe the problem in this selection or the solutions, and write each word on the appropriate clipboard. (If any of the words seem to fit both categories, find them in the selection and then make your choice.)

3. Save your work. You will refer to it again in the Vocabulary Check.

Strategy Builder

Identifying Problems and Solutions

- In most fictional stories, the main character or characters have a **problem**. Throughout the story, the characters work to solve the problem. They often try more than one **solution**. By the end of the story, they usually come up with the solution that works—the **end result**.

- Although the characters in historical fiction are often people who actually lived, they too face problems and try to find solutions. In the story you are about to read, for example, the main character is a boy named Kali, who really did travel to the United States aboard the *Amistad* and later tried to gain his freedom.

- As you read about Kali's experiences, you will learn how to record them on a **problem-solution frame**. To see how a problem-solution frame works, first read the following paragraphs and notice the problems and solutions:

Scott and Grant met for lunch at their usual table. "Oh no," said Grant when he saw what his mother had packed. "Peanut butter and jelly again!"

"You think you've got it bad," said Scott. "I have a tuna-salad sandwich, and everyone knows I hate tuna. I'd rather have a peanut butter-and-jelly sandwich any day."

The boys studied their lunches for a moment. Then they had an idea. Grant took Scott's tuna-salad sandwich. Scott took Grant's peanut butter-and-jelly sandwich. As the boys ate, they both agreed that their sandwiches tasted great.

- If you wanted to show the boys' situation on a **problem-solution frame**, it would look like this:

What is the problem?
Grant has a peanut butter-and-jelly sandwich, and Scott has a tuna-salad sandwich.

Why is it a problem?
Neither boy likes his lunch.

Solutions	Results
1. Grant takes Scott's tuna-salad sandwich.	1. Grant has a lunch he likes.
2. Scott takes Grant's peanut butter and jelly.	2. Scott has a lunch he likes.
3. The boys eat each other's sandwiches.	3. **END RESULT:** They both agree that their sandwiches taste great.

The Story of the Amistad Africans

by Mary Ann Limauro

As you read the first part of this selection, apply the strategies that you just learned. Look for the problem that Kali and the others face—and why.

Locked in a crowded Connecticut **jail cell** with thirty-two fellow West Africans, a world away from his village in Sierra Leone, eleven-year-old Kali longed for the familiar surroundings of his homeland. He missed the wide blue sky and tall palm trees of Mendeland. He missed running and playing with his friends. He wished he could be back home with them, fishing in the river again. A tear glistened in Kali's dark eyes as he thought about his family—his sister and brother, his mother and father. So much time had passed since he had seen them.

The date was January 4, 1841. Kali and the other prisoners, all of whom had been **kidnapped** in Africa and sold into slavery, had been fighting for their **freedom** for almost two years. Their fierce **determination** to return home, coupled with the efforts of a group of **supporters** who believed in the right of freedom for all, would soon make them the first slaves ever to gain their freedom through the U.S. courts.

The Amistad Africans, as Kali and his group were known, first came together in the spring of 1839 at an **illegal** slave market in Havana, Cuba. There, two Spanish slave traders had purchased the original group of fifty-three, planning to bring them to a sugar cane plantation on the other side of the island.

Once aboard the *Amistad*, the Africans revolted against their captors. After an ill-fated attempt to sail back to Africa, both ship and Africans were taken into U.S. custody in Long Island Sound. The group was charged with murder and **mutiny** and jailed in New Haven.

Kali, though only nine, was kept with the men. The three girls in the group—Teme, age twelve, Kagne, age ten, and Margru, age seven—were sent to live with the jailer and his wife. Criminal charges were soon dropped because of a lack of jurisdiction, but the ship's owners then claimed that the Africans should be returned to them as "cargo."

Finally, after two trials and several months' imprisonment, the court ruled that the group be freed and returned to their homeland. The U.S. attorney, acting on the orders of President Martin Van Buren, appealed that decision, and the case was now pending before the Supreme Court.

 Stop here for the Strategy Break.

Strategy Break

If you were to create a problem-solution frame for this selection so far, it might look like this:

What is the problem?
Kali and the other prisoners had been fighting for their freedom for almost two years.

Why is it a problem?
Many people—including President Van Buren—believed that the slaves should stay in prison and were fighting to keep them there.

 Go on reading.

Looking around at his companions in the damp cell, Kali, a small, dark-skinned boy with a stout build, felt a deep love for these brave men. Cinque, who had led the revolt aboard the *Amistad*, was acknowledged as the group's leader. A strong, powerfully built man in his mid-twenties, Cinque also was kind and gentle and showed much concern for Kali and the others. He, like the small, wiry Grabeau, had been a rice planter at home. Several of the others were blacksmiths. Almost all were married and had been snatched away from their families. Young Kali, who had been taken while walking along a road in his village, shared their pain of separation from loved ones.

The past two years, though difficult, had held some moments of happiness, thought Kali. Many of the townspeople in New Haven had **befriended** the captives, visiting them and bringing them food and clothing. Professors and students from Yale University had come regularly to instruct the captives in religion and English, bringing them Bibles and books to read. And several local clergymen who strongly disapproved of slavery had banded together with other **abolitionists** from around the United States to raise funds for the Africans' defense.

These supporters, who called themselves the Amistad Committee, had hired several of the best local attorneys for the captives' earlier trials. Now that the case was going before the Supreme Court, the committee members felt that an attorney with a national reputation was needed. They decided on former president John Quincy Adams.

Though not an abolitionist, Adams was a strong foe of slavery, and even though he was seventy-three years old and had not appeared before the Supreme Court in thirty years, "Old Man Eloquent" agreed to take the case. Now Kali, a bright boy who had quickly learned English, was chosen by Cinque and the others to write a letter to Mr. Adams.

"Dear Friend Mr. Adams," he began. "I want to write a letter to you because you love Mendi people, and you talk to the grand court." Speaking for all the captives, Kali poured out his heart, ending with a plea to "make us free."

The next month, Adams successfully argued the Africans' case. On March 9, 1841, the Supreme Court justices ruled that the Amistad Africans were free men and should be returned to their homeland. Six months later, Kali and his countrymen returned to Sierra Leone. ●

Strategy Follow-up

Now complete the following problem-solution frame with information from the second part of this selection. Some of the frame has been filled in for you.

What is the problem?
Kali and the other prisoners had been fighting for their freedom for almost two years.

Why is it a problem?
Many people—including President Van Buren—believed that the slaves should stay in prison and were fighting to keep them there.

Solutions

1. When the captives' case was about to go to the Supreme Court,

2. Kali

3. On March 9, 1841,

Results

1.

2.

3. END RESULT:

✓Personal Checklist

Read each question and put a check (✓) in the correct box.

1. How well do you understand what happened in this selection?
    - ☐ 3 (extremely well)
    - ☐ 2 (fairly well)
    - ☐ 1 (not well)

2. In Building Background, how well were you able to trace a route from Sierra Leone to Cuba to the United States?
    - ☐ 3 (extremely well)
    - ☐ 2 (fairly well)
    - ☐ 1 (not well)

3. In the Vocabulary Builder, how well were you able to put each word on the appropriate clipboard?
    - ☐ 3 (extremely well)
    - ☐ 2 (fairly well)
    - ☐ 1 (not well)

4. How well were you able to complete the problem-solution frame in the Strategy Follow-up?
    - ☐ 3 (extremely well)
    - ☐ 2 (fairly well)
    - ☐ 1 (not well)

5. How well do you understand why the Amistad Committee took such an active role in helping the captives?
    - ☐ 3 (extremely well)
    - ☐ 2 (fairly well)
    - ☐ 1 (not well)

Vocabulary Check

Look back at the work you did in the Vocabulary Builder. Then answer each question by circling the correct letter.

1. Which of these words is related to the problem that the Amistad Africans faced?
    - a. befriended
    - b. supporters
    - c. kidnapped

2. Which of these words is related to the solution to their problem?
    - a. freedom
    - b. jail cell
    - c. illegal

3. The imprisoned captives were charged with murder and mutiny. What does *mutiny* mean?
    - a. destroying someone's property
    - b. rebelling against authority
    - c. making someone deaf

4. Which phrase describes the abolitionists in this selection?
    - a. people fighting to uphold slavery
    - b. people fighting to become slaves
    - c. people fighting to end slavery

5. What does the word *befriended* mean?
    - a. had a fight with
    - b. made friends with
    - c. defeated

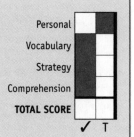

Add the numbers that you just checked to get your Personal Checklist score. Fill in your score here. Then turn to page 217 and transfer your score onto Graph 1.

Personal
Vocabulary
Strategy
Comprehension
TOTAL SCORE
✓ T

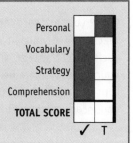

Check your answers with your teacher. Give yourself 1 point for each correct answer, and fill in your Vocabulary score here. Then turn to page 217 and transfer your score onto Graph 1.

Personal
Vocabulary
Strategy
Comprehension
TOTAL SCORE
✓ T

Strategy Check

Review the problem-solution frame that you completed in the Strategy Follow-up. Also review the selection if necessary. Then answer the following questions:

1. What was the result when the Amistad Committee asked John Quincy Adams to represent the captives?

    a. Adams agreed to take the case.

    b. Adams told them he was too old.

    c. Adams told them he was for slavery.

2. What did the captives have Kali do to try to ensure that Adams would fight hard for them?

    a. They had Kali write him a song.

    b. They had Kali call him on the phone.

    c. They had Kali write him a letter.

3. What happened after Adams successfully argued the captives' case?

    a. The Supreme Court ruled that the captives should be returned to their jail cells.

    b. The Supreme Court ruled that the captives should be returned to Cuba and sold.

    c. The Supreme Court ruled that the captives should be returned to their homeland.

4. How long after the Supreme Court's ruling was the captives' problem finally solved?

    a. six days

    b. six months

    c. six years

5. How long did it actually take the captives to gain their freedom?

    a. about two years

    b. about three years

    c. about four years

Comprehension Check

Review the selection if necessary. Then answer these questions:

1. When did the Amistad Africans revolt against their captors?

    a. when they were going from Africa to Cuba

    b. when they were being carried from one side of Cuba to the other

    c. when they were being carried from Cuba to Connecticut

2. How can you tell that the Africans killed at least some of the crew on the ship when they revolted?

    a. They were arrested for murder and mutiny.

    b. The Spanish slave traders demanded their return as "cargo."

    c. The court ruled that the group should be freed.

3. Which of these statements is false?

    a. The abolitionists wanted to abolish, or put an end to, slavery.

    b. In the 1840s, the only people against slavery were abolitionists.

    c. John Quincy Adams was not an abolitionist but was against slavery.

4. Why did the abolitionists ask John Quincy Adams to represent the captives during their last trial?

    a. They felt the captives needed an attorney with a national reputation.

    b. They knew that Adams wanted slavery and wouldn't fight for the captives.

    c. Both of the above answers are correct.

5. Which of the following does this selection prove?

    a. Everyone in the United States approved of the practice of slavery.

    b. Nobody in the United States approved of the practice of slavery.

    c. There was much disagreement in the United States about slavery.

Check your answers with your teacher. Give yourself 1 point for each correct answer, and fill in your Strategy score here. Then turn to page 217 and transfer your score onto Graph 1.

Personal
Vocabulary
Strategy
Comprehension
TOTAL SCORE
✓ T

Check your answers with your teacher. Give yourself 1 point for each correct answer, and fill in your Comprehension score here. Then turn to page 217 and transfer your score onto Graph 1.

Personal
Vocabulary
Strategy
Comprehension
TOTAL SCORE
✓ T

Extending

Choose one or both of these activities:

INVESTIGATE THE ABOLITIONISTS

Work with a group of students to find out more about the abolitionists, both white and black, who struggled to end slavery. Draw up a list of men and women who worked for the abolitionist cause between 1800 and 1861. Then have each member of your group choose one of the abolitionists and do further research on that person. Write a short report on the person's life and contribution to the cause of freeing the slaves. If possible, copy a photograph of the person. Then combine all the group members' reports into a single presentation, such as a panel discussion, a series of short speeches, a bulletin board, a booklet, or an original play.

WRITE A POEM

If you were imprisoned in a strange country, threatened with slavery or death, how would you describe your longing for your native land? your desire for freedom? your anger at those who stole you from your home? your appreciation for those who helped you? Write a poem that would express your feelings.

Resources

Books

Katz, William Loren. *Breaking the Chains: African-American Slave Resistance*. Bt Bound, 1999.

Wepman, Dennis. *The Struggle for Freedom: African-American Slave Resistance*. Library of African-American History. Facts on File, 1996.

Zeinert, Karen. *The Amistad Slave Revolt and American Abolition*. Linnet Books, 1997.

Web Sites

http://www.amistad.org
You can find links to pages about the *Amistad* on this Web site.

http://www.nationalgeographic.com/railroad/
This is an interactive exhibit by National Geographic Online about the Underground Railroad, which abolitionists used to bring slaves from the South to freedom in the North.

http://www.tulane.edu/~amistad/
This is the Web site of the Amistad Research Center at Tulane University.

Audio Recording

Owens, William A. *Black Mutiny: The Revolt of the Schooner Amistad* (abridged). Brilliance Audio, 1998.

Videos/DVDs

Amistad. Morgan Freeman, Anthony Hopkins, and Steven Spielberg, dir. Universal Studios, 2000.

The Amistad Revolt. Amistad Committee, 1995.

The Voyage of La Amistad: A Quest for Freedom. Alfre Woodard. MPI Home Video, 1998.

Passage to Mishima

Building Background

Yoshi, the boy in "Passage to Mishima," has been charged with a very important task. If he succeeds in helping his father, Yoshi will gain his father's respect. If he fails, however, he will lose his father's respect.

How important is it for you to have other people's respect, and what would you do to get it? Is it more important to have the respect of some people over others? Why?

Think about the people on the following list. On the lines provided, write what you would have to do to gain their respect.

Your friends_____

Your parents _____

Your grandparents _____

Your teachers_____

Your younger brother(s) &/or sister(s) _____

Your older brother(s) &/or sister(s) _____

aft deck

bulkhead

deck

galley

helm

pitched

port

wheelhouse

yawed

Vocabulary Builder

1. In this story, Yoshi story takes a trip on a fishing boat. While relating Yoshi's experience, the author uses many words to describe the boat and the way it moves. Knowing these words in advance will help you better understand what is happening.

2. Before you begin reading "Passage to Mishima," see if you can match the words in Column 1 to their definitions in Column 2. Use a dictionary or other reference book for the words you don't know.

COLUMN 1	COLUMN 2
aft deck	ship's kitchen
bulkhead	the wheel used to steer a ship
deck	rose up and then fell down
galley	the part of a deck near the back of a ship
helm	turned from a straight course
pitched	enclosed place that protects the captain and helm
port	the left side of a ship
wheelhouse	wall that divides a ship into compartments
yawed	the floor, or sole, of a ship

3. As you come across the words in the story, use their definitions and context to help you visualize what is happening.

4. Save your work. You will use it again in the Vocabulary Check.

Strategy Builder

Drawing Conclusions About Characters

- When you read "Taking Sides" in Lesson 5, you learned to draw conclusions about a character named Lincoln. As you recall, a **conclusion** is a decision that you reach after thinking about certain facts or information.

- You can draw conclusions about the **characters** in a story by paying attention to their words, thoughts, feelings, and actions. Paying attention to these clues will help you see the characters' **traits**, or qualities, and will help you understand the characters better. It also will help you understand why the characters do what they do.

- Read the following description of a character named Gregory. Then look at the **character map** below the description. It shows the conclusions that one reader drew about Gregory—and why.

Amber's little brother Gregory is always trying to go everywhere with her. If Amber asks him not to go, he will follow her anyway. Gregory also spies on Amber and her friends. He makes up songs about what Amber and her friends do, and then he teases her by singing them over and over. But worst of all, Gregory always tells their parents everything that Amber and her friends are doing. If he doesn't know anything that will get Amber into trouble, he will make something up.

CHARACTER TRAIT:
tag-along
Example:
He always follows Amber around, even when she asks him not to.

CHARACTER TRAIT:
nosy
Example:
He spies on Amber and her friends and then makes up songs about what they do.

CHARACTER: Gregory

CHARACTER TRAIT:
tattletale
Example:
He tells their parents everything that Amber and her friends are doing.

CHARACTER TRAIT:
troublemaker
Example:
If he doesn't know anything that will get Amber into trouble, he will make something up.

Passage to Mishima

by William J. Buchanan

As you read this story, you will focus on two main characters: Yoshi and Captain Nakai. Look for clues that the author provides to help you draw conclusions about each character.

Entrusted to carry out family business, young Yoshi must endure a violent sea voyage or suffer a worse fate—dishonor.

Fourteen-year-old Yoshi Fujiwara stared nervously at the old boat that lay moored to a backside wharf at Nagato, Japan. Weather-beaten, older by decades than he, the small craft had seen better days. On the **aft deck**, the boat's scurvy-looking skipper cast a heavy mooring rope ashore and looked at Yoshi. "Time to come aboard, boy," he barked, "if you intend to."

The air was thick with the sharp stench of the dock. Struggling to keep his fear under control, Yoshi sucked in his breath and approached the old boat.

When Yoshi had arrived by train from Yokohama that morning, the sky had been leaden with storm clouds. He'd gone directly to the station to ask directions to the ferry to Mishima.

"End of the dock," the station master said. "But there'll be no ferry in these heavy seas. They will sail tomorrow."

"Tomorrow!" Yoshi's heart sank. Desperate, he poured out his story to the station master: how his father, a food broker, taken ill at the last moment, had entrusted him to purchase the entire rice crop from Wamatsu Farm on Mishima; how payment must be made by sundown today; how if he failed, his father would lose a premium crop.

"And . . ." his voice trailed off.

"And," the station master said, "you will lose your father's trust."

So it was that Yoshi learned of a captain who sailed when others feared to leave the harbor. "Captain Nakai," the station master said. "He is going to Mishima today. I can arrange passage for you. It will cost you 2,800 yen."

Twice the fare for a ferry, Yoshi thought. *For a decrepit fishing boat, against an angry sea*. With no alternative, he agreed.

 Stop here for the Strategy Break.

Strategy Break

What conclusions can you draw about Yoshi so far? If you were to begin a character map to list some of his traits, it might look like the one below. When you get to the end of the story, you will finish the map.

CHARACTER TRAIT:
determined
Example:
When the station master tells Yoshi that no ferries will sail that day, Yoshi doesn't give up. He decides to travel with Captain Nakai, even though it will cost him twice as much.

CHARACTER TRAIT:
brave
Example:
Yoshi is nervous about traveling on Captain Nakai's old boat in such bad conditions, but he overcomes his fear and goes anyway.

CHARACTER: Yoshi

CHARACTER TRAIT:

Example(s):

CHARACTER TRAIT:

Example(s):

As you continue reading, keep drawing conclusions about Yoshi. You will finish his character map later. Also draw conclusions about Captain Nakai. You will create a character map for him in the Strategy Follow-up.

 Go on reading to see what happens.

Now, as he boarded the boat, he glanced again at the skipper. Captain Nakai was one of the ugliest men Yoshi had ever seen. The burly seaman stood well over six feet tall. Unkempt tufts of white hair protruded beneath the sides of his soiled knit cap. His sea jacket, greasy canvas pants and rubber boots looked as if he had not taken them off for weeks.

Yoshi felt again beneath his jacket to make sure the money pouch was secure. Inside were his travel receipts, his audit sheet and 2 million yen, more money than his father's employees earned in an entire year. He patted the pouch nervously. Then he went aft to a bench that allowed him to keep the menacing Captain Nakai in sight.

The captain mounted the wheel house. "Cast off!" he shouted to the crew, his voice like a klaxon horn. With a belch of black smoke, the old engine roared to life and the boat began to move.

Just beyond the breakwater, heavy waves began to pound them with fury. A wind-driven spray blurred Yoshi's vision, the salt burning his eyes. Surely, he thought, they would turn back. Instead, Captain Nakai held a steady **helm** while his vessel **pitched** and **yawed** through a mounting sea.

Drenched to the skin, fearful of being washed overboard, Yoshi held on for dear life as they plowed through the giant swells. At the peak of each crest the little boat teetered for breathless seconds. Then, like a runaway roller coaster, it made a stomach-wrenching plunge into the next deep trough. Twenty minutes after casting off, he was dreadfully seasick. And there were miles of raging sea yet to cross.

Clutching the rail, he turned and vomited into the sea. Suddenly, a vise-like hand pulled him to his feet. Captain Nakai dragged him across the **deck**. *Does he know about the money pouch?* Yoshi thought. *Did the station master tell him? Am I going to be thrown overboard?*

At the base of the **wheelhouse**, Captain Nakai opened a small wooden door and shoved Yoshi inside. "You stay," he bellowed above the roar of the storm, and slammed the door shut.

At that moment, the little boat pitched hard to **port** and Yoshi sprawled facedown on the deck. He saw that he was in the **galley**. The small enclosure was suffocating. He crawled to the door and banged on it, to no avail. He was the trapped captive of a madman on a dilapidated boat that could founder and sink beneath any one of the relentlessly pounding waves. Heart racing, he lay back on the deck, helpless.

Mustering his last dregs of strength, he dragged himself across the deck to the **bulkhead**. Something was constricting his chest. Opening his shirt, he untied the money pouch and withdrew it. Beside him a heavy trolling net hung from the ceiling to the deck. He hid the pouch beneath the folds of the net, then let his arms drop limply at his sides. With tears in his eyes, he prayed to the ancient deities whom legend claimed formed Japan from the primordial mud: *"Izanagi . . . Izanami . . . deliver me. . . . "*

Suddenly the galley door flew open and the massive bulk of Captain Nakai filled the entryway. He glanced once at Yoshi, then crossed the room on steady legs and retrieved a bottle from the cabinet. Kneeling, he grasped the back of Yoshi's head, shoved the bottle neck into his mouth and tipped it high. *Poison!* Yoshi thought. Too sick to care, he let the thick white liquid slide down his throat.

Hours later he awoke to the clang of bells. The boat was riding calm waters. Rising on rubber legs, he pushed the galley door open and saw that the sky was clear. Crewmen were casting lines toward a dock.

After a moment, Captain Nakai descended the wheelhouse ladder. He helped Yoshi through the little door, then lifted him effortlessly and set him ashore on the dock. Without a word the captain pointed toward a waiting truck.

A sign on the truck read Wamatsu Farm. The driver, not much older than Yoshi, bowed and opened the passenger door. Yoshi returned the bow and got in. The seat was crushed, and wire springs protruded through the fabric. To Yoshi it was pure comfort. He glanced at the rutted dirt road leading up a steep hill. "How far?" he asked.

"Ten kilometers," the driver replied.

Still drowsy from Captain Nakai's seasick potion, Yoshi rolled down the window, rested his head against the back of the seat and closed his eyes.

Sometime later he awakened to see the gate to a large farm. He gave a sigh of relief. He could make the final payment, obtain a room at the farm for the night and catch the morning ferry back to Nagato. He reached beneath his shirt—and his blood turned to ice water. The money pouch was gone!

"No!" he cried.

Startled, the driver stared at him.

"Turn around!" Yoshi exclaimed. "Back to the dock. Hurry!"

The driver whipped the truck around.

Visions of his father filled Yoshi's mind. *How can I explain that I was careless? That I was robbed by a seafaring bandit?* Minutes before, he'd been trapped in a nightmarish storm at sea. This was worse. He had dishonored his father. For the remainder of his life he would be known as the Fujiwara who disgraced his family.

"Faster! Faster!" he cried.

The driver sped on, struggling to hold the jolting truck on the road. On the final descending curve Yoshi got a clear view of the harbor far below. Captain Nakai's boat was still moored to the dock. Yoshi bit his lip. How would he handle the situation? Were there police nearby? Then, something else caught his eye. A lone figure trudging uphill along the side of the road. Captain Nakai!

The captain waved the truck down. When it skidded to a stop, he handed something through the open window to Yoshi. The pouch!

Frantically, Yoshi yanked it open. Inside were his receipts, his audit sheet—and the money. Keenly aware of what had taken place, he jumped from the truck and bowed lower than he had ever bowed to another person. "I . . . I am indebted. . . . "

"You are a careless boy," Captain Nakai said. "You must be more responsible." Without another word, the big man turned and walked down to his boat.

Within the hour, Yoshi had made payment to the manager at Wamatsu Farm. He folded the promissory note for grain into the pouch and pulled out his audit sheet. Just then another grievous thought struck him. He had not paid for his passage to Mishima!

Once more he pressed the dismayed truck driver into racing to the harbor. But the mooring slip was empty. He dismissed the driver, then all that night sat on a waterfront bench, watching for Captain Nakai to return. By dawn it was obvious the vigil was futile. At midmorning he bought passage on the return ferry to Nagato, then caught the train to Yokohama. Late that night he placed the pouch on his father's desk. Exhausted, he went to his room, unrolled his futon and collapsed into a deep sleep.

Hours later, he was awakened by his mother. "Your father wishes to speak with you."

Ogi Fujiwara put down his abacus when Yoshi entered. "Your account is short by 2,800 yen."

"Short? But I. . . ." He stopped. 2,800 yen! Suddenly it was clear. Captain Nakai had collected his fare from the money pouch. And had not taken one yen more. All Yoshi would have had to do was enter the fare on his audit sheet—but he'd been too exhausted to even notice the missing yen.

Yet how could he explain without revealing the whole story? No, it all would remain his secret. "I regret the error. I am truly sorry."

"You must be more responsible."

The words echoed in his mind. He'd heard them from a crusty old sea captain yesterday and now from his father today.

"Next time, be more careful with your accounts."

"Yes, Father. I will work to repay the shortage." He turned to leave.

"Yoshi."

He turned back.

"The receipt is in good order. You did well, my son."

Yoshi beamed. "Thank you, Father." He left, grateful for his father's trust and the lasting memory of his passage to Mishima. ●

Strategy Follow-up

First go back and complete the character map for Yoshi. Then complete the following character map for Captain Nakai.

CHARACTER TRAIT:

Example(s):

CHARACTER TRAIT:

Example(s):

CHARCTER: Captain Nakai

CHARACTER TRAIT:

Example(s):

CHARACTER TRAIT:

Example(s):

✓Personal Checklist

Read each question and put a check (✓) in the correct box.

1. How well were you able to use what you wrote in Building Background to understand how Yoshi feels in this story?
    ☐ 3 (extremely well)
    ☐ 2 (fairly well)
    ☐ 1 (not well)

2. In the Vocabulary Builder, how well were you able to match the vocabulary words and their definitions?
    ☐ 3 (extremely well)
    ☐ 2 (fairly well)
    ☐ 1 (not well)

3. How well were you able to use your knowledge of the vocabulary words to help you understand what happens on the boat?
    ☐ 3 (extremely well)
    ☐ 2 (fairly well)
    ☐ 1 (not well)

4. How well were you able to complete the character maps for Yoshi and Captain Nakai?
    ☐ 3 (extremely well)
    ☐ 2 (fairly well)
    ☐ 1 (not well)

5. How well do you understand why Yoshi doesn't explain about the missing 2,800 yen?
    ☐ 3 (extremely well)
    ☐ 2 (fairly well)
    ☐ 1 (not well)

Vocabulary Check

Look back at the work you did in the Vocabulary Builder. Then answer each question by circling the correct letter.

1. Where on a boat is the aft deck?
    a. at or near the front of a ship
    b. at or near the back of a ship
    c. at or near the middle of a ship

2. Which word describes a movement that a ship makes?
    a. yawed
    b. helm
    c. port

3. What does the word *port* mean in the context of this story?
    a. a strong, sweet wine
    b. a harbor
    c. the left side of a ship

4. Which vocabulary word describes what is located in the wheelhouse?
    a. helm
    b. galley
    c. bulkhead

5. What does the word *galley* mean in the context of this story?
    a. ship used in Medieval times
    b. the kitchen of a ship
    c. warship of the ancient Greeks

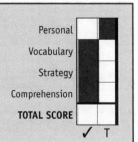

Add the numbers that you just checked to get your Personal Checklist score. Fill in your score here. Then turn to page 217 and transfer your score onto Graph 1.

Personal
Vocabulary
Strategy
Comprehension
TOTAL SCORE
✓ T

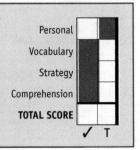

Check your answers with your teacher. Give yourself 1 point for each correct answer, and fill in your Vocabulary score here. Then turn to page 217 and transfer your score onto Graph 1.

Personal
Vocabulary
Strategy
Comprehension
TOTAL SCORE
✓ T

Strategy Check

Review your character maps for Yoshi and Captain Nakai. Then answer these questions:

1. Which of the following character traits would you *not* include on a character map for Captain Nakai?

   a. gentle

   b. fearless

   c. skilled seaman

2. Which example supports the conclusion that Captain Nakai is honorable?

   a. He sails when other people are afraid to leave the harbor.

   b. He takes only the cost of the fare from Yoshi's money pouch.

   c. He holds the helm steady while the boat pitches and yaws.

3. Which of the following traits would *not* belong on a character map for Yoshi?

   a. brave

   b. respectful

   c. careful

4. Which example supports the conclusion that Yoshi is careless?

   a. He does his father's bidding and doesn't talk back.

   b. He leaves his money pouch on Captain Nakai's ship.

   c. He doesn't give up when he finds out there's no ferry.

5. What is one character trait that Yoshi and Captain Nakai seem to have in common?

   a. They are both determined.

   b. They are both careless.

   c. They are both good seamen.

Comprehension Check

Review the story if necessary. Then answer these questions:

1. How does Yoshi learn that Captain Nakai might take him as a passenger?

   a. His father tells him to look for the captain at Nagato.

   b. Yoshi sees a poster advertising rides on Nakai's boat.

   c. The station master at the docks tells him about the captain.

2. Why does Captain Nakai drag Yoshi across the deck and push him into the cabin?

   a. He wants to remind Yoshi who is in charge.

   b. He wants to trap Yoshi and keep him prisoner.

   c. He doesn't want Yoshi to fall overboard.

3. If Captain Nakai means Yoshi no harm, why does he yell at him when he pushes him into the cabin?

   a. Nakai is deaf and doesn't know he is yelling.

   b. Nakai wants to be heard above the wind and rain.

   c. Nakai is angry with Yoshi for being out in the storm.

4. What does Captain Nakai take from Yoshi's money pouch?

   a. the cost of the voyage

   b. nothing at all

   c. everything but the audit sheet

5. Why doesn't Yoshi explain to his father why the audit sheet is incorrect?

   a. He is too tired and can't explain it.

   b. He knows his father won't believe his story anyway.

   c. He doesn't want his father to know that he forgot the money pouch.

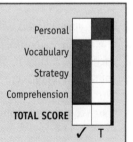

Check your answers with your teacher. Give yourself 1 point for each correct answer, and fill in your Strategy score here. Then turn to page 217 and transfer your score onto Graph 1.

Check your answers with your teacher. Give yourself 1 point for each correct answer, and fill in your Comprehension score here. Then turn to page 217 and transfer your score onto Graph 1.

Extending

Choose one or more of these activities:

DISCOVER JAPAN!

Use the resources listed on this page or ones you find yourself to research modern Japan to find out what cities and scenic areas you might like to visit. Find pictures of these sites and maps showing how to get to them. Then put together a travel brochure publicizing a tour to the sites. Give potential clients all the reasons they should consider taking the tour.

FIND OUT WHAT IT'S WORTH

In the story, Yoshi pays 2,800 yen for his voyage. How much is that worth in U.S. currency? Use the Internet, call a bank, or look in a newspaper to find the exchange rates between countries. Using today's rate of exchange, figure out how much Yoshi's trip would cost in U.S. dollars. If possible, do some research about inflation in both countries. If the story took place 20 years ago, would the exchange rate then have made the trip more costly in U.S. dollars or less costly?

STORMY SKIES

Investigate Japan's long history of struggle with the seas. Report on your findings in a written report or through a poster with pictures with captions. Include shipwrecks and floods, typhoons and tidal waves caused by volcanoes or earthquakes.

Resources

Books

Brown, Azby. *Japan: A Living Portrait.* Kodansha International, 2000.

Harris, Bill. *Japan: A Photographic Journey.* Random House, 1993.

Pictorial Encyclopedia of Japanese Life and Events. Farrer Straus & Giroux, 1999.

Web Sites

http://www.currency-conversion.info/
This Web site provides an exchange-rate converter that allows you to calculate how much Japanese yen (or other currencies) are worth in U.S. dollars.

http://www.jnto.go.jp/eng/
This is the home page of the Japan National Tourist Organization.

Videos/DVDs

Japan. Travelview International, 1995.

Japan. Maureen Zrike and Michael Jewell. Rand McNally Video Traveller, 1995.

The World's Biggest Ship

Building Background

The article you are about to read describes the life and some of the accomplishments of Isambard Kingdom Brunel, "a man who loved to do things that ordinary people thought were impossible." Brunel was not alone in his quest to do extraordinary things. As a matter of fact, record books are filled with people who have tried to do things that hadn't—or still haven't—been done before.

With a partner or two, think of at least five people who tried to do something that had or has never done before. Then complete the chart below.

Person	What he or she tried to accomplish	Result or Outcome

collapsed

christened

enormous

launched

rivets

vessels

Vocabulary Builder

1. The words in the margin are all found in the following article. Use your knowledge of the words to decide if the boldfaced words in the sentences below are used correctly or incorrectly. If a word is used correctly, put a **C** next to the sentence. If a word is used incorrectly, put an **I** next to the sentence.

    _____ When the bridge **collapsed**, it fell into the water.

    _____ The great ship *Titanic* is one of the most famous **vessels** on earth.

    _____ Someone or something that has been **christened** has no name yet.

    _____ Construction workers building tall buildings use **rivets** frequently.

    _____ When the ship was **launched**, it was removed from the water for repairs.

    _____ An **enormous** ship could easily fit into a small space.

2. Save your work. You will refer to it again in the Vocabulary Check.

Strategy Builder

Following Sequence While You Read

- You know that an **informational article** is nonfiction that gives facts and details about a particular topic. You also know that a **biography** is nonfiction that tells the story of a real person's life, as written by someone else.

- The selection you are about to read is a combination of both of these types of nonfiction. The author combines the organizational patterns of **sequence** and **description** as he tells the story of Isambard Brunel's life and describes several of his accomplishments.

- In order to make the sequence of events as clear as possible in this selection, the author uses **signal words**. Some signal words—such as *then*, *next*, and *a few days later*—help you link one smaller event to the next. However, signal words such as *in 1841* or *on January 30* help you see the sequence of the major, or most important, events.

- The following paragraph is from an article about Robert Fulton and his inventions. Notice how the signal words help you track the sequence in this paragraph.

> Robert Fulton was a great inventor of the 18th century. <u>Born in 1765</u> in Lancaster County, Pennsylvania, he showed early talent for inventing. <u>In 1786</u>, Fulton traveled to England. There he studied art while working with a jeweler. <u>After a few years</u>, in 1793, Fulton switched his attention from art to engineering. <u>In 1801</u>, Fulton built an early submarine which he called the *Nautilus*. <u>Then</u> Fulton became interested in steamboats. <u>After designing and building a successful steamboat</u>, he returned to the United States <u>in 1806</u>. <u>In 1807</u>, he oversaw the launch of the first steamboat to carry passengers on the Hudson River—the *Clermont*. Robert Fulton died <u>in 1815</u>, in the midst of a project to build a steam-powered warship.

- If you wanted to show the sequence of the events described in the paragraph, you could put them on a **time line.** It would look like this:

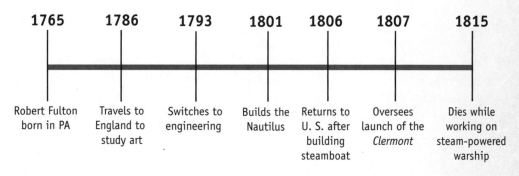

1765	1786	1793	1801	1806	1807	1815
Robert Fulton born in PA	Travels to England to study art	Switches to engineering	Builds the Nautilus	Returns to U. S. after building steamboat	Oversees launch of the *Clermont*	Dies while working on steam-powered warship

The World's Biggest Ship

by John Koster

Now use what you've learned to track the major events in the first part of this selection. Notice the signal words. They will help make the sequence clearer.

In the 1850s, a man who loved to do things that ordinary people thought were impossible built the biggest ship in the world on the Isle of Dogs in London's Thames River.

Isambard Kingdom Brunel was the son of a French-born engineer named Marc Brunel and an Englishwoman, Sophie Kingdom. Born in 1806, Isambard began assisting his father on "impossible" projects while he was still in his teens.

In 1825 Marc and "Sam" Brunel started work on a tunnel under the Thames. Marc Brunel had invented a sort of capsule that could tunnel through earth and mud, laying out an iron pipe behind it that allowed workers to move around underwater without drowning or being buried alive. Brunel got the idea while studying a shipworm, a kind of sea creature that bores through the wood of ocean-going **vessels**.

On five occasions the pipe broke, and the river Thames burst into the tunnel. The workmen and engineers escaped by running up the pipe, pursued by a roaring whirlpool of dirty brown water.

 Stop here for the Strategy Break.

Strategy Break

If you were to show the major events described in this selection so far, your time line might look like this:

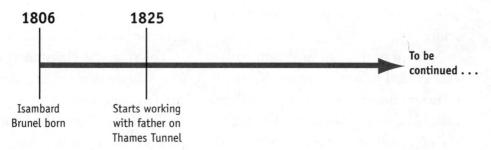

1806   **1825**

Isambard   Starts working
Brunel born   with father on
                  Thames Tunnel

To be
continued . . .

As you continue reading, keep paying attention to the order of events. At the end of this selection, you will complete the time line on your own. (Be careful—one of the events is out of order. Use the signal words to help you decide which one it is.)

 Go on reading.

Once, when the pipe burst, Isambard Brunel was caught in the head of the capsule. He was able to squeeze through the hole and swim to the surface, but the two workmen behind him weren't so lucky and drowned. Cave-ins and financial problems stopped the Thames Tunnel for years at a time, but in 1841 it was finally completed. It's still in use today.

When his father retired, Isambard K. Brunel became interested in steamships. British steamships burned coal, but they couldn't carry enough fuel to get them across the Atlantic without danger of running out. The ships all carried masts and sails in case they had to use the wind, as vessels had done for thousands of years. Sometimes, when the wind and the coal both failed, the ships' crews burned the deck planks to keep the boilers hot.

Brunel realized that a big ship could carry more coal than a small one. He began building a steamship 236 feet long, which was 32 feet longer than the biggest ship afloat at that time. The *Great Western* was built of iron plates, not wood, and had two big paddle wheels, one on each side, to push it through the water. When the *Great Western* was **launched** in 1838, it crossed the Atlantic easily and safely, carrying plenty of coal, mail, and passengers.

The *Great Britain*, launched in 1845, was bigger yet—322 feet long and powered by a "screw," a propeller that turned underwater behind the ship. The *Great Britain* was the first ship with a screw propeller to cross the Atlantic, and it has set the fashion up until the present time.

But the ship being built on the Isle of Dogs in the 1850s was the biggest yet—692 feet long, twice the length of any ship that had ever existed. The double hull, with an inner and an outer "skin" of iron plates, was 85 feet wide.

No ship of this size or design had ever existed before. The two "skins" were far enough apart so that workers, called "bashers," could stand inside the hull while it was being built. Their job was to hammer at the hot **rivets** as they were poked through from the outside. Boys as young as nine or ten years old ran around inside the twin hulls, carrying tools for the bashers and bringing them food and water. As the great iron ship took shape, 2,000 workmen and boys swarmed over it like termites over a gigantic log.

Three people were killed while building the ship. Two others, a man and a boy, never showed up for their pay. Most people assumed that they'd had enough and had quit without giving notice. But some workers said that they'd heard muffled cries and the dull banging of a hammer after one section of the iron hull was closed.

On November 3, 1857, the huge 12,000-ton hull was ready to be launched. But its weight was so **enormous** that no force on earth could budge it. A winch, a sort of giant spool cranked with poles, was hooked to the ship. The gears broke, the winch reversed, and the workers who didn't let go fast enough were thrown into the air. Two were killed.

Brunel tried using hydraulic jacks. At one time he had 19 of the heaviest jacks he could find pushing at the huge iron hull. One by one, the jacks burst, spurting oil.

Finally, on January 30, an extremely high tide rose in the Thames, and the wooden frame that held the huge ship washed loose and **collapsed**. The giant vessel had launched itself.

The ship was **christened** *Leviathan*, but nobody ever called it anything but the *Great Eastern*.

The *Great Eastern* had both a screw propeller and paddle wheels. It also had five funnels, or smokestacks, and six masts with sails, just in case. To prevent confusion, the six masts were named for the days of the week—Monday, Tuesday, Wednesday, Thursday, Friday, and Saturday. If children asked what happened to Sunday, they were told that there was no Sunday at sea. This was a joke among sailors who had to work on Sundays while people at home read the Bible, went to church, or simply rested.

Most ships of the *Great Eastern*'s day had a crew of 18 or 20 men. The *Great Eastern* had a crew of 300 and room for 4,000 passengers.

During the ship's first tests, a crewman shut down a steam safety valve by mistake. When the excess steam couldn't escape, a boiler blew up and a smokestack collapsed. Five men were killed, and many others were hurt. The mistake wasn't Brunel's fault. But the stress and strain of trying to launch the huge ship had weakened his health, and the shock of the fatal explosion and the investigation that followed led to a heart attack. Isambard Brunel died before the world's biggest ship had completed its first Atlantic voyage.

Without his guiding genius, the *Great Eastern* became a bad-luck ship—what sailors call a "Jonah." When the huge vessel came into harbors, its paddle wheels chewed up docks and piers. The ship crushed tugboats and struck rocks because it rode so low in the water.

In a fog off Long Island, New York, the *Great Eastern* struck one underwater rock that tore her outer hull open and let the sea flood in. But the inner hull wasn't broken, and the great ship stayed afloat.

When a diver in his waterproof canvas suit and round brass helmet went down to inspect the damage, the crew heard a strange noise that sounded like something banging against the hull from the inside. Suddenly the sailors remembered the missing basher and basher's boy.

"The basher's ghost is hammering inside the hull," the sailors whispered.

Then the diver saw a piece of tackle banging against the hull. The workers laughed at their fear and went down to seal the hole, and the *Great Eastern* sailed on.

For the next thirty years, the *Great Eastern* proved that it could survive any storm, carry any load, steam across any ocean. But the most important thing the *Great Eastern* did was to help lay the first telegraph cable across the bottom of the Atlantic Ocean. Only the giant *Great Eastern* was big enough to carry more than 2,000 miles of rubber-coated copper cable in one enormous length.

Although the *Great Eastern* was one of the fastest ships in the world, there was one thing it couldn't do—it couldn't make a profit for its owners. By 1888, the ship had lost so much money that the last group of stockholders sold the *Great Eastern* for scrap. It was still the biggest ship in the world, but nobody wanted it.

When the breakers who took ships apart for scrap were tearing the iron hull open, a workman screamed. The other men shuddered as they gathered around the hole. The skeletons of the basher and the basher's boy were found caught between the two iron hulls, where they had been trapped thirty years before.

Some sailors said that the *Great Eastern* had been the victim of a curse. But most people took a more practical view. They said that the biggest ship in the world had simply been too big for anyone but the man who had designed it. ●

Strategy Follow-up

Now complete the time line with major events from the second part of this selection. Use a separate sheet of paper if you need more room to write.

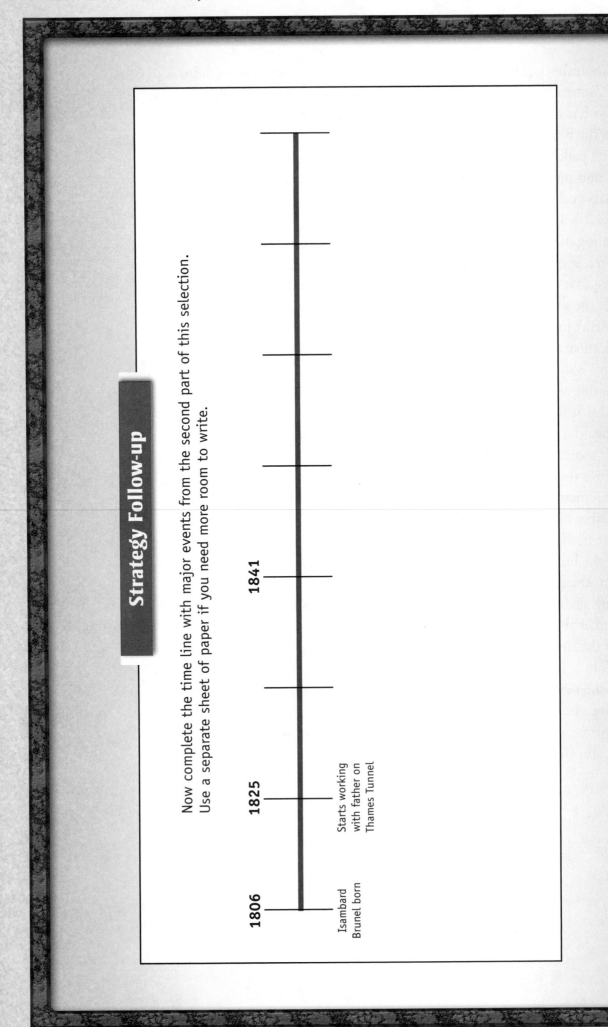

1806

Isambard Brunel born

1825

Starts working with father on Thames Tunnel

1841

✓Personal Checklist

Read each question and put a check (✓) in the correct box.

1. How well were you able to complete the chart in Building Background?
    - ☐ 3 (extremely well)
    - ☐ 2 (fairly well)
    - ☐ 1 (not well)

2. How well were you able to use the information on the chart to understand the personality and accomplishments of Sam Brunel?
    - ☐ 3 (extremely well)
    - ☐ 2 (fairly well)
    - ☐ 1 (not well)

3. In the Vocabulary Builder, how many words were you able to identify as being used correctly or incorrectly?
    - ☐ 3 (5–6 words)
    - ☐ 2 (3–4 words)
    - ☐ 1 (0–2 words)

4. How well were you able to complete the time line in the Strategy Follow-up?
    - ☐ 3 (extremely well)
    - ☐ 2 (fairly well)
    - ☐ 1 (not well)

5. How well do you understand what caused Brunel's death?
    - ☐ 3 (extremely well)
    - ☐ 2 (fairly well)
    - ☐ 1 (not well)

Vocabulary Check

Look back at the work you did in the Vocabulary Builder. Then answer each question by circling the correct letter.

1. Which vocabulary word is a synonym of *huge*?
    a. enormous
    b. collapsed
    c. christened

2. Which meaning of the word *vessels* fits the context of this article?
    a. containers for holding something
    b. tubes that carry bodily fluids
    c. boats

3. What is the purpose of a rivet?
    a. to steer a ship
    b. to hold things together
    c. to be used as a hammer

4. Which word could you use to describe what happens when a mine caves in?
    a. launch
    b. collapse
    c. christen

5. Which of these things is not usually launched?
    a. a ship
    b. a rocket
    c. a bridge

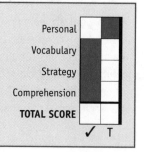

Add the numbers that you just checked to get your Personal Checklist score. Fill in your score here. Then turn to page 217 and transfer your score onto Graph 1.

Check your answers with your teacher. Give yourself 1 point for each correct answer, and fill in your Vocabulary score here. Then turn to page 217 and transfer your score onto Graph 1.

Strategy Check

Review the time line that you completed in the Strategy Follow-up. Also review the rest of the article. Then answer these questions:

1. How many years did Brunel work on the Thames Tunnel with his father?
   a. 32
   b. 20
   c. 16

2. About how old was Brunel when the *Great Eastern* was ready to be launched?
   a. 51
   b. 39
   c. 35

3. Which of these events happened first?
   a. Brunel completes the Thames Tunnel.
   b. Brunel launches the *Great Western*.
   c. The *Great Eastern* is scrapped.

4. Which of these events happens last?
   a. Skeletons are found in the *Great Eastern's* hull.
   b. The world's biggest ship is ready to be launched.
   c. The *Great Eastern* launches itself.

5. Which event is described out of sequence in this article?
   a. Brunel launches the *Great Western*.
   b. Brunel completes the Thames Tunnel.
   c. Brunel launches the *Great Britain*.

Comprehension Check

Review the selection if necessary. Then answer these questions:

1. With whom did Sam Brunel work on the Thames Tunnel?
   a. his father
   b. his mother
   c. his brother

2. Why couldn't British steamships make it all the way across the Atlantic Ocean?
   a. They were too heavy and would begin to sink.
   b. They had no sails, so they'd get blown off course.
   c. They couldn't carry enough coal to power their engines.

3. According to this article, what is a "basher"?
   a. a large iceberg
   b. a worker who bashes hot rivets inside the hull
   c. someone who criticizes inventors

4. Why was the *Great Eastern* thought to be unlucky?
   a. It had six masts.
   b. It caused the deaths of many people over the years.
   c. It launched itself at high tide on January 30.

5. What surprising discovery did the breakers make when they tore open the hull of the *Great Eastern*?
   a. a telegraph cable that was hidden there
   b. the body of Sam Brunel
   c. the skeletons of two workers

Check your answers with your teacher. Give yourself 1 point for each correct answer, and fill in your Strategy score here. Then turn to page 217 and transfer your score onto Graph 1.

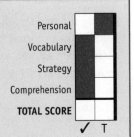

Check your answers with your teacher. Give yourself 1 point for each correct answer, and fill in your Comprehension score here. Then turn to page 217 and transfer your score onto Graph 1.

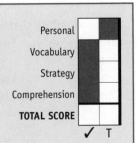

Extending

Choose one or both of these activities:

LEARN MORE ABOUT ISAMBARD KINGDOM BRUNEL

"Sam" Brunel was an engineer who worked on several other projects besides the *Great Eastern*. Use some of the resources listed on this page to find out more about Brunel. Present an oral report about him and his other famous engineering feats. You might create a time line first to help you keep track of important events.

MAKE A COMPARISON GRAPH

At 692 feet, the *Great Eastern* was the longest boat that had ever existed. But how does its length compare to the length of other ships, such as the *Titanic* or modern-day aircraft carriers or passenger ships? Consult an encyclopedia or other source to find out the lengths of these ships. Then, on graph paper, draw scale drawings of the *Great Eastern* and at least three other ships. (For example, if each square represents 100 feet, your drawing of the *Great Eastern* would be almost seven squares long.) Let your graph show how much longer or shorter the *Great Eastern* was than the other ships. Label each ship by name.

Resources

Books

Falconer, John. *Sail and Steam—A Century of Maritime Enterprise, 1840–1935: Photographs from the National Maritime Museum, Greenwich.* David R. Godine, 1993.

Jenkins, David, and Hugh Jenkins. *Isambard Kingdom Brunel, Engineer Extraordinary.* Priory Press, 1977.

Rolt, L. T. C. *The Story of Brunel.* Metheun, 1965.

Web Sites

http://pc-78-120.udac.se:8001/WWW/Nautica/Ships/Ships.html
This Web site provides information, including dimensions, on ships that sailed from the 1500s to the 1900s.

http://web.ukonline.co.uk/b.gardner/brunel/kingbrun.html
The biography of Brunel on this Web page includes images of the architect and some of his works.

http://www.greatbuildings.com/architect/Isambard_Kingdom_Brunel.html
A brief biography of Brunel on this Web site includes links to information on two of his engineering projects.

Learning New Words

Compound Words

A compound word is made up of two words put together. In "Passage to Mishima," for example, Captain Nakai's boat has a wheelhouse. A *wheelhouse* is the enclosed area, or *house,* that protects the captain while he steers the *wheel,* or helm.

Fill in each blank with a compound word by combining a word from Row 1 with a word from Row 2.

Row 1: shop   wheel   story   weather
Row 2: teller   person   barrow   keeper

1. one-wheeled cart for carrying loads = _____

2. person who manages a store = _____

3. person who "spins yarns" = _____

4. person who states atmospheric conditions = _____

Multiple-Meaning Words

A single word can have several meanings. For example, a *tick* can be a sound a clock makes or an animal that attaches to the skin or a muscle twitch. When you read "Duffy's Jacket," you used context to figure out that the tick in that story is an animal that attaches to the skin. Now use context to figure out the meaning of each underlined word.

1. Susan poured the <u>port</u> into small crystal glasses.

    a. harbor for ships

    b. strong, sweet wine

2. Walter <u>pitched</u> an incredible game last night.

    a. rose up and then fell down

    b. threw a ball to a batter

3. The magician told me to cut the <u>deck</u> in half.

    a. stack of playing cards

    b. floor of a ship

Suffixes

A suffix is a word part that is added to the end of a root word. When you add a suffix, you often change the root word's meaning and function. For example, the suffix *-less* means "without," so the root word *pain* changes from a noun to an adjective meaning "without pain."

-er

The suffix *-er* turns a verb into a noun that means "a person who _____." In Lesson 13 you learned that the Amistad Africans had many supporters who tried to helped them gain their freedom. In this context, a *supporter* is a person who supports, or tries to help, someone else.

Write a description for each person below.

1. writer   _____

2. teacher   _____

3. player   _____

4. defender _____

5. builder   _____

-ist

The suffix *-ist* has a similar function to *-er*. It, too, turns words into nouns that mean "a person who _____." For example, in Lesson 13 you learned that *abolitionists* were people who wanted to abolish, or put an end to, slavery.

Now write the word that describes each person below.

1. a person who tours a place   _____

2. a person who terrorizes others   _____

3. a person who plays the piano   _____

4. a person who makes or performs art   _____

5. a person who's an expert in chemistry _____

VOCABULARY

From Lesson 13
• supporters

From Lesson 13
• abolitionists

The Woman Who Loves Bones

Building Background

The woman described in this article not only loves bones, she loves her job. That's because her job is finding and studying things—something she has loved to do since she was a child.

What have you loved to do since you were a child? sing? draw? play an instrument? write short stories? play a sport? study bugs? keep tropical fish? If you could turn your passion into your dream job, what would that job be? Think for a moment about what type of work you would do, and where and how you would do it. For example, would your "office" be a high rise in the city, a concert hall, a football field, or the great outdoors? Would you travel in your job or stay in the same place? Would you work by yourself or with other people? On the lines below, describe your dream job, and explain why and how you would do it.

_____

_____

_____

_____

_____

_____

_____

_____

beach-combing

calcium

catalog

finch

humerus

osteologist

Vocabulary Builder

1. Many of the words you will read in this article are explained in **context**. This means that the surrounding words and phrases contain examples or definitions that help explain the words.

2. Read the following sentences, which are taken from the article. Underline the context clues that help you understand each boldfaced word.

3. Then save your work. You will refer to it again in the Vocabulary Check.

a. As a child in Texas, she loved **beach-combing** with her mother, looking for things washed up on the shore.

b. Tortoises and rodents may need **calcium**—an important ingredient of bones, teeth, and muscle.

c. She also helps **catalog**—make a detailed list of—all the finds and the exact place they were discovered.

d. For instance, if a **finch** (a very small bird) dies and a leaf falls on top of it, Pillaert won't see it when she walks by.

e. Pillaert says her favorite bone will probably always be the **humerus** (the upper arm bone) of a mole.

f. Actually, Pillaert is an **osteologist**, a scientist who studies bones.

Strategy Builder

Asking Questions While You Read

- Textbooks and informational articles give you lots of unfamiliar information at once. To keep that information straight—and to remember it better—there are some things you can do. One thing that you already know how to do is summarize. When you **summarize** a portion of text, you list or retell the most important ideas in your own words.

- Another thing that you can do is ask yourself questions about what you read. **Self-questioning** works a lot like summarizing. First you ask yourself a question to get at the **main idea** of a section of text. Then you answer the question with **details** from that section.

- To understand how self-questioning works, read the following section of text from "The Printer's Apprentice." Then read one student's question and answers about it.

But hard work and rough treatment couldn't keep apprentices from having fun. In the evening, they played the accordion and sang. They played chess and perhaps cards in secret, since a strict master might believe that cards were sinful. Apprentices were even known to roam the streets or visit taverns.

Sometimes they played tricks on each other. One shy country boy named Horace Greeley had his blond hair inked black by the other apprentices. But they must not have discouraged him too badly. He kept working at the printer's craft, learning how to edit and publish a newspaper. Later he became the most famous newspaper editor of his time.

Q: What did printers' apprentices do for fun?
—They played the accordion and sang.
—They played chess and cards.
—Some even roamed the streets and went to taverns.
—They also played tricks on each other, like inking Horace Greeley's blond hair black.

The Woman Who Loves Bones

by Marguerite Holloway

As you read the first part of this article, underline the information that you would use for your questions and answers. When you get to the Strategy Break, you will have a chance to compare what you've underlined to the sample questions and answers.

"Bones are beautiful," says E. Elizabeth Pillaert. "They are little works of art, each one of them." So Pillaert spends a lot of her time hunting for dead bodies in order to get her hands on their skeletons. She doesn't kill anything, though. She just waits and waits and patiently waits until something dies. Or until someone brings her a carcass, or a bunch of bones, or even a single bone.

From this description it may sound as though Pillaert has a strange, morbid job—that perhaps she works in a morgue or moonlights as a graverobber. Actually, Pillaert is an **osteologist**, a scientist who studies bones. She looks at bones and teeth in order to tell what their owners ate, how they moved, how big they were, why they died, what diseases they had, and when they lived. Bones can tell you a lot if you know what to look for.

But Pillaert's job is a little unusual, even for an osteologist. This is because she does a lot of work in a place inhabited by some of the rarest animals in the world: the Galápagos Islands. Isolated in the Pacific Ocean, the islands are 600 miles west of Ecuador, a country in South America.

The islands are part of a vast national park that was set up by the Ecuadoran government to help save the creatures that live there; even the waters around these beautiful islands are legally protected. And they need to be: many creatures on the Galápagos don't live anywhere else. Only on these remote islands can you find lava gulls, Galápagos penguins, flightless cormorants, Darwin's finches, marine iguanas, and 11 subspecies of giant tortoise. Some of the creatures are very, *very* rare: Lonesome George, a giant tortoise that lives at the Charles Darwin Research Station on Santa Cruz Island, is the last of his kind on the planet.

Every other year or so, Pillaert leaves her office at the University of Wisconsin Zoological Museum and travels to Quito, the capital of Ecuador. From there she flies to the Galápagos, where she spends her days scaling cliffs, peering into caves, and hiking over lava flows and beaches looking for dead creatures. What Pillaert does is called salvage collecting.

Pillaert's work in the Galápagos isn't easy. There are 19 islands and 42 tiny islands called islets for her to search.

There's no way to know where to find a dead animal. It can be hard to see carcasses. For instance, if a **finch** (a very small bird) dies and a leaf falls on top of it, Pillaert won't see it when she walks by. And, of course, bodies don't last long in the wild: there are plenty of animals around who eat them. Tortoises and rodents may need **calcium**—an important ingredient of bones, teeth, and muscle—and so they may gnaw or eat bones to get it.

Recently, Pillaert's work was made a little less difficult. The University of Wisconsin is the only institution that has permission from the Ecuadoran government to do salvage collecting on the Galápagos. But the government just gave other scientists working on the islands permission to bring Pillaert any bones or carcasses that they may come across. These field biologists can now carry the material back to the Charles Darwin Research Station.

 Stop here for the Strategy Break.

Strategy Break

As you read, did you underline information for your questions and answers? If you did, see if your information matches these:

Q: Why is Pillaert's job unusual?
—She studies animal bones.
—She does a lot of her work in the Galápagos Islands.
—She studies some of the rarest creatures in the world.

Q: Why is Pillaert's job difficult?
—She must search 19 islands and 42 islets.
—There's no way to know where to find carcasses.
—Carcasses don't last long.

Q: How was her work made easier?
—Her university got permission to do salvage work in the Galápagos.
—Other scientists can now bring Pillaert the bones that they find.

Go on reading.

Pillaert is always looking for complete skeletons, because those can give scientists the most information. But they are also the hardest to find. "Penguins are one thing I don't have a lot of specimens of," she says. "The penguins feed way out at sea, so when they die they are not necessarily going to come in on the current. I won't necessarily find them on beaches. So I have to go into the nesting holes for those that died there. But if they died in the nesting holes it is probably because a rock fell on their heads, and then I have a specimen without a skull. So we are right back where we started."

But Pillaert knows that if she waits long enough she'll eventually find, or be given, what she needs. For example, ever since she started working on the islands in 1979, she's been looking for more albatross skeletons. Luckily, a scientist who was working in the islands recently found some, and brought them in for Pillaert. So she was finally able to get the bones she was missing.

About 60,000 tourists visit the Galápagos each year and it's crucial that they don't disturb the environment; visitors are prohibited from touching or picking up anything. So whenever Pillaert pokes around she has to be careful that tourists don't see what she's doing. The only collecting allowed on the islands is for scientific study, and she doesn't want to give anyone ideas. As Pillaert puts it, "they can take nothing but pictures and leave nothing but footprints." So Pillaert stays away from the main trails. If a tour group comes by she tries to look like a tourist. She stares into space and always carries a camera.

Pillaert has had some close calls. Once "we had already collected for the day and we had bags filled with carcasses. A small boat came, and we didn't know what to do because we were going down the path and they were coming up the path," laughs Pillaert. "As they passed by, my assistant said, 'Boy, you have a lot of camera equipment!' I said to her, 'Do you really think they are going to believe all those bags are filled with camera equipment?' But it worked. They didn't even look at us!"

Those plastic bags allow Pillaert to get the smelly stuff back to Wisconsin. Because the Galápagos are hot, bodies rot quickly. "When I find them, they are usually pretty dry. It's a bag of bones: a skin filled with bones on the inside," explains Pillaert. She packs this sack of bones in a plastic bag—often with a poison to kill any insects that might eat the skin—and closes it up. "Once it is sealed the bugs don't come out of it; they should be dead anyway. And no smell comes out."

Much of the material found—by Pillaert or anyone else—stays in Ecuador. Pillaert gives half of her specimens to the country and gets to keep the rest for the university's collection. She also helps **catalog**—make a detailed list of—all the finds and the exact place they were discovered. Before she can leave the islands with her specimens, Pillaert has to fill out piles of permission forms. It's a crucial part of her job. Every specimen must be recorded and registered with both the Ecuadoran and the American governments; this procedure is one way of protecting the islands from illegal collecting. If travelers can't produce papers for their specimens, the material may be taken from them and they may be fined. When Pillaert has filled out the proper permission slips, the shipment is ready to go. She packs the plastic bags in trunks and sends them to the zoological museum in Wisconsin.

Sometimes she has to resort to unusual methods to get specimens back safely. Once she found a giant tortoise shell that she was worried would break. So she stuffed it with clothes. "I have never been able to wear those clothes again, needless to say, and this was not a tortoise that was rotten or anything. But there was a wild smell that I just couldn't get rid of. It didn't go away with the wash."

Once everything is back at the zoological museum, Pillaert examines it carefully. Bones need a lot of attention. If a specimen has dried flesh on it, Pillaert must put it in the "bug room." Most natural history museums have a sealed room for flesh-eating bugs called dermestid beetles; they pick the bones clean. Or sometimes Pillaert cooks the carcasses in warm water so the flesh disintegrates. She has to be very careful not to overcook them, though, because the bones can suddenly turn to mush. After they have been cleaned, the bones are whitened, waterproofed, and numbered.

They are then officially part of the University of Wisconsin's collection of more than 17,000 specimens. And Pillaert is free to study them, which she loves to do. For instance, just by looking at foot bones, Pillaert can tell the difference between birds such as the blue-footed, red-footed, and masked boobies. But even though she has found some wonderful bones on the Galápagos over the years, Pillaert says her favorite bone will probably always be the **humerus** (the upper arm bone) of a mole, because it is rounder and stubbier than ours is. That shape allows the mole to burrow using a swimming motion, its powerful forelimbs propelling it through the earth.

Pillaert didn't always know that she loved bones so much. She just thought she liked finding things and being outside. As a child in Texas, she loved **beach-combing** with her mother, looking for things washed up on the shore. At first, she thought she wanted to study ancient people and places. But while she was in graduate school, she realized that she wasn't really happy doing that kind of work. So she started studying the animal remains found at ancient sites instead. One day, Pillaert visited the zoology collection at the University of Wisconsin and almost immediately discovered "that I loved skeletons more than anything else in the world." She has been there ever since, touching bones, waiting for more skeletons to come her way. ●

Strategy Follow-up

Work with the whole class or a group of students to complete this activity. First, skim the second part of "The Woman Who Loves Bones," and divide it into several sections. Assign each section to a pair or group of students. Then write questions and answers for your particular section of text. Be sure to use your own words, and include only the most important information.

When everyone is finished, put all the questions and answers in order and review them together. Revise any information as necessary.

✓Personal Checklist

Read each question and put a check (✓) in the correct box.

1. Now that you've read this article, how well would you be able to explain what an osteologist does?
   - ☐ 3 (extremely well)
   - ☐ 2 (fairly well)
   - ☐ 1 (not well)

2. In Building Background, how well were you able to describe your dream job?
   - ☐ 3 (extremely well)
   - ☐ 2 (fairly well)
   - ☐ 1 (not well)

3. How well are you able to use the description of your dream job and the information in this article to understand why Elizabeth Pillaert loves *her* job?
   - ☐ 3 (extremely well)
   - ☐ 2 (fairly well)
   - ☐ 1 (not well)

4. How well were you able to underline the context clues in the Vocabulary Builder?
   - ☐ 3 (extremely well)
   - ☐ 2 (fairly well)
   - ☐ 1 (not well)

5. In the Strategy Follow-up, how well were you able to write questions and answers for your section of text?
   - ☐ 3 (extremely well)
   - ☐ 2 (fairly well)
   - ☐ 1 (not well)

Vocabulary Check

Look back at the work you did in the Vocabulary Builder. Then answer each question by circling the correct letter.

1. Which word best completes the analogy A *zoologist* is to *animals* as an *osteologist* is to _____?
   - a. birds
   - b. bones
   - c. islands

2. What is another way of saying "a humorous humerus"?
   - a. a skeleton key
   - b. a clean carcass
   - c. a funny bone

3. In the context of this selection, how is the word *catalog* used?
   - a. as a verb
   - b. as a noun
   - c. as an adjective

4. As a child, Pillaert loved beach-combing with her mother. What does *beach-combing* mean?
   - a. looking for things that have washed up on the shore
   - b. sifting through the sand with a tiny plastic comb
   - c. combing your hair with a comb made of sand

5. Which of these words from the article describes a very small bird?
   - a. islet
   - b. finch
   - c. albatross

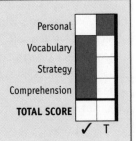

Add the numbers that you just checked to get your Personal Checklist score. Fill in your score here. Then turn to page 217 and transfer your score onto Graph 1.

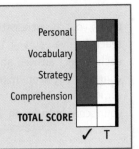

Check your answers with your teacher. Give yourself 1 point for each correct answer, and fill in your Vocabulary score here. Then turn to page 217 and transfer your score onto Graph 1.

Strategy Check

Review the questions and answers that your class or group wrote for this article. Then answer these questions:

1. Why does Pillaert look for complete skeletons?
    a. because they give scientists the most information
    b. because they make the best museum displays
    c. because they are hardest to find

2. Which question does the statement *She stays away from the main trails* answer?
    a. How does Pillaert get her camera equipment past the tourists?
    b. How does Pillaert get bones back to the University of Wisconsin?
    c. How is Pillaert careful not to let tourists see what she is doing?

3. What must Pillaert do before she can leave the island with her specimens?
    a. She must fill out piles of permission forms.
    b. She must pack the specimens carefully.
    c. She must do both of the above.

4. Which question does the statement *Sometimes she boils the carcasses in warm water* answer?
    a. How does Pillaert get the bones back to Wisconsin?
    b. How does Pillaert get the flesh off the bones?
    c. How did Pillaert get a giant tortoise shell home?

5. Which question best summarizes the main idea of this entire article?
    a. Why does Elizabeth Pillaert spend a lot of time hunting for bones?
    b. Where does Elizabeth Pillaert spend a lot of time hunting for bones?
    c. What kinds of bones does Elizabeth Pillaert like to hunt?

Comprehension Check

Review the selection if necessary. Then answer these questions:

1. What does Elizabeth Pillaert do with the bones she collects?
    a. She carves them into the shapes of animals.
    b. She catalogs them and puts them into storage.
    c. She studies them to learn about the lives of the animals.

2. Which of the following statements is false?
    a. Pillaert always knew that she wanted to study bones.
    b. Pillaert has studied bones since graduate school.
    c. Pillaert can tell different kinds of birds from their foot bones.

3. Which of the following do you suppose might be discovered from the bones of an animal?
    a. how the animal walks, swims, or flies
    b. how the animal blends into its surroundings
    c. whether the animal can be tamed

4. To which animal does Pillaert's favorite bone belong?
    a. the blue-footed booby
    b. the mole
    c. the giant tortoise

5. Why does the Ecuadoran government take such a strong stand against souvenir hunters on the Galápagos Islands?
    a. They are trying to preserve the home of some of the world's rarest animals.
    b. They want to profit from selling the souvenirs in their own country.
    c. The Ecuadoran government doesn't want visitors there at all.

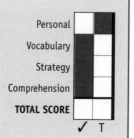

Check your answers with your teacher. Give yourself 1 point for each correct answer, and fill in your Strategy score here. Then turn to page 217 and transfer your score onto Graph 1.

Personal
Vocabulary
Strategy
Comprehension
TOTAL SCORE
✓ T

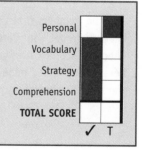

Check your answers with your teacher. Give yourself 1 point for each correct answer, and fill in your Comprehension score here. Then turn to page 217 and transfer your score onto Graph 1.

Personal
Vocabulary
Strategy
Comprehension
TOTAL SCORE
✓ T

Extending

Choose one or more of these activities:

COMPARE ANIMAL BONES

Visit a science museum or zoo that has displays of the bones of various creatures—either those alive today or prehistoric ones. Choose two very different creatures and compare one type of bone, such as their leg bones or their skulls. What differences do you notice? Write a short comparison of the bones of the two animals. Illustrate your comparison with sketches of the bones.

MAKE A TRAVEL BROCHURE

Using the resources listed on this page or ones you find yourself, create a travel brochure for the Galápagos Islands. Be sure your brochure includes a map, some photos, a chart of year-round weather conditions, and descriptions of the main attractions.

INVESTIGATE CAREERS RELATED TO BONES

The article you just read focuses on the work of an osteologist. Here are some other people with careers that relate to bones: osteopath, osteoplastic surgeon, physical therapist. Find out what each of these people does, as well as the preparation that a person must go through for that particular career. Report your findings in the form of a job description that you write for each career.

Resources

Books

Humann, Paul. *Galápagos: A Terrestrial and Marine Phenomenon.* New World Publications, 1994.

Parker, Steve, and Philip Dowell. *Skeleton.* Eyewitness. DK Publishing, 2000.

Rogers, Barbara Radcliffe. *Galápagos.* Mallar Press, 1990.

Taylor, Barbara. *Skeleton.* DK Pockets. DK Publishing, 1998.

Web Sites

http://career.berkeley.edu/Article/030502a.stm
Read about careers in osteopathic medicine on this Web site.

http://www.apta.org/
This is the Web site of the American Physical Therapy Association.

http://www.galapagospark.org/en/home.htm
This is the official Web site of the Galapagos National Park.

http://www.nmnh.si.edu/VirtualTour/Tour/Second/Bones/index.html
Take a virtual tour of the Osteology Hall at the National Museum of Natural History.

Video/DVD

Beneath the Sea: The Galápagos. Mutual of Omaha's Spirit of Adventure. MPI Home Video, 1991.

Riding the Raptor (Part 1)

Building Background

The title of a story is usually intended to give readers a clue to what the story is about. Some titles can tell you the **mood**, or feeling, of a story before you even read a word—that is, *if* the title has meaning for you. For example, take the title "Riding the Raptor." In order to understand the importance of this title, you need to know what a raptor is.

According to its dictionary definition, a raptor is a bird of prey. A bird of prey is a bird that hunts and kills other animals for food. Now what feeling does this title suggest? fear? terror? excitement? thrills? That depends on whether you identify with the raptor or its victim.

As you begin reading "Riding the Raptor," you will learn what the Raptor is. Start looking for clues that help you predict whether the narrator sees himself as the Raptor or its victim—or neither. When you get to the end of Part 2 in Lesson 18, you'll have a chance to check your prediction.

bearings

furtively

indescribably

intimidating

register

shimmers

unharnessed

Vocabulary Builder

1. The boldfaced vocabulary words below are from Part 1 of "Riding the Raptor." Read each boldfaced word, and then underline the word or phrase that best describes it. If you need help with any of the words, find them in context and then choose your answers.

bearings	wild animals	sense of direction	pieces of jewelry
furtively	sneakily	openly	shyly
indescribably	ready to explain	easy to explain	impossible to explain
intimidating	exciting	frightening	humorous
register	scare	amuse	sink in
shimmers	freezes	shines	disappears
unharnessed	unhappy	wild	strapped

2. Save your work. You will refer to it again in the Vocabulary Check.

Drawing Conclusions About Characters

- Every story is told from a particular point of view. The **point of view** reveals the thoughts and feelings of the **narrator**—the one who is telling the story. When the narrator is a character in the story, that story is told from a **first-person point of view**. A first-person narrator uses words such as *I, me, my,* and *mine* to describe what is happening.

- Since Brent, the first-person narrator of "Riding the Raptor," tells the story from his own point of view, he can only describe what he is seeing, thinking, and feeling himself. He does not know—and therefore cannot explain—what the other characters are seeing, thinking, and feeling. He can only explain what he hears them say and sees them do. It is then up to you, the reader, to take that information and draw your own conclusions about the characters.

- As you learned earlier in this book, when you draw **conclusions** about a character, you make decisions or judgments about him or her. As you read Part 1 of this story, you will draw conclusions about Brent and his brother, Trevor. As you read Part 2, you will use some of those conclusions to predict what the brothers might do.

Riding the Raptor (Part 1)

by Neal Shusterman

As you read Part 1 of "Riding the Raptor," note details that describe the mood. Also note details that help you draw conclusions about Brent and Trevor. Are the boys alike, or are they different?

"This is gonna be great, Brent!" says my older brother, Trevor. "I can feel it."

I smile. Trevor always says that.

The trip to the top of a roller coaster always seems endless, and from up here the amusement park seems much smaller than it does from the ground. As the small train clanks its way up the steel slope of a man-made mountain, I double-check the safety bar across my lap to make sure it's tight. Then, with a mixture of terror and excitement, Trevor and I discuss how deadly that first drop is going to be. We're roller coaster fanatics, my brother and I—and this brand-new, sleek, silver beast of a ride promises to deliver ninety incredible seconds of **unharnessed** thrills. It's called the Kamikaze, and it's supposed to be the fastest, wildest roller coaster ever built. We'll see . . .

We crest the top, and everyone screams as they peer down at the dizzying drop. Then we begin to hurl downward.

Trevor puts up his hands as we pick up speed, spreading his fingers and letting the rushing wind slap against his palms. But I can never do that. Instead I grip the lap bar with sweaty palms. And I scream.

You can't help but scream at the top of your lungs on a roller coaster, and it's easy to forget everything else in the world as your body flies through the air. That feeling is special for me, but I know it's even more special for Trevor.

We reach the bottom of the first drop, and I feel myself pushed deep down into the seat as the track bottoms out and climbs once more for a loop. In an instant there is no up or down, no left or right. I feel my entire spirit become a ball of energy twisting through space at impossible speeds.

I turn my head to see Trevor. The corners of his howling mouth are turned up in a grin, and it's good to see him smile. All his bad grades, all his anger, all his fights with Mom and Dad—they're all gone when he rides the coasters. I can see it in his face. All that matters is the feel of the wind against his hands as he thrusts his fingertips into the air.

We roll one way, then the other—a double forward loop and a triple reverse corkscrew. The veins in my eyes bulge, my joints grind against each other, my guts climb into my throat. It's great!

One more sharp turn, and suddenly we explode back into the real world as the train returns to the station. Our car stops with a jolt, the safety bar pops up, and an anxious crowd pushes forward to take our seats.

"That was unreal!" I exclaim, my legs like rubber as we climb down the exit stairs. But Trevor is unimpressed.

"Yeah, it was okay, I guess," he says with a shrug. "But it wasn't as great as they said it would be."

I shake my head. After years of riding the rails, Trevor's become a roller coaster snob. It's been years since any coaster has delivered the particular thrill that Trevor wants.

"Well, what did you expect?" I ask him, annoyed that his lousy attitude is ruining my good time. "It's a roller coaster, not a rocket, you know?"

"Yeah, I guess," says Trevor, his disappointment growing with each step we take away from the Kamikaze. I look up and see it towering above us—all that **intimidating** silver metal. Somehow, now that we've been on it, it doesn't seem so intimidating.

Then I get to thinking how we waited six months for them to build it and how we waited in line for two hours to ride it, and I get even madder at Trevor for not enjoying it more.

 Stop here for the Strategy Break.

Strategy Break

Use these questions to help you draw conclusions about the two brothers:

1. In what ways are the two brothers alike? _____

_____

_____

2. What are some clues that help you understand Brent's personality? (Think about his thoughts, feelings, and actions.) _____

_____

_____

_____

_____

3. What are some clues that help you understand Trevor's personality? (Think about his thoughts and actions, as well as what Brent says about him.) _____

_____

_____

_____

_____

Go on reading to see what happens.

We stop at a game on the midway, and Trevor angrily hurls baseballs at milk bottles. He's been known to throw rocks at windows with the same stone-faced anger. Sometimes I imagine my brother's soul to be like a shoelace that's all tied in an angry knot. It's a knot that only gets loose when he's riding rails at a hundred miles an hour. But as soon as the ride is over, that knot pulls itself tight again. Maybe even tighter than it was before.

Trevor furiously hurls another baseball, missing the stacked gray bottles by a mile. The guy behind the counter is a dweeb with an Adam's apple the size of a golf ball that bobs up and down when he talks. Trevor flicks him another crumpled dollar and takes aim again.

"Why don't we ride the Skull-Smasher or the Spine-Shredder," I offer. "Those aren't bad rides—and the lines aren't as long as the Kamikaze's was."

Trevor just hurls the baseball even harder, missing again. "Those are baby rides," he says with a sneer.

"Listen, next summer we'll find a better roller coaster," I say, trying to cheer him up. "They're always building new ones."

"That's a whole year away," Trevor complains, hurling the ball again, this time nailing all three bottles at once.

The dweeb running the booth hands Trevor a purple dinosaur. "Nice shot," he grunts.

Trevor looks at the purple thing with practiced disgust.

Great, I think. *Trevor's already bored out of his mind, and it's only this amusement park's opening day.* As I watch my brother, I know what'll happen now; five more minutes, and he'll start finding things to do that will get us into trouble, deep trouble. It's how Trevor is.

That's when I catch sight of the tickets thumbtacked to the booth's wall, right alongside the row of purple dinosaurs—two tickets with red printing on gold paper.

"What are those?" I ask the dweeb running the booth.

"Beats me," he says, totally clueless. "You want' em instead of the dinosaur?"

We make the trade, and I read the tickets as we walk away: GOOD FOR ONE RIDE ON THE RAPTOR.

"What's the Raptor?" I ask Trevor.

"Who knows," he says. "Probably some dumb kiddie-go-round thing, like everything else in this stupid place."

I look on the amusement park map but can't find the ride anywhere. Then, through the opening-day crowds, I look up and see a hand-painted sign that reads THE RAPTOR in big red letters. The sign is pointing down toward a path that no one else seems to be taking. That alone is enough to catch Trevor's interest, as well as mine.

He glances around **furtively**, as if he's about to do something he shouldn't, then says, "Let's check it out."

He leads the way down the path, and as always, I follow.

The dark asphalt we are on leads down into thick bushes, and the sounds of the amusement park crowd get farther and farther away, until we can't hear them at all.

"I think we made a wrong turn," I tell Trevor, studying the map, trying to get my **bearings**. Then suddenly a deep voice booms in the bushes beside us.

"You're looking for the Raptor, are you?"

We turn to see a clean-shaven man dressed in the gray-and-blue uniform that all the ride operators wear, only his doesn't seem to be made of the same awful polyester. Instead, his uniform **shimmers** like satin. So do his eyes, blue-gray eyes that you can't look into, no matter how hard you try.

I look at Trevor, and tough as he is, he can't look the man in the face.

"The name's DelRio," the man says. "I run the Raptor."

"What is the Raptor?" asks Trevor.

DelRio grins. "You mean you don't know?" He reaches out his long fingers and pulls aside the limbs of a dense thornbush. "There you are, gentlemen—the Raptor!"

What we see doesn't **register** at first. When something is so big—so indescribably huge—sometimes your brain can't quite wrap around it. All you can do is blink and stare, trying to force your mind to accept what it sees.

There's a valley before us, and down in the valley is a wooden roller coaster painted black as night. But the amazing thing is that the valley itself is part of the roller coaster. Its peaks rise on either side of us in a tangle of tracks that stretch off in all directions as if there is nothing else but the Raptor from here to the ends of the earth.

"No way," Trevor gasps, more impressed than I've ever seen him. "This must be the biggest roller coaster in the world!"

"The biggest *anywhere*," corrects DelRio.

In front of us is the ride's platform with sleek red cars, ready to go.

"Something's wrong," I say, although I can't quite figure out what it is. "Why isn't this ride on the map?"

"New attraction," says DelRio.

"So how come there's no crowd?" asks Trevor.

DelRio smiles and looks through us with those awful eyes. "The Raptor is by invitation only." He takes our tickets, flipping them over to read the back. "Trevor and Brent Collins," he says. "Pleased to have you aboard." ●

Strategy Follow-up

Use these questions to help you draw more conclusions about the brothers:

1. What does Trevor do to vent, or express, his anger? _____

_____

_____

_____

2. How does Brent describe Trevor's soul? _____

_____

_____

3. How can you tell that Brent is feeling uneasy? _____

_____

_____

_____

_____

✓Personal Checklist

Read each question and put a check (✓) in the correct box.

1. How well do you understand what has happened in this story so far?
    - ☐ 3 (extremely well)
    - ☐ 2 (fairly well)
    - ☐ 1 (not well)

2. In the Vocabulary Builder, how many words were you able to correctly match with their definitions?
    - ☐ 3 (6–7 words)
    - ☐ 2 (3–5 words)
    - ☐ 1 (0–2 words)

3. In the Strategy Break and Strategy Follow-up, how well were you able to draw conclusions about the brothers?
    - ☐ 3 (extremely well)
    - ☐ 2 (fairly well)
    - ☐ 1 (not well)

4. How well could you explain why Trevor is always disappointed with his roller coaster rides?
    - ☐ 3 (extremely well)
    - ☐ 2 (fairly well)
    - ☐ 1 (not well)

5. Using what you know about Brent so far, how well could you explain his personality?
    - ☐ 3 (extremely well)
    - ☐ 2 (fairly well)
    - ☐ 1 (not well)

Vocabulary Check

Look back at the work you did in the Vocabulary Builder. Then answer each question by circling the correct letter.

1. What does the word *register* mean in this story?
    a. a printed list of names
    b. device through which air enters a room
    c. to sink in or be recorded in the mind

2. Which of these situations would be intimidating?
    a. ice cream melting in your mouth
    b. a UFO hovering over your house
    c. a baby sleeping peacefully in his crib

3. What happens when you lose your bearings?
    a. You lose your sense of direction.
    b. You can't find your teddy bears.
    c. Neither of the above happens.

4. Which of these things might appear to be shimmering?
    a. the sun shining down on a dirt road
    b. the moon shining down on a lake
    c. Neither of the above shimmers.

5. When Trevor glances around furtively, how does he feel?
    a. as if someone is hunting him down
    b. as if he can't get his sense of direction
    c. as if he's about to do something he shouldn't

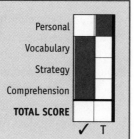

Add the numbers that you just checked to get your Personal Checklist score. Fill in your score here. Then turn to page 217 and transfer your score onto Graph 1.

Personal
Vocabulary
Strategy
Comprehension
TOTAL SCORE
✓ T

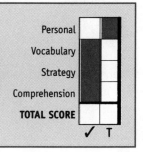

Check your answers with your teacher. Give yourself 1 point for each correct answer, and fill in your Vocabulary score here. Then turn to page 217 and transfer your score onto Graph 1.

Personal
Vocabulary
Strategy
Comprehension
TOTAL SCORE
✓ T

Strategy Check

Review what you wrote in the Strategy Break and Strategy Follow-up. Also review the rest of Part 1 if necessary. Then answer these questions:

1. What clue does the author give about the boys' personalities by the way they ride roller coasters?

   a. Brent grips the lap bar, but Trevor throws his hands in the air.

   b. Brent hates coasters, but Trevor loves them.

   c. Brent screams while riding the Kamikaze, but Trevor doesn't.

2. Which word does Brent use that best describes Trevor?

   a. bored

   b. snob

   c. angry

3. Why do you think Brent doesn't yell at Trevor for ruining his good time on the Kamikaze?

   a. It's not worth mentioning.

   b. He doesn't want Trevor to take his anger out on him.

   c. He's too excited about the next ride.

4. Which clue helps you conclude that Brent cares about his brother?

   a. He double-checks Trevor's safety bar to make sure it's tight.

   b. He is annoyed with Trevor for ruining his good time.

   c. He tries to cheer Trevor up and keep him from being bored.

5. Trevor can't look DelRio in the face. What does this clue help you conclude?

   a. DelRio's shimmering clothes are too bright for Trevor to look at.

   b. Even Trevor senses that there is something wrong with DelRio.

   c. DelRio's eyes are impossible to look into.

Comprehension Check

Review the story if necessary. Then answer these questions:

1. Which phrase best describes the mood of this story?

   a. cheerful and exciting

   b. uncertain and threatening

   c. confusing and humorous

2. What does Brent mean when he calls Trevor a "roller coaster snob"?

   a. Trevor is too proud to ride a roller coaster.

   b. Trevor rides only fancy, expensive roller coasters.

   c. Trevor has high standards for roller coasters.

3. Which statement best describes the relationship between the brothers?

   a. Trevor is the leader, and Brent is the follower.

   b. Brent is the leader, and Trevor is the follower.

   c. The two brothers are equals.

4. How can you tell that Brent doesn't enjoy getting into trouble because of his brother?

   a. He goes on the roller coaster rides with Trevor.

   b. He is annoyed that Trevor ruins his good time.

   c. He tries to distract Trevor when he sees that Trevor is bored.

5. At the end of Part 1, Brent feels that there is something wrong. Which clue does *not* make him feel that way?

   a. He can't find the Raptor on the map.

   b. Trevor isn't excited about riding it.

   c. There are no crowds waiting to ride it.

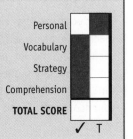

Check your answers with your teacher. Give yourself 1 point for each correct answer, and fill in your Strategy score here. Then turn to page 217 and transfer your score onto Graph 1.

Personal
Vocabulary
Strategy
Comprehension
TOTAL SCORE
✓ T

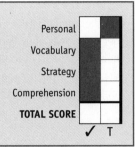

Check your answers with your teacher. Give yourself 1 point for each correct answer, and fill in your Comprehension score here. Then turn to page 217 and transfer your score onto Graph 1.

Personal
Vocabulary
Strategy
Comprehension
TOTAL SCORE
✓ T

LESSON 17: RIDING THE RAPTOR (PART 1)

Extending

Choose one or both of these activities:

MAKE A FACT BOOK OF ROLLER COASTERS

When was the first roller coaster built? How many roller coasters are there in the United States today? How big is the biggest roller coaster? How fast is the fastest one? Which one can carry the most people at one time? How many different kinds of roller coasters are there? How long does it take to design a coaster? How much does it cost to build one? How much do riders pay in a single year to ride them? Using the resources on this page, do some research on roller coasters to find answers to some or all of these questions. If you can, find pictures of different roller coasters. Use your facts and pictures to make a booklet about roller coasters. Take it along with you the next time you go to an amusement park, and read it to your friends while you wait in line for your favorite roller coaster.

RATE YOUR FAVORITE AMUSEMENT PARK RIDES

You probably have visited an amusement park or two. Which rides in those parks would you recommend to others? Using a scale that you create yourself, rate your favorite rides in various categories, such as roller coasters, rides that spin, water rides, and so on. Write one-paragraph descriptions of the rides. Be as precise as possible in pointing out what makes one ride different from—and better or worse than—the others.

Resources

Books

Urbanowicz, Steven J. *The Roller Coaster Lover's Companion: A Thrill-Seeker's Guide to the World's Best Coasters.* Citadel Press, 2002.

Wyatt, Mark. *White Knuckle Ride: The Illustrated Guide to the World's Biggest and Best Roller Coaster and Thrill Rides.* Random House, 2001.

Web Sites

http://search.eb.com/coasters/
Learn about the history and the future of roller coasters on this Britannica.com Web site.

http://www.coasters.net/
This site provides information on roller coasters around the world.

http://www.pbs.org/wnet/nature/eagles/masters.html
Check out this Web site for information on another kind of raptor—the eagle.

Videos/DVDs

America Screams. Vincent Price. Rhino Video, 1990.

America's Greatest Roller Coaster Thrills in 3-D. Ned Rodgers, dir. Goldhil Home Media, 1994.

Roller Coaster Thrills. Eastman Kodak, 1988.

LESSON 18 Riding the Raptor (Part 2)

Building Background

From "Riding the Raptor" (Part 1):
There's a valley before us, and down in the valley is a wooden roller coaster painted black as night. But the amazing thing is that the valley itself is part of the roller coaster. Its peaks rise on either side of us in a tangle of tracks that stretch off in all directions as if there is nothing else but the Raptor from here to the ends of the earth.

"No way," Trevor gasps, more impressed than I've ever seen him. "This must be the biggest roller coaster in the world!"

"The biggest anywhere," corrects DelRio.

In front of us is the ride's platform with sleek red cars, ready to go.

"Something's wrong," I say, although I can't quite figure out what it is. "Why isn't this ride on the map?"

"New attraction," says DelRio.

"So how come there's no crowd?" asks Trevor.

DelRio smiles and looks through us with those awful eyes. "The Raptor is by invitation only." He takes our tickets, flipping them over to read the back. "Trevor and Brent Collins," he says. "Pleased to have you aboard."

Read on to find out what happens to Brent and Trevor. Keep looking for clues to help you draw conclusions about the boys and make predictions about what they will do.

anticipation

dismantling

extending

gawking

infinite

superstructure

tentatively

unflinching

Vocabulary Builder

1. Each word in the margin has a base word, or root word. A **root word** is a complete word by itself. However, you can add other words or word parts to a root word to make new words. For example, *build* is a root word. You can add *re-*, *-er*, and *-ing* to *build* to make *rebuild*, *builder*, and *building*. Identifying the root word of an unfamiliar word can sometimes help you figure out the word's meaning.

2. After each boldfaced word below, write its meaning. Then write its root word. (You may have to add a letter to make some of the root words.)

3. If you have trouble with any of the meanings or root words, find them in the story and use context to figure them out. If context does not help, use a dictionary. The first word has been done for you.

anticipation   meaning: _____expectation_____

root word: _____anticipate_____

dismantling   meaning: _____

root word: _____

extending   meaning: _____

root word: _____

gawking   meaning: _____

root word: _____

infinite   meaning: _____

root word: _____

superstructure   meaning: _____

root word: _____

tentatively   meaning: _____

root word: _____

unflinching   meaning: _____

root word: _____

4. Save your work. You will refer to it again in the Vocabulary Check.

Strategy Builder

Making Predictions While Reading

- When you try to figure out what might happen next in a story, you are making a **prediction**. You can predict what might happen in Part 2 of "Riding the Raptor" by thinking about what happened in Part 1.

- You also can use the **conclusions** that you drew about Brent and Trevor to help you predict what each character will do. If necessary, go back and read the conclusions that you wrote in Lesson 17. Then, in the space below, write what you predict might happen in Part 2 of "Riding the Raptor." Don't worry if your predictions don't match what actually happens. You will have chances to make new ones at the Strategy Breaks.

I predict that in Part 2 of "Riding the Raptor,"

_____

_____

_____

_____

Riding the Raptor (Part 2)

by Neal Shusterman

As you read, keep looking for clues that help you make predictions. Also keep drawing conclusions about Brent and Trevor. Does either of the boys change from Part 1 to Part 2? If so, how?

Trevor and I look at each other, then at the torn ticket stubs DelRio has just handed back to us. Sure enough, our names are printed right there on the back, big as life.

"Wait! How did—" But before I can ask, Trevor cuts me off, his eyes already racing along the wildly twisting tracks of the gigantic contraption.

"That first drop," he says, "that's three hundred feet."

"Oh, the first one's grand!" DelRio exclaims. "But on this ride, it's the last drop that's special."

I can see Trevor licking his lips, losing himself in the sight of the amazing ride. It's good to see him excited like this . . . and *not* good, too.

Every time DelRio talks, I get a churning feeling in my gut—the kind of feeling you get when you find half a worm in your apple. Still, I can't figure out what's wrong.

"Are we the only ones invited?" I ask **tentatively**.

DelRio smiles. "Here come the others now."

I turn to see a group of **gawking** kids coming through the bushes, and DelRio greets them happily. The look in their eyes is exactly like Trevor's.

They don't just want to ride the coaster—they *need* to ride it.

"Since you're the first, you can ride in the front," DelRio tells us. "Aren't you the lucky ones!"

While Trevor psyches himself up for the ride and while DelRio tears tickets, I slip away into the **superstructure** of the great wooden beast. I'm searching for something—although I'm not sure what it is. I follow the track with my eyes, but it's almost impossible to stick with it. It twists and spins and loops in ways that wooden roller coasters aren't supposed to be able to do—up and down, back and forth, until my head gets dizzy and little squirmy spots appear before my eyes. It's like a huge angry knot.

Before long I'm lost in the immense web of wood, but still I follow the path of the rails with my eyes until I come to that last drop that DelRio claimed was so special. I follow its long path up . . . and then down . . .

In an instant I understand just what it is about this ride I couldn't put my finger on before. Now I *know* I have to stop Trevor from getting on it.

 **Stop here for Strategy Break #1.**

Strategy Break #1

1. What do you predict will happen next? _____

_____

2. Why do you think so? _____

_____

3. What clues from the story helped you make your prediction(s)? _____

_____

_____

 Go on reading to see what happens.

In a wild panic I race back through the dark wooden frame of the Raptor, dodging low-hanging beams that poke out at odd angles.

When I finally reach the platform, everyone is sitting in the cars, ready to go. The only empty seat is in the front car. It's the seat beside Trevor. DelRio waits impatiently by a big lever **extending** from the ground.

"Hurry, Brent," DelRio says, scowling. "Everyone's waiting."

"Yes! Yes!" shout all the kids. "Hurry! Hurry! We want to RIDE!"

They start cheering for me to get in, to join my brother in the front car. But I'm frozen on the platform.

"Trevor!" I finally manage to say, gasping for breath. "Trevor, you have to get off that ride."

"What are you, nuts?" he shouts.

"We can't ride this coaster!" I insist.

Trevor ignores me, fixing his gaze straight ahead. But that's not the direction in which he should be looking. He should be looking at the track behind the last car—because if he does, he'll see that there is no track behind the last car!

"The coaster doesn't come back!" I shout at him. "Don't you see? It doesn't come back!"

Trevor finally turns to me, his hands shaking in **infinite** terror and ultimate excitement . . . and then he says . . .

"I know."

I take a step back.

I can't answer that. I can't accept it. I need more time, but everyone is shouting at me to get on the ride, and DelRio is getting more and more impatient. That's when Trevor reaches out his hand toward me, his fingers bone white, trembling with **anticipation**.

"Ride with me, Brent," he pleads desperately. "It'll be great. I can feel it!"

I reach out my hand. My fingers are an inch from his.

"Please . . ." Trevor pleads.

He's my brother. He wants me to go. They *all* want me to go. What could be better than riding in the front car, twisting through all those spins and drops? I can see it now: Trevor and

me—the way it's always been—his hands high in the air, wrestling the wind, and me gripping the safety bar.

Only thing is, the Raptor *has* no safety bar.

 Stop here for Strategy Break #2.

Strategy Break #2

1. What do you predict will happen next? _____

   _____

2. Why do you think so? _____

   _____

3. What clues from the story helped you make your prediction(s)? _____

   _____

   _____

 Go on reading to see what happens.

I pull my hand back away from his. *I won't follow you, Trevor!* my mind screams. *Not today. Not ever again.*

When Trevor sees me backing away, his face hardens—the way it hardens toward our parents or his teachers or anyone else who's on the outside of his closed world. "Wimp!" he shouts at me. "*Loooooser!*"

DelRio tightly grips the lever. "This isn't a ride for the weak," he says, his hawk eyes judging me, trying to make

me feel small and useless. "Stand back and let the big kids ride."

He pulls back on the lever, and slowly the Raptor slides forward, catching on a heavy chain that begins to haul it up to the first big drop. Trevor has already turned away from me, locking his eyes on the track rising before him, preparing himself for the thrill of his life.

The coaster clacketty-clacks all the way to the top. Then the red train begins to fall, its metal wheels throwing sparks and screeching all the way down. All I can do is watch as Trevor puts up his hands and rides. The wooden beast of a roller coaster groans and roars like a dragon, and the tiny red train rockets deep inside the black wooden framework stretching to the horizon.

Up and down, back and forth, the Raptor races. Time is paralyzed as its trainload of riders rockets through thrill after terrifying thrill, until finally, after what seems like an eternity, it reaches that last mountain.

DelRio turns to me. "The grand finale," he announces. "You could have been there—*you* could have had the ultimate thrill if you weren't a coward, Brent."

But I know better. This time *I* am the brave one.

The red train climbs the final peak, defying gravity, moving up and up until it's nothing more than a tiny red sliver against a blue sky . . . and then it begins the trip down, accelerating faster than gravity can pull it. It's as if the ground itself were sucking it down from the clouds.

The Raptor's whole wooden framework rumbles like an earthquake. I hold on to a black beam, and I feel my teeth rattle in my head. I want to close my eyes, but I keep them open, watching every last second.

I can see Trevor alone in the front car. His hands are high, slapping defiantly against the wind, and he's screaming louder than all the others as the train plummets straight down . . . into that awful destiny that awaits it.

I can see that destiny from here now, looming larger than life— a bottomless, blacker-than-black pit.

I watch as my brother and all the others are pulled from the sky, down into that emptiness . . . and then they are swallowed by it, their thrilled screams silenced without so much as an echo.

The ride is over.

I am horrified, but DelRio remains unmoved. He casually glances at his watch, then turns and shouts deep into the superstructure of the roller coaster. "Time!"

All at once hundreds of workers crawl from the woodwork like ants. Nameless, faceless people, each with some kind of tool like a hammer or wrench practically growing from their arms. They all set upon the Raptor, **dismantling** it with incredible speed.

"What is this?" I ask DelRio. "What's going on?"

"Surely you don't expect an attraction this special to stay in one place?" he scoffs. "We must travel! There are worlds of people waiting for the thrill of a lifetime!"

When I look again at the roller coaster, it's gone. Nothing remains but the workers carrying its heavy beams off through the thick underbrush.

DelRio smiles at me. "We'll see you again, Brent," he says. "Perhaps next time you'll ride."

As the last of the workers carry away the final rail of the Raptor on their horribly hunched backs, I stare DelRio down. I can look him in the eyes now, **unflinching**.

"Tell your friends about the Raptor," he says, then he pauses and adds, "No . . . on second thought, don't tell them a thing. Wouldn't want to spoil their surprise."

Then he strolls after the workers, who are carrying the Raptor to its next location. I just stand there.

No, I won't tell anyone—ever. What could I possibly say? And if I encounter the Raptor again someday, I can only hope I will have the strength to stare DelRio down once more, dig my heels deep into the earth beneath my feet . . . and refuse to ride. ●

Strategy Follow-up

Now go back and look at the predictions that you wrote in this lesson. Do any of them match what actually happened in this story? Why or why not?

✓Personal Checklist

Read each question and put a check (✓) in the correct box.

1. In Building Background, how well were you able to use your conclusions from Part 1 of "Riding the Raptor" to predict what Brent and Trevor might do in Part 2?
   - ☐ 3 (extremely well)
   - ☐ 2 (fairly well)
   - ☐ 1 (not well)

2. How well were you able to complete the activity in the Vocabulary Builder?
   - ☐ 3 (extremely well)
   - ☐ 2 (fairly well)
   - ☐ 1 (not well)

3. How well were you able to make predictions at each of the Strategy Breaks?
   - ☐ 3 (extremely well)
   - ☐ 2 (fairly well)
   - ☐ 1 (not well)

4. How well do you understand why Brent doesn't ride the Raptor?
   - ☐ 3 (extremely well)
   - ☐ 2 (fairly well)
   - ☐ 1 (not well)

5. Now that you've read Parts 1 and 2 of this selection, how well do you understand why the roller coaster is called the Raptor?
   - ☐ 3 (extremely well)
   - ☐ 2 (fairly well)
   - ☐ 1 (not well)

Vocabulary Check

Look back at the work you did in the Vocabulary Builder. Then answer each question by circling the correct letter.

1. Which of these words has both a prefix and a suffix added to its root word?
   - a. anticipation
   - b. unflinching
   - c. superstructure

2. What is the root word of *superstructure*?
   - a. super
   - b. struct
   - c. structure

3. What is the root word of *dismantling*?
   - a. dismantle
   - b. mantle
   - c. mantling

4. Brent turns to see a group of gawking kids coming through the bushes. What does *to gawk* mean?
   - a. run clumsily
   - b. chatter loudly
   - c. stare in amazement

5. If you were doing something tentatively, how would you be doing it?
   - a. hesitantly
   - b. boldly
   - c. angrily

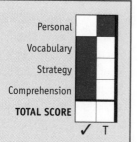

Add the numbers that you just checked to get your Personal Checklist score. Fill in your score here. Then turn to page 217 and transfer your score onto Graph 1.

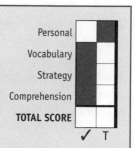

Check your answers with your teacher. Give yourself 1 point for each correct answer, and fill in your Vocabulary score here. Then turn to page 217 and transfer your score onto Graph 1.

Strategy Check

Review the predictions that you wrote in this lesson. Then answer these questions:

1. If you had predicted that Brent would tell Trevor what was wrong with the Raptor, which clue would have best supported your prediction?

    a. I'm searching for something—although I'm not sure what it is.

    b. I understand just what it is about this ride I couldn't put my finger on before.

    c. It's like a huge angry knot.

2. Which clue could you have used to predict that the Raptor doesn't come back?

    a. I follow the track with my eyes, but it's almost impossible to stick with it.

    b. I follow its long path up . . . and then down.

    c. It twists . . . in ways that wooden roller coasters aren't supposed to.

3. Which clue would have indicated that Brent would not be able to stop Trevor?

    a. Every time DelRio talks, I get a churning feeling in my gut.

    b. Now I *know* I have to stop Trevor.

    c. They don't just want to ride the coaster— they *need* to ride it.

4. At Strategy Break #2, if you had predicted that Brent would ride the Raptor, which clue would *not* have supported your prediction?

    a. My fingers are an inch from his.

    b. Trevor and me—the way it's always been.

    c. Only thing is, the Raptor *has* no safety bar.

5. If you had predicted that Brent would *not* ride the Raptor, which clue would have best supported your prediction?

    a. "Ride with me, Brent," he pleads desperately.

    b. "The coaster doesn't come back!" I shout.

    c. He's my brother. He wants me to go.

Comprehension Check

Review the story if necessary. Then answer these questions:

1. When Brent examines the superstructure of the Raptor, what does he discover about the ride?

    a. It's not put together well, and will probably break down soon.

    b. There's no track behind the last car, so the coaster doesn't return.

    c. The coaster is set up so its riders will keep going around in circles.

2. Which statement is probably true about all the children who ride Raptor?

    a. They are all very brave and strong.

    b. They are all very smart.

    c. They are all looking for the thrill of their life.

3. What do Trevor and DelRio think of Brent?

    a. They look down upon him as a coward.

    b. They respect him for his decision.

    c. They are concerned about his safety.

4. To what does Brent compare both Trevor's soul and the Raptor?

    a. a huge, angry knot

    b. a gigantic, twisting contraption

    c   the biggest roller coaster in the world

5. Why do you think the Raptor roller coaster was named after the raptor bird?

    a. Both soar high into the sky.

    b. Both hook and kill their prey.

    c. Both fly away and never return.

Check your answers with your teacher. Give yourself 1 point for each correct answer, and fill in your Strategy score here. Then turn to page 217 and transfer your score onto Graph 1.

Personal
Vocabulary
Strategy
Comprehension
TOTAL SCORE
✓ T

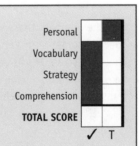

Check your answers with your teacher. Give yourself 1 point for each correct answer, and fill in your Comprehension score here. Then turn to page 217 and transfer your score onto Graph 1.

Personal
Vocabulary
Strategy
Comprehension
TOTAL SCORE
✓ T

Extending

Choose one or more of these activities:

WRITE AN ANALYSIS

"Riding the Raptor" begins as a realistic story, but ends more like a fantasy. At what point in the story did you begin to realize that something supernatural is happening? Do you think the main characters react to the strange happenings in believable ways? Write two or three paragraphs telling what you think of this story, and how it made you feel. Point out specific passages in the story that support your opinions and reactions.

LOOK AT REAL-LIFE APPLICATIONS

Certainly "Riding the Raptor" is fiction; these events could never really happen. But there are real-life thrills that could easily result in injury or death, and yet they still attract people. When Brent describes the other riders of the Raptor, he notes that "They don't just want to ride the coaster—they *need* to ride it." Can you think of any situations in which a person knowingly gets involved in an activity that is likely to harm him or her? Write a description of such an activity. (The resources listed on this page might give you a place to start.) Include an explanation of why a person might engage in the activity even though it is risky.

WRITE A SEQUEL TO "RIDING THE RAPTOR"

DelRio tells Brent that he'll see him again someday, and that, "Perhaps next time you'll ride." Write the sequel to "Riding the Raptor," in which Brent faces DelRio again. Explain what happens and what Brent decides to do. Use the conclusions that you drew about Brent in this story to help you develop the plot. Read your completed story to a group of classmates. If you'd like, stop once or twice and ask them to predict what might happen next.

Resources

*See also **Resources** for Lesson 17, "Ride the Raptor, Part 1."*

Web Site

http://www.s-t.com/daily/01-96/01-02-96/a3person.htm
The news article on this Web page reports on scientific research related to why people engage in impulsive or risky activity.

Video/DVD

Extreme Rides. Unapix, 1998.

Dealing with Dirt

Building Background

Dirt is always a problem. Most of the time we pay as little attention to it as possible, but it still won't go away. The title of this informational article suggests another approach to dirt: facing it head on and finding out how to handle it. Before reading the article, think about your own problems with dirt. Where does dirt most bother you? What sort of information would you need in order to deal with that dirt? In the box, write three questions that you hope this article will answer so you can learn to make your life a little cleaner.

> **My top three questions about dealing with dirt:**
>
> 1. _____
>   _____
>
> 2. _____
>   _____
>
> 3. _____
>   _____

As you read "Dealing with Dirt," look for answers to your questions. If your questions aren't answered directly, can you use what's discussed to figure out the answers?

bacteria

detergent

disinfectants

shampoo

substance

surface

Vocabulary Builder

1. The vocabulary words in the margin are all specialized vocabulary words. As you recall, **specialized vocabulary** words all relate to the same topic. For example, as you learned in Lesson 10, the words *apprentice, craftsman, lever,* and *press* are all specialized vocabulary words related to the trade of printing. The specialized vocabulary words in this selection are all related to dirt.

2. Match the words in the Column 1 to their definitions in Column 2. Use a dictionary if you need help.

3. Save your work. You will refer to it again in the Vocabulary Check.

COLUMN 1	COLUMN 2
bacteria	soap used to clean clothes or dishes
detergent	outside covering
disinfectants	matter or material that something consists of
shampoo	soap used to clean the hair
substance	soaps used to kill germs
surface	tiny creatures seen under a microscope

Strategy Builder

How to Read an Informational Article

- As you know, an **informational article** gives readers information about a particular topic. The **topic** of the article usually can be found in its **title**. For example, the topic of the article you are about to read is dirt—or more specifically, how to deal with it.

- Like all other nonfiction, this article follows a particular pattern of organization. The pattern of "Dealing with Dirt" is description. **Descriptions** usually tell what things are, what they do, or how and why they work. In the case of this article, the author describes what dirt is and what we can do to get rid of it.

- Descriptions are usually organized according to **main ideas** and **supporting details**. Read the following excerpt from an article about bears and try to locate its main ideas and supporting details.

> All bears are large and stocky with short, thick legs. They have short tails, small ears, pointed muzzles, and eyes that look straight ahead. Each bear foot has five toes. Bears walk the way we do, on the flat of the foot. When a bear stands up on its hind legs, it looks a lot like a furry person.
>
> Bears are usually born in the winter den of the mother. They are tiny at birth; a newborn black bear cub, for example, weighs less than a pound. But the cubs grow fast on their mother's rich milk and are ready to explore when the time comes to leave the den. Young bears depend on their mother to teach them what they need to know to survive. They learn from her how to avoid danger and where to find food.

- If you wanted to arrange this excerpt's main ideas and supporting details on a graphic organizer, you could use a **concept map**, or web. It would look something like this:

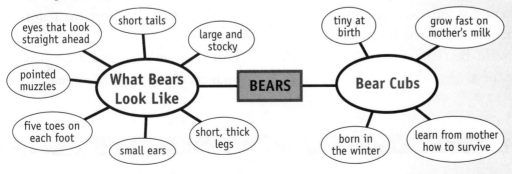

Dealing with Dirt

by Lesley Newson

As you begin reading this article, apply some of the strategies that you just learned. Look for the main ideas and supporting details in this description, and think about how you might organize them on a concept map.

If you traveled back in time to see how people lived in the past, what do you think would be the first thing you noticed as you stepped out of your time machine? The clothes? The buildings? The old-fashioned way that people spoke? No, the first thing you'd notice would probably be the smell.

You would find that everyone, even the richest people in their finest clothes, was very grubby. The only cleaning chemical around when Elizabeth I was queen was soap, and she probably didn't use it very often. She had no **shampoo**, toothpaste, or **detergent**. And if she spilled gravy on her favorite gown during a banquet, she couldn't send it to the dry cleaners.

Today we keep ourselves and our homes cleaner than any other people in history, and many new chemicals have been invented to help us get rid of dirt.

Dirt can be made of almost anything. That's because dirt is any **substance** that ends up where we don't want it to be. Most dirt is perfectly all right as long as it stays in the right place.

Mud is fine in the garden. It turns into dirt as soon as it gets on your shoes. And if it gets from your shoes onto the best carpet, it becomes a real mess.

If you want to get rid of dirt, you have to think about what it's made of. The different kinds of chemical cleaning tools each work on a different kind of dirt.

Some dirt is very easy to get rid of and just washes away with water. The sticky, sugary mess babies and toddlers make if they're allowed to get their hands on some sweets is like this. It can usually be wiped away with a wet cloth. That's because sugar mixes easily with water, especially warm water.

If the babies have been trying to eat chocolate, the mess they make is harder to clean up. Chocolate contains sugar, but it also contains other substances that don't mix so easily with water. If a cleaning chemical, such as soap, is used with the water, the chocolate washes away more easily.

The most stubborn dirt of all is usually made of substances that were invented by humans. House paint, for example, is made to stick to walls and ceilings and stay there for years; no one would want paint that could be easily wiped or washed off. The problem is that spills and splatters of paint are difficult to clean up. Your best bet is to wipe them up before the paint dries.

Dirt is sometimes more than just a substance. If you look at some dirt with a microscope, you will often see tiny creatures, such as **bacteria**, molds, and insects. Many of the substances we think of as dirt serve as food for these microorganisms. If the dirt is particularly nutritious and the microscopic creatures eat quickly and give off a lot of waste, it can all begin to smell after a while. Some cleaners contain **disinfectants** to kill bacteria and help get rid of the smell.

 Stop here for the Strategy Break.

Strategy Break

If you were to create a concept map for the first part of this article, it might look like this:

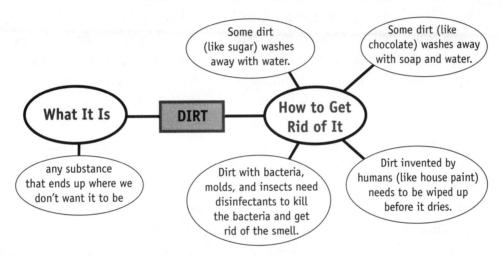

As you continue reading, keep looking for the main ideas and supporting details that describe dirt and how to deal with it. At the end of this article, you will use some of those main ideas and details to create a concept map of your own.

Go on reading.

Cleaning Us

If you look on the shelves in a drugstore or supermarket, you'll find an enormous number of different products for removing dirt from our bodies. These are often called toiletries.

Each bottle, jar, tube, bar, or box contains a mixture of chemicals. Not all of these chemicals are for cleaning. Some are there to make the product look, feel, smell, and sometimes taste good to the consumer. The scientists who choose the cleaning chemicals to go into toiletries must look for ones that are strong enough to get rid of dirt quickly without the need for painful scrubbing. But they must also find chemicals that will not harm our skin or our eyes.

Although the chemicals we use to clean ourselves have to be carefully chosen, they actually work in the same way as the chemicals in some of the products we use to clean the house or our clothes. For instance, our hair is made of almost exactly the same material as a wool sweater, and the shampoo we use to clean our hair is like the detergent powders and liquids we use for cleaning sweaters. Our teeth are made of the same sort of material as bathroom sinks; toothpaste is very similar to the cleaners we use on sinks and bathtubs.

Try using a little toothpaste to clean the bathroom sink. You should find it works quite well. Don't use too much though. Toothpaste is more expensive than ordinary bathroom cleaners because it's specially made to be safe to use in your mouth.

Your Dirty Skin

Your skin is a strange thing to clean because it's alive and growing. Your hair grows, too, but only its roots are alive. All of your skin is alive except a very thin layer on the **surface**. In one way, because your skin is alive, it is very easy to clean.

Have you ever tried writing on your skin with a ballpoint pen? Ballpoints leave marks that are very difficult to remove, and when you get the ink on your skin, it seems as though it's on there for good. It won't come off at first, no matter how hard you scrub.

Even so, your hands don't get inkier and inkier as you go through school. You've probably noticed that ink marks just fade away after a few days.

You may be surprised to know that this isn't because the ink has rubbed off your skin. It's because the surface of your skin has rubbed off and taken the ink marks with it. When your skin grows, it isn't just growing bigger along with the rest of your body. It's also growing outward: a replacement layer is always growing just underneath the surface of the skin. Once this replacement layer is ready, the skin on the surface flakes off.

All the dirt that gets on your skin in ordinary ways comes off quite easily in a few days. You don't need to use strong cleaning chemicals. And if you do use them, your skin may not feel right afterward.

Skin is covered with a thin coating of oil to protect it, keep it waterproof, and make it soft and flexible. This oil is made all the time inside the skin and oozes out of tiny holes in the surface. Every time you wash, you not only wash away any dirt that has landed on your skin, you also wash away some of the oil, as well as sweat, flakes of dead skin, and bacteria that live on the skin. If you stopped washing your skin, all these substances would begin to build up, and the bacteria would multiply. They eat the oil, sweat chemicals, and dead skin and leave some quite smelly waste. If you stopped washing, this waste would build up and you would begin to reek.

Nowadays, most people think it's a good idea to wash often enough to keep themselves from becoming smelly. But it's also a good idea not to wash too much of the oil from your skin. For most people's skin, soap is the ideal cleaning chemical. ●

Strategy Follow-up

Now create a concept map for the section of this article called "Cleaning Us." The topic and main ideas have been filled in for you.

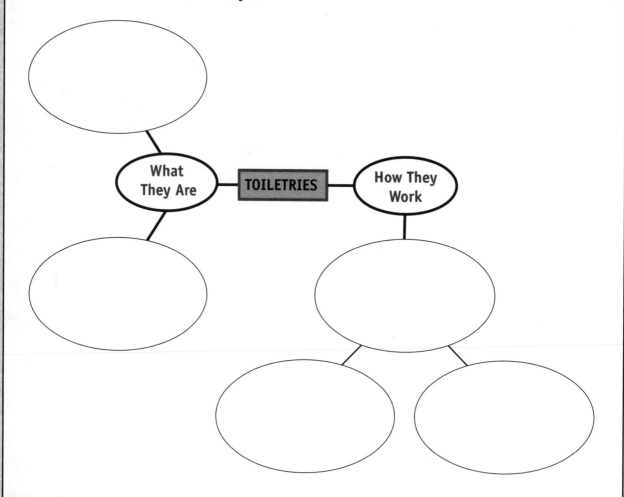

✓Personal Checklist

Read each question and put a check (✓) in the correct box.

1. How well do you understand the information presented in this article?
   - ☐ 3 (extremely well)
   - ☐ 2 (fairly well)
   - ☐ 1 (not well)

2. In Building Background, you listed questions that you had about dirt. How well were you able to decide if this article answered your questions?
   - ☐ 3 (extremely well)
   - ☐ 2 (fairly well)
   - ☐ 1 (not well)

3. In the Vocabulary Builder, how well were you able to match the words and their definitions?
   - ☐ 3 (extremely well)
   - ☐ 2 (fairly well)
   - ☐ 1 (not well)

4. How well were you able to complete the concept map in the Strategy Follow-up?
   - ☐ 3 (extremely well)
   - ☐ 2 (fairly well)
   - ☐ 1 (not well)

5. How well would you be able to explain why different kinds of dirt require different cleaning products?
   - ☐ 3 (extremely well)
   - ☐ 2 (fairly well)
   - ☐ 1 (not well)

Vocabulary Check

Look back at the work you did in the Vocabulary Builder. Then answer each question by circling the correct letter.

1. Which of these statements is true?
   a. Bacteria are smaller than ants.
   b. Bacteria are about the same size as ants.
   c. Bacteria are larger than ants.

2. What kind of cleaning chemical would you use if you wanted to kill bacteria?
   a. detergent
   b. shampoo
   c. disinfectant

3. Which of the following is *not* an example of a substance?
   a. mud
   b. ink
   c. music

4. Which vocabulary word describes the outer layer of something?
   a. surface
   b. substance
   c. bacteria

5. Which of the following are specialized vocabulary words about airplanes?
   a. wing, cockpit, landing gear
   b. bat, diamond, bases
   c. microscope, laboratory, experiment

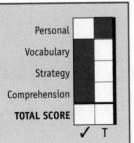
Add the numbers that you just checked to get your Personal Checklist score. Fill in your score here. Then turn to page 217 and transfer your score onto Graph 1.

Personal
Vocabulary
Strategy
Comprehension
TOTAL SCORE
✓ T

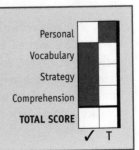
Check your answers with your teacher. Give yourself 1 point for each correct answer, and fill in your Vocabulary score here. Then turn to page 217 and transfer your score onto Graph 1.

Personal
Vocabulary
Strategy
Comprehension
TOTAL SCORE
✓ T

Strategy Check

Review the concept map that you created for "Cleaning Us" (Toiletries). Also review the rest of the article. Then answer the following questions.

1. Which detail belongs under the main idea "What Toiletries Are"?
   a. products for removing dirt from our bodies
   b. products for cleaning the toilet and tub
   c. products for removing the smell from substances

2. Which detail describes how toiletries work?
   a. by removing the layer of oil from our skin
   b. in the same way as products that we use on our house and clothes
   c. as disinfectants that kill bacteria and get rid of smells

3. Which detail provides an example of how toiletries work?
   a. Toothpaste is similar to sink cleaners.
   b. Shampoo is like the detergents we use for cleaning sweaters.
   c. Both details above are examples of how toiletries work.

4. If you were to create a concept map for "Your Dirty Skin," what is one main idea that you would include?
   a. Your skin is strange to clean because it alive and growing.
   b. Your hands don't get inkier as you go through school.
   c. Toiletries contain chemicals that will not harm your skin.

5. Which word best describes the main idea of this entire article?
   a. skin
   b. dirt
   c. chemicals

Comprehension Check

Review the selection if necessary. Then answer these questions:

1. If you want to get rid of dirt, what do you have to do?
   a. Think about how it smells and use the right cleaning tool.
   b. Think about what it's made of and use the right cleaning tool.
   c. Think about what looks like and use the right cleaning tool.

2. Which word best completes this comparison: *Toothpaste* is to *bathtub* as *shampoo* is to _____?
   a. teeth
   b. skin
   c. sweater

3. Which of these statements is false?
   a. It's very easy to clean up any kind of dirt.
   b. Disinfectants in a cleaner are there to kill bacteria.
   c. Chemicals that clean people work like chemicals that clean houses.

4. What is the best way to handle dirt on your skin?
   a. Wait until your next layer of skin grows out.
   b. Use a soap that is not too strong.
   c. Use very strong soap to scrub off the dirt and oil.

5. Why are bacteria on skin so much of a problem?
   a. They eat the dead skin and leave smelly waste.
   b. They eat the skin that is alive but leave the dirt.
   c. They look dreadful.

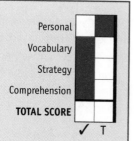

Check your answers with your teacher. Give yourself 1 point for each correct answer, and fill in your Strategy score here. Then turn to page 217 and transfer your score onto Graph 1.

Personal
Vocabulary
Strategy
Comprehension
TOTAL SCORE
✓ T

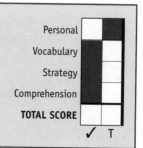

Check your answers with your teacher. Give yourself 1 point for each correct answer, and fill in your Comprehension score here. Then turn to page 217 and transfer your score onto Graph 1.

Personal
Vocabulary
Strategy
Comprehension
TOTAL SCORE
✓ T

Extending

Choose one or both of these activities:

MAKE A GUIDE TO CLEANING

Beginning with the resources on this page and the information in this article, put together a useful guide to cleaning agents that should be in every household. If you'd like, use a question-and-answer format. Or create a chart with one column listing various kinds of dirt—dirty windows, floors, clothes, woodwork, etc.—and the next two columns listing the best cleaners for those kinds of dirt and why they work best. Do research on the topic in the library, on the Internet, and in supermarket aisles that contain cleaning products.

PRACTICAL CHEMISTRY

Who invents the cleaners we use today? How do they do their work? Find out from the companies that produce the cleaning products you use in your home. Brainstorm a list of questions to ask, such as "Who came up with the idea, and why?" and "How long does development of a product take?" Then write to the company and see if they answer. If you have access to a computer and the company has an Internet address, consider sending your letter via e-mail.

Resources

Books

Chapman, Eugenia, and Jill C. Major. *More Clean Your House and Everything in It.* Perigee Books, 1985.

Consumer Reports. *How to Clean Practically Anything.* Consumer Reports, 2002.

Phillips, Barty. *How to Clean Absolutely Everything.* Avon, 1995.

Wylie, Harriet. *420 Ways to Clean Everything.* Bonanza Books, 1989.

Web Sites

http://doityourself.com/clean/index.htm
This Web site offers tips on household cleaning.

http://www.barwonwater.vic.gov.au/index.cfm?h2o=environment.hints
This site provides hints on household cleaning using natural materials instead of chemical cleaners.

http://www.chem.duke.edu/~bonk/Careers/ProdDevChem.html
This article explains the work of chemists who develop household chemical products.

LESSON 20 Speed Cleen

Building Background

The main character in the short story you are about to read is not very remarkable or special. Yet he has an opinion about everyone else, and it's usually a low opinion. Have you run into people like that? How do they make you feel?

Recall a time when you've had to deal with a demanding, unpleasant person. Then fill in the chart below.

Brief description of the person (what makes him or her annoying or difficult):	
What the person thinks of himself/herself:	What other people think of him/her:
What the person wants from other people:	What other people want from him/her:
What the person would like to give others:	What others would like to give him/her:

As you read "Speed Cleen," look for ways in which the main character is like or unlike the person you just described. Do you approve of the way others in the story react to this character? Why or why not?

attendant

blank

crouched

demanded

desolate

presently

visible

Vocabulary Builder

1. As you recall, **synonyms** are words with the same or similar meanings. Knowing a word's synonym can help you learn and remember the word more easily.

2. Read each boldfaced word below, and then underline its synonym. If you don't know a boldfaced word, find it in the story and use context to figure it out. If using context doesn't help, use a dictionary.

3. Save your work. You will refer to it again in the Vocabulary Check.

attendant	employee	bride
blank	lively	expressionless
crouched	stooped	fell
demanded	ordered	answered
desolate	empty	crowded
presently	later	now
visible	hidden	seeable

Strategy Builder

Mapping the Elements of a Short Story

- "Speed Cleen" is a **short story**—a piece of fiction that usually can be read in one sitting. Because it is much shorter than a novel, a short story often has fewer characters and takes place over a briefer period of time.

- A short story often takes place in a single **setting**, since the action moves so quickly. For example, in "Speed Cleen," the entire story takes place at a car wash.

- One of the main elements of every short story is its **plot**, or sequence of events. In most stories, the plot revolves around a problem and what the main characters do to solve it. Sometimes a problem's solution is satisfactory to the main characters—and sometimes it's not. Either way, it leads to the **conclusion**, or ending, of the story.

- Another story element that you'll encounter as you read "Speed Cleen" is irony. Often when a story contains **irony**, the plot will move along in a predictable way right up until the end. Then without warning, it will take an unexpected turn, leaving readers both surprised and amused.

- A good way to keep track of what happens in a short story is to record its elements on a **story map**. Study the story map below. It lists and defines the elements that you should look for as you read.

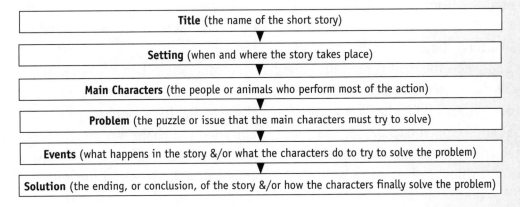

| **Title** (the name of the short story) |
| **Setting** (when and where the story takes place) |
| **Main Characters** (the people or animals who perform most of the action) |
| **Problem** (the puzzle or issue that the main characters must try to solve) |
| **Events** (what happens in the story &/or what the characters do to try to solve the problem) |
| **Solution** (the ending, or conclusion, of the story &/or how the characters finally solve the problem) |

Speed Cleen

by James Stevenson

As you begin reading this short story, apply the strategies that you just learned. Keep track of the characters, the setting, and other elements. You may want to underline them as you read.

"Don't forget those little ashtrays in the back, my friend!" called Harry Joe Shreve, holding open the front door of his white Chrysler Imperial. The windows of the car were shut, so he couldn't call through the window ("TURN OFF ENGINE. LEAVE CAR IN NEUTRAL. CLOSE WIN-DOWS," said the sign above the door of the Speed Cleen Car Wash), but the car-wash **attendant** who was **crouched** down vacuuming the floor behind the front seat gave no sign of hearing.

"Ashtrays, boy!" called Shreve, loud-er, and when the man turned his dark, **blank** face toward him Shreve pointed at the ashtrays. Then he closed the door and stepped back. A second attendant—a tall, skinny man wearing Army-surplus clothes, a cap, and black rubber boots—was shooting steam from a hose at the wheels of the Chrysler, and Shreve, walking around to the front of his car, tried to call his attention to the left headlight, which had a small mark on it—a black, V-shaped smear that looked like oil—but the man, when he looked over, merely nodded.

"Well, come on take a *look!*" called Shreve. "I'm showing you what I'm talking about." The man continued to

shoot steam at the wheels, so Shreve, his face reddening, strode over and grabbed him by the arm. "Come here," he said, and led him around the front of the car. "See what I'm talking about?" he said, pointing to the mark on the rim of the light. "You see?" The man gazed evenly at it, the steam hose spitting at the ground beside him. Shreve made a rubbing motion with his free hand. "You clean that good, hear?" Then he let go of the man's arm and stepped back, shaking his head. "What's the use?" he said to himself.

Another attendant, this one in a faded sweatshirt, was attaching a small chain to the front bumper of the Chrysler; the chain was attached in turn to a thicker, heavier chain that crawled forward—gleaming with grease—along the floor of the car wash. **Presently**, the white Chrysler began to inch slowly into the build-ing, following a bright-red Buick Riviera. The Buick disappeared into the steam clouds, and Shreve's car moved after it. Shreve had a last glimpse of his Alabama plate, and then a black Cadillac Eldorado was hauled by, blocking his view. Shreve watched for a moment, staring at the churning clouds, the shower of hot

LESSON 20: SPEED CLEEN   207

water, and—when the steam parted for an instant—the giant spinning brushes.

Shreve turned away and walked along the side of the building toward the front of the car wash. Beyond a chain fence was the deserted parking lot of a frozen-custard stand. "SEE YOU IN THE SPRING," said a sign on one of the big windows, but the place had a **desolate**, bankrupt look. Across the highway was a discount furniture store. At the end of the fence, by the front of the car wash, there were several black oil drums with wringers, and men with rolled-up sleeves, breathing steam, were plunging rags into the drums, wringing them out, and then scrubbing and polishing the chrome on the newly washed cars that emerged from the building. The car owners stood around, watching, waiting.

Shreve glanced into the car wash. The red Buick was just **visible**, covered with soapsuds, behind several other cars, but the Chrysler was still out of sight. The nearest car—a green Ford—was moving under the hot air dryer, flecks of water leaping from its roof and hood.

Shreve walked along the sidewalk, lighting a cigarette. Next to the car wash was an auto-parts store, its windows smeared with dirt; there were stacks of tires and bumpers and accessories piled in the dimness. Two hundred yards down the highway were the big blue turnpike signs. Shreve glanced at his watch. A few minutes more—five maybe—and he'd be back on the turnpike, homeward bound.

 Stop here for the Strategy Break.

Strategy Break

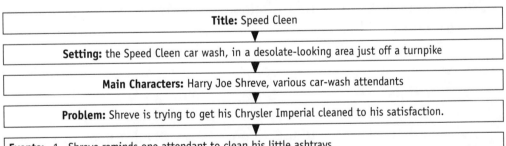

If you were to create a story map for the this selection so far, it might look like this:

Title: Speed Cleen

Setting: the Speed Cleen car wash, in a desolate-looking area just off a turnpike

Main Characters: Harry Joe Shreve, various car-wash attendants

Problem: Shreve is trying to get his Chrysler Imperial cleaned to his satisfaction.

Events:
1. Shreve reminds one attendant to clean his little ashtrays.
2. He rudely tells another attendant to clean his left headlight.
3. Another attendant hooks up Shreve's car, and it moves into the car wash behind a red Buick.
4. As Shreve checks out the area, he notices an auto-parts store next to the car wash.

To be continued . . .

As you continue reading, keep paying attention to the events in this selection. You will complete the story map in the Strategy Follow-up.

➡ Go on reading to see what happens.

He turned back to the car wash just in time to see the red Buick emerging, gleaming in the sunlight. He strode over and peered into the building to see how his Chrysler looked. There, a few feet behind the rear of the red Buick coming slowly along the chain, was the black Cadillac. Behind it was a blue Volkswagen, and behind that a gray Rover. "Where's my car?" said Shreve, almost to himself. Then he yelled, "Where's my car!"

He ran into the building. The floor was slippery with oil and water, and it was hot inside. "My car!" he yelled. "Where is it?" The faces of the attendants were blank, puzzled. He ran all the way through the building, past the unfamiliar cars, past the hot-air dryer and the hot-water rinse and the soapy brushes and the steam, and then he was outdoors again, where he had started a few minutes before. "Where is my car?" he **demanded** of the tall, thin man in the Army-surplus clothes. "What's the big idea?"

"What car?" said the man.

"My Imperial!" yelled Shreve. "My Chrysler Imperial!"

The man looked puzzled, and shook his head slowly. "I didn't see no Chrysler Imperial," he said.

"You cleaned it!" yelled Shreve. "I saw you clean it! I saw you clean my car!"

The man shook his head. "I don't recall no Imperial," he said.

Shreve spun around and pointed at the man with the vacuum. "You

cleaned it, too," he said. "I told you 'Clean the ashtrays'! Remember—the ashtrays!"

The attendant frowned. "Don't remember no Imperial today," he said.

"But it went on the chain!" Shreve shouted. "I saw it hooked on right in front of that black Caddy. One of you must have taken it off while it was inside there."

"You can't take no car off that chain, Mister," the attendant said. "That chain's movin' all the time. It's hot in there. All that steam and stuff—you can't see." He shook his head and turned slowly away, opening the door of the next car in line.

"Where's the manager?" demanded Shreve, running back inside the building. No one paid any attention. When he emerged on the front sidewalk, his clothes damp from the sprays, the men were putting final touches on the black Cadillac. Shreve grabbed a short, stout man who was polishing the rear bumper. "Where's the manager?"

"He went away for a while."

"My car's gone," said Shreve.

"You got your ticket?" asked the short man.

"What ticket?" yelled Shreve. "I didn't get any ticket!"

"Got to have a ticket," said the man. "Didn't nobody give you the ticket when you come in?"

"No!" Shreve was beginning to feel dizzy.

The short man glanced around and caught the eye of the Cadillac owner—a man in a dark suit and hat, wearing glasses. "You got *your* ticket, Mister?" he asked.

The man pulled his hand from his coat pocket and held up a small, pink ticket.

Shreve stepped over to him. "They didn't *give* me a ticket," he said.

The man turned away, shrugging slightly.

"They took my car," said Shreve.

"I don't know anything about that," said the man.

"All set, sir," said the short attendant, and the man handed him the ticket and two dollars, and got into the Cadillac, slamming the door. Shreve ran over to the car.

"Listen, friend," he said, "I'm from out of state. They—"

The window of the Cadillac rolled quietly and quickly closed, and then the car was moving away, out onto the highway. Shreve watched it drive away down the road, and then he turned back. The attendants were all busy now on the Volkswagen. No one looked at him. Shreve yelled, "I'm going to get the police, you hear? The police!"

He turned and started to stride down the sidewalk, not caring which way he was going, just getting out of there, going to find a phone. He was in front of the auto-parts store now— they might have a phone he could use—and he grabbed the door handle. It was locked. "CLOSED FOR VACATION," said a hand-lettered sign on the door. Shreve peered through the dirty window of the dark store, swearing, and he was about to turn away when he saw, on top of a heap of bumpers and tires, a single headlight—one with a small V-shaped black smear that looked like oil. ●

Strategy Follow-up

By now, you have realized the irony in this story: the solution to the problem isn't very satisfactory . . . unless you look at it from the attendants' point of view!

Now complete the story map for "Speed Cleen," starting with Event 5. Use a separate sheet of paper if you need more room to write.

Problem: Shreve is trying to get his Chrysler Imperial cleaned to his satisfaction.

▼

Event 5: When Shreve sees the red Buick emerging from the car wash,

▼

Event 6:

▼

Event 7:

▼

Event 8: After an attendant tells him

▼

Solution/Conclusion: As Shreve looks into the auto-parts store,

✓Personal Checklist

Read each question and put a check (✓) in the correct box.

1. In Building Background, you listed details about a real-life person who is unpleasant. How well were you able to find ways in which Shreve is like or unlike that person?

   ☐ 3 (extremely well)
   ☐ 2 (fairly well)
   ☐ 1 (not well)

2. How many synonyms were you able to correctly identify in the Vocabulary Builder?

   ☐ 3 (6–7 synonyms)
   ☐ 2 (3–5 synonyms)
   ☐ 1 (0–2 synonyms)

3. How well were you able to complete the story map in the Strategy Follow-up?

   ☐ 3 (extremely well)
   ☐ 2 (fairly well)
   ☐ 1 (not well)

4. How well do you understand Shreve's situation at the end of the story?

   ☐ 3 (extremely well)
   ☐ 2 (fairly well)
   ☐ 1 (not well)

5. How well do you understand the irony in this story?

   ☐ 3 (extremely well)
   ☐ 2 (fairly well)
   ☐ 1 (not well)

Vocabulary Check

Look back at the work you did in the Vocabulary Builder. Then answer each question by circling the correct letter.

1. If something is happening presently, when is it happening?

   a. right now
   b. very soon
   c. tomorrow

2. At the end of the story, what is visible to Shreve through the dirty window of the auto-parts store?

   a. the tires of his Chrysler
   b. the bumper of his Chrysler
   c. the headlight of his Chrysler

3. The attendants all have blank expressions on their faces when Shreve speaks to them. Which phrase best describes a blank expression?

   a. a smiling face
   b. a fearful look
   c. no expression at all

4. Which phrase best describes a person in a crouched position?

   a. lying down
   b. stooped over
   c. sitting on the couch

5. Which of the following could best be described as desolate?

   a. a crowded apartment building
   b. a ghost town
   c. a stadium during a football game

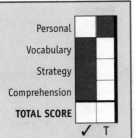

Add the numbers that you just checked to get your Personal Checklist score. Fill in your score here. Then turn to page 217 and transfer your score onto Graph 1.

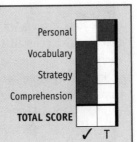

Check your answers with your teacher. Give yourself 1 point for each correct answer, and fill in your Vocabulary score here. Then turn to page 217 and transfer your score onto Graph 1.

Strategy Check

Review the story map that you completed for "Speed Cleen." Also review the story itself. Then answer the following questions:

1. Which story element does the sentence *The place had a desolate, bankrupt look* describe?

   a. setting

   b. event

   c. problem

2. Which story element is *not* introduced in the first paragraph of "Speed Cleen"?

   a. the main character

   b. the setting

   c. the solution

3. What does Shreve do when he sees the red Buick emerging from the car wash?

   a. He goes to see how his Chrysler looks.

   b. He demands to talk to the manager of the car wash.

   c. He tells the attendants he is going to get the police.

4. What could you have written for Event 6?

   a. Shreve leaves the car wash to call the police.

   b. Shreve looks for his car but doesn't see it.

   c. Shreve sees his car's headlight in the auto-parts store.

5. Which sentence tells the conclusion of this story?

   a. Shreve asks the attendants where his car is.

   b. Shreve leaves the car wash to call the police.

   c. Shreve sees his car's headlight in the auto-parts store.

Comprehension Check

Review the story if necessary. Then answer these questions:

1. What do you think the lesson of this story is?

   a. Treat others the same way you want to be treated.

   b. Never take your car to an unfamiliar car wash.

   c. Chrysler Imperials are undependable cars.

2. How does Shreve recognize his headlight in the auto-parts store?

   a. It looks like the headlights on other Chrysler Imperials.

   b. It has a mark like the one that he told the attendant to clean.

   c. He didn't really recognize it; he was just imagining things.

3. Why do you think the writer includes so much detail about the makes and colors of the cars?

   a. He's a car fanatic and likes to describe them in detail.

   b. Knowing which car is where is important to understanding the plot.

   c. He's trying to make the story sound as up-to-date as possible.

4. What is ironic about the solution to Shreve's problem?

   a. The solution is satisfying to the attendants but not to Shreve.

   b. The attendants clean Shreve's car so well that it disappears.

   c. Both of the above statements could describe the irony.

5. Which of these sentences best describes the plot of this story?

   a. This could never happen.

   b. This probably could not happen.

   c. This could happen very easily.

Check your answers with your teacher. Give yourself 1 point for each correct answer, and fill in your Strategy score here. Then turn to page 217 and transfer your score onto Graph 1.

Personal
Vocabulary
Strategy
Comprehension
TOTAL SCORE
✓ T

Check your answers with your teacher. Give yourself 1 point for each correct answer, and fill in your Comprehension score here. Then turn to page 217 and transfer your score onto Graph 1.

Personal
Vocabulary
Strategy
Comprehension
TOTAL SCORE
✓ T

Extending

Choose one or more of these activities:

RETELL THE STORY IN PICTURES

Obtain pictures of the cars described in "Speed Cleen," and arrange them in the order in which the cars went into the car wash. Then use the pictures to read or retell the story to a group of classmates or younger students.

WRITE A SEQUEL

If "Speed Cleen" were a chapter in a novel, what do you predict might happen next? Will any other patrons lose their cars in the car wash? Are the car-wash attendants regular humans, or are they magical or alien beings? Will they be found out? By yourself or with a partner, write a sequel to "Speed Cleen" that answers at least one of these questions. Share your sequel with others in your class. If you'd like, put it on as a play.

SHARE OTHER STORIES

Using the resources on this page as a start, watch or read other scary or surprising stories. Write a brief review of each story on a 3 x 5 card, then put the cards on display in your school or classroom library. Encourage other students to add their reviews too.

Resources

Book

Serling, Rod. *The Twilight Zone: Complete Stories.* TV Books, 1999.

Web Sites

http://www.car.com
This Web site lets you search for particular makes and models of cars for sale. It includes photographs of many of the cars.

http://www.scifi.com/twilightzone/
This Web site focuses on *The Twilight Zone,* the famous television series featuring eerie science fiction stories.

Audio Recording

Serling, Rod. *The Odyssey of Flight 33* (abridged). Twilight Zone. HarperAudio, 1993.

Learning New Words

Prefixes

A prefix is a word part that is added to the beginning of a root word. (*Pre-* means "before.") When you add a prefix, you often change the root word's meaning and function. For example, the prefix *re-* means "again." So adding *re-* to the root word *make* changes meaning of the word to "make again."

in- and *un-*

The prefixes *in-* and *un-* have the same meaning: "not" or "the opposite of." For example, in Lesson 17 Brent calls the Raptor roller coaster "indescribably huge." *Indescribably* means "not able to be described" or impossible to explain."

Match each word with its definition.

1. inadmissible   not convincing or final
2. inaccurate   not allowable
3. inconclusive   not the same
4. indecent   not correct or precise
5. inconsistent   not proper

super-

The prefix *super-* can mean "beyond" or "superior to." It also can mean "over or above." For example, when Brent examines the *superstructure* of the Raptor, he is looking at the part of the roller coaster that is above the ground.

Match each word with its definition.

1. superabundant   person who oversees schools
2. supernatural   beyond what's human
3. superintendent   more than enough
4. superhuman   put on top of something
5. superimpose   beyond what's natural

Suffixes

A suffix is a word part that is added to the end of a root word. When you add a suffix, you often change the root word's meaning and function. For example, the suffix *-ful* means "full of," so the root word *joy* changes from a noun to an adjective meaning "full of joy."

-ly

The suffix *-ly* can turn words into adverbs meaning "in a _____ way, or manner." Or it can turn words into adjectives meaning "like a/the _____." In "Riding the Raptor," Brent asks tentatively if he and Trevor are the only ones invited to ride the roller coaster. *Tentatively* means "in a tentative, or hesitant, manner."

   Write the definition for each word below.

1. friendly   _____

2. cautiously   _____

3. cheerfully   _____

4. brotherly   _____

Prefixes and Suffixes

Some root words have both a prefix and a suffix added to them. For example, in the word *indefinitely, in-* means "not" and *-ly* means "in a _____ way." So *indefinitely* means "in a way that is not definite or clear."

   Match each word with its definition.

1. dislocation   not willing

2. incompletely   in a way that's not complete

3. unwilling   in a way that's not convenient

4. inconveniently   a putting out of place or joint

VOCABULARY

From Lesson 17
- furtively
- indescribably

From Lesson 18
- tentatively

From Lesson 20
- presently

From Lesson 17
- indescribably
- unharnessed

From Lesson 18
- dismantling
- unflinching

From Lesson 19
- disinfectants

Graphing Your Progress

The graphs on page 217 will help you track your progress as you work through this book. Follow these directions to fill in the graphs:

Graph 1

1. Start by looking across the top of the graph for the number of the lesson you just finished.

2. In the first column for that lesson, write your Personal Checklist score in both the top and bottom boxes. (Notice the places where *13* is filled in on the sample.)

3. In the second column for that lesson, fill in your scores for the Vocabulary, Strategy, and Comprehension Checks.

4. Add the three scores, and write their total in the box above the letter *T*. (The *T* stands for "Total." The ✓ stands for "Personal Checklist.")

5. Compare your scores. Does your Personal Checklist score match or come close to your total scores for that lesson? Why or why not?

Graph 2

1. Again, start by looking across the top of the graph for the number of the lesson you just finished.

2. In the first column for that lesson, shade the number of squares that match your Personal Checklist score.

3. In the second column for that lesson, shade the number of squares that match your total score.

4. As you fill in this graph, you will be able to check your progress across the book. You'll be able to see your strengths and areas of improvement. You'll also be able to see areas where you might need a little extra help. You and your teacher can discuss ways to work on those areas.

Graph 1

For each lesson, enter the scores from your Personal Checklist and your Vocabulary, Strategy, and Comprehension Checks. Total your scores and then compare them. Does your Personal Checklist score match or come close to your total scores for that lesson? Why or why not?

Go down to Graph 2 and shade your scores for the lesson you just completed.

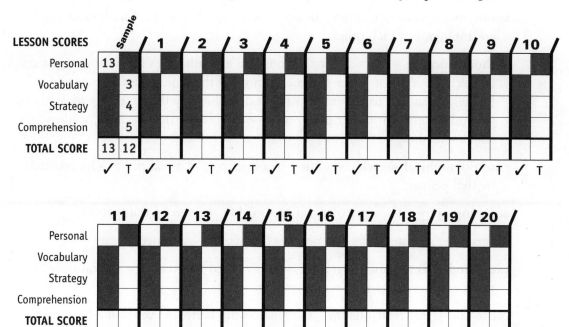

Graph 2

Now record your overall progress. In the first column for the lesson you just completed, shade the number of squares that match your Personal Checklist score. In the second column for that lesson, shade the number of squares that match your total score. As you fill in this graph, you will be able to check your progress across the book.

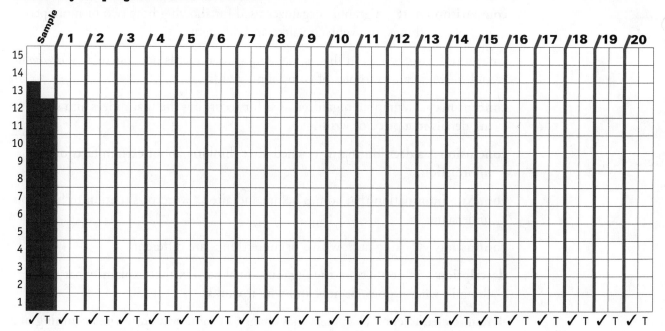

Glossary of Terms

This glossary includes definitions for important terms introduced in this book.

antonym   a word that means the opposite of another word. *Quickly* and *slowly* are antonyms of each other.

author's purpose   the reason or reasons that an author has for writing a particular selection. Authors write for one or more of these purposes: to *entertain* (make you laugh), to *inform* (explain or describe something), to *persuade* (try to get you to agree with their opinion), to *express* (share their feelings or ideas about something).

autobiographical sketch   the story of a brief part of a real person's life, written by that perosn.

autobiography   the story of a real person's life, written by that perosn.

biography   the story of a real person's life, written by someone else.

cause-and-effect chain   a graphic organizer used for recording the cause-and-effect relationships in a piece of writing.

cause-and-effect relationship   the relationship between events in a piece of writing. The cause in a cause-and-effect relationship tells *why* something happened; the effect tells *what* happened.

character map   a graphic organizer used for recording a character's traits, as well as examples that illustrate those traits.

characters   the people or animals that perform the action in a story.

character wheel   a graphic organizer used for recording the changes that a character goes through from the beginning to the end of a story.

comparing   looking at how two or more things are alike.

comparison chart   a graphic organizer used for showing how two or more people, places, things, or events are alike and different.

compound word   a word that is made up of two words put together. *Wheelhouse* and *bulkhead* are examples of compound words.

concept map   a graphic organizer used for recording the main ideas and supporting details in a piece of writing.

conclusion   a decision that is reached after thinking about certain facts or information.

context   information that comes before and after a word or situation to help you understand it.

contrasting   looking at how two or more things are different.

description   in nonfiction, the organizational pattern that explains what something is, what it does, or how and why it works.

dynamic characters   characters that change in some way from the beginning of a story to the end

end result   the solution a character or characters try that finally solves the problem in a story.

event   a happening. The plot of any story contains one or more events during which the characters try to solve their problems.

fact   a statement that can be proved.

fiction   stories about made-up characters or events. Forms of fiction include short stories, historical fiction, fantasy, and folktales.

first-person point of view   the perspective, or viewpoint, of one of the characters in a story. That character uses words such as *I, me, my,* and *mine* to tell the story.

flashback   an event that is told out of sequence and describes something that happened in the past.

graphic organizer   a chart, graph, or drawing used to show how the main ideas in a piece of writing are organized and related.

headings   the short titles given throughout a piece of nonfiction. The headings often state the main ideas of a selection.

historical ficton   fiction that tells made-up stories based on historical facts.

informational article   a piece of writing that gives facts and details about a particular subject, or topic.

irony   the contrast between what is expected and what really happens in a story.

legend   a traditional tale that has been passed from generation to generation by word of mouth. Legends often contain magical elements, such as talking objects or animals, or characters that can change form.

main idea   the most important idea of a paragraph, section, or whole piece of writing.

mood   the feeling that a piece of writing conveys.

multiple-meaning word   a word that has more than one meaning. The word *cell* is a multiple-meaning word whose meanings include "a small room," "the matter that living things are made of," and "a box-shaped arrangement of dots."

narrator   the person or character who is telling a story.

nonfiction   writing that gives facts and information about real people, events, and topics. Informational articles, autobiographies, and biographies are some forms of nonfiction.

opinion   a statement, or belief, that cannot be proved as fact.

organizational pattern   in nonfiction, the pattern in which the text is written and organized. Common organizational patterns include description, cause-effect, sequence, compare-contrast, and problem-solution.

outline   a framework for organizing the main ideas and supporting details in a piece of writing. Some outlines are organized according to a system of Roman numerals (I, II, III, IV, V, and so on), capital letters (A, B, C, D, E, and so on), and Arabic numerals (1, 2, 3, 4, 5, and so on).

plot   the sequence of events in a piece of writing.

point of view   the perspective, or viewpoint, from which a story is told.

prediction   a kind of guess that is based on the context clues given in a story.

problem   difficulty or question that a character must solve or answer.

problem-solution frame   a graphic organizer used for recording the problem, solutions, and end result in a piece of writing.

root word   a word to which prefixes and suffixes are added to make other words.

self-questioning   the process of asking yourself questions as a way of summarizing what you read.

sequence   the order of events in a piece of writing. The sequence shows what happens or what to do first, second, and so on.

setting   the time and place in which a story happens.

short story   a work of fiction that usually can be read in one sitting.

signal words   words and phrases that tell when something happens or when to do something. Examples of signal words are *first, next, finally, after lunch, two years later,* and *in 1820.*

solution   the things that characters or people do to solve a problem.

specialized vocabulary   words that are related to a particular subject, or topic. Specialized vocabulary words in the selection "Dealing with Dirt" include *bacteria, detergent,* and *disinfectants.*

static characters   characters that stay the same from the beginning of a story to the end.

story map   a graphic organizer used for recording the main parts of a story: its title, setting, character, problem, events, and solution.

suffix   a word part that is added to the end of a word. Adding a suffix usually changes the word's meaning and function. For example, the suffix *-less* means "without," so the word *painless* changes from the noun *pain* to an adjective meaning "without pain."

summary   a short description. A summary describes what has happened so far in a piece of fiction, or what the main ideas are in a piece of nonfiction.

supporting details   details that describe or explain the main idea of a paragraph, section, or whole piece of text.

synonym   a word that has the same meaning as another word. *Fast* and *quick* are synonyms of each other.

third-person point of view   the perspective, or viewpoint, of a narrator who is not a character in a story. That narrator uses words such as *she, her, he, his, they,* and *their* to tell the story.

time line   a graphic organizer used for recording the sequence of events in a piece of writing. Time lines are used mostly for longer periods of time, and sequence chains are used mostly for shorter periods of time.

title   the name of a piece of writing.

topic   the subject of a piece of writing. The topic is what the selection is all about.

Acknowledgments

Acknowledgment is gratefully made to the following publishers, authors, and agents for permission to reprint these works. Every effort has been made to determine copyright owners. In the case of any omissions, the Publisher will be pleased to make suitable acknowledgments in future editions.

"Alex, the Talking Parrot" by Dorothy Hinshaw Patent from *Spider*, September 1996. Reprinted by permission of the author.

"Concha" by Mary Helen Ponce. Reprinted by permission of author.

"Dancer" by Vickie Sears from *Simple Songs*. Reprinted by permission of Firebrand Books, Ithaca, New York. Copyright © 1990 by Vicki Sears.

"Dealing With Dirt" by Lesley Newson from *Dealing with Dirt*, 1993. Reprinted by permission of A & C Black Publishers.

"Do Animals Think?" by Ellen Lambeth from the March 1997 issue of *Ranger Rick* magazine, with the permission of the publisher, the National Wildlife Federation. Copyright 1997 by the National Wildlife Federation.

"Duffy's Jacket" by Bruce Coville originally published in *Things That Go Bump in the Night*, 1989, edited by Jane Yolen and Martin H. Greenburg. Reprinted by permission of the Ashley Grayson Literary Agency.

"Faces in Sports: Jackie Joyner-Kersee" by Judith P. Josephson from *Children's Digest*, copyright © 1994 by Children's Better Health Institute, Benjamin Franklin Literary and Medical Society, Inc., Indianapolis, Indiana. Used by permission.

"The Faithful Sister" by Madhur Jaffrey from *Seasons of Splendor* as appeared in *Cricket*, May 1991, Vol. 18, No. 9. Copyright © 1985 by Madhur Jaffrey. Reproduced by permission of the author c/o Rogers, Coleridge & White Ltd., 20 Powis Mews, London W11 1JN.

"The Mysterious Mr. Lincoln" from *Lincoln, A Photobiography*. Copyright © 1987 by Russell Freedman. Reprinted by permission of Clarion Books/Houghton Mifflin Company. All rights reserved.

"Passage to Mishima" by William J. Buchanan. By permission of William J. Buchanan and *Boys' Life*, May 1998, published by the Boy Scouts of America.

"The Printer's Apprentice" by Linda Roberts as appeared in *Cricket*, September 1993, Vol. 21, No. 1.

"Riding the Raptor" by Neal Shusterman, from *Beware, Your Wish Could Come True*. Copyright 1997 by Jamestown Publishers, Inc., a division of NTC/Contemporary Publishing Group, Inc.

"The Silent Storm" reprinted by permission of Maureen Crane Wartski and *Boy's Life*, published by the Boy Scouts of America.

"Speed Cleen" by James Stevenson originally published in *The New Yorker*, 1968. Reprinted by permission of the author.